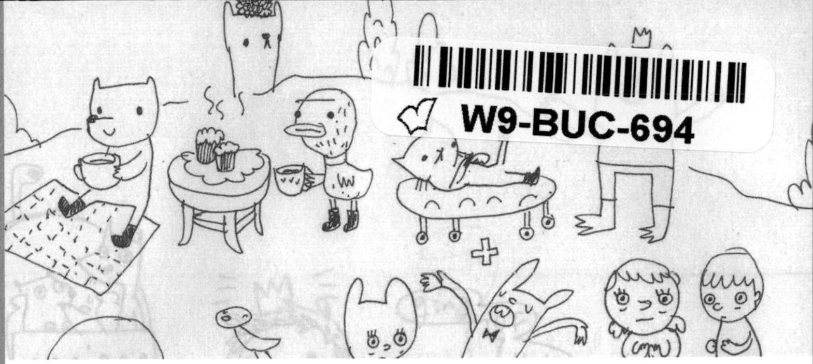

contents

Vol. 15: Summer 2009

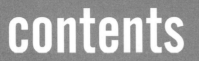

Cover images by Andrice Arp Incidental drawings by Kaela Graham

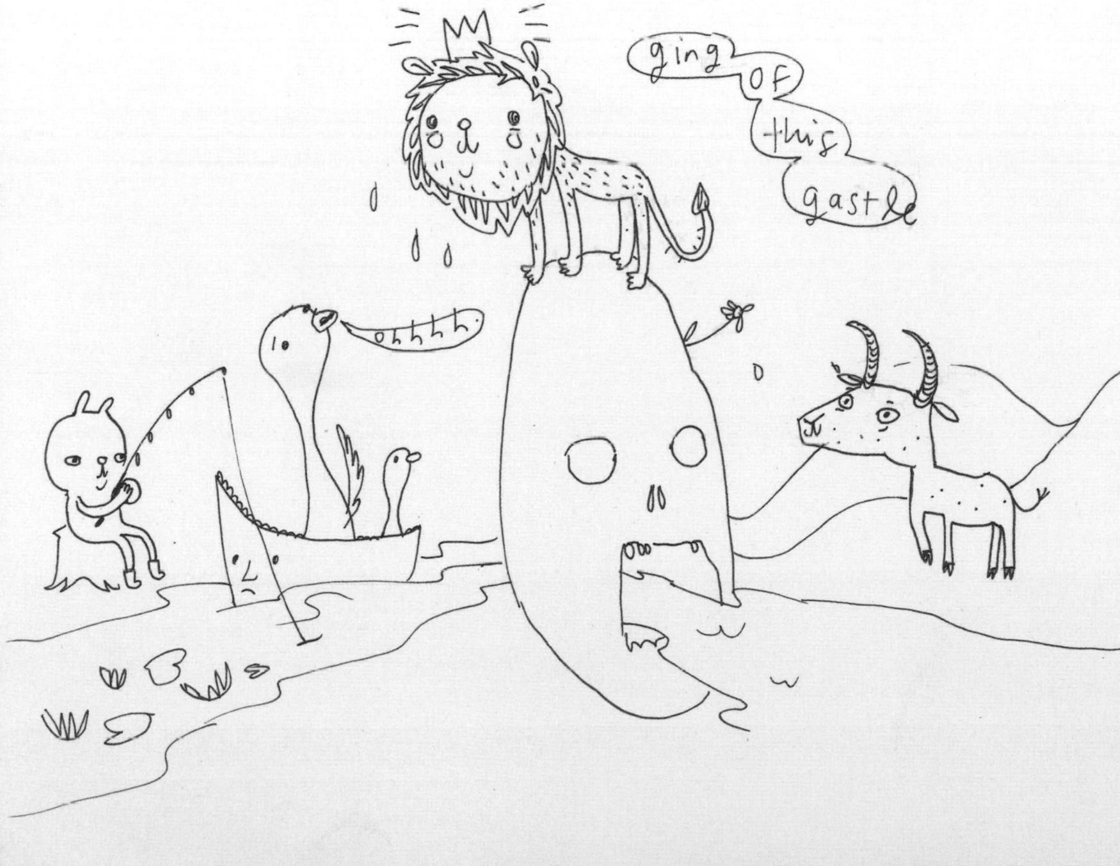

ging of this gastle
ohhhh.

particulars

Information / notes from the editors

MOME 15: SUMMER 2009

Published by Fantagraphics Books, 7563 Lake City Way Northeast, Seattle, Washington, 98115. MOME is copyright © 2009 Fantagraphics Books. Individual stories and images are copyright © 2009 the respective artist. All rights reserved. Permission to reproduce material from this book, except for purposes of review and/or notice, must be obtained by the publisher. Edited by Eric Reynolds and Gary Groth. Art direction by Adam Grano. Original MOME design by Jordan Crane.

First edition: May 2009
ISBN: 978-1-60699-152-7
Printed in Singapore

VISIT THE FANTAGRAPHICS BOOKSTORE & GALLERY:

1201 S. Vale St. (at Airport Way) in the Georgetown neighborhood of Seattle, Washington.

FOR A FREE CATALOG OF COMICS AND CARTOONING:

Please telephone 1-800-657-1100 or consult www.fantagraphics.com.

PLEASE NOTE:

• Mea Cupla Dept.: In our last issue, we made the most egregiously idiotic mistake in MOME's history. In Dash Shaw's story, "The Making of the Abyss," the very last page of the story was inadvertently run as the second page of the story. The reasons for this are too embarrassing to mention, but suffice it to say that we would not have objected if Mr. Shaw had flown to Seattle to beat us within an inch of our life. If you read the piece and thought, "Hm, that second page felt like it should have been the ending," then you might want to send your editorial resumé to Fantagraphics because you are clearly smarter than us. Our sincere apologies to Mr. Shaw. Please go re-read this story immediately, in its correct order.

• This issue of MOME features the final three chapters of Tim Hensley's Wally Gropius, which has appeared in MOME since our fifth issue (Fall 2006). We are grateful to have had the opportunity to midwife this masterpiece into the world, and are proud to announce that a Wally Gropius collection will be published by Fantagraphics in 2010. We'll miss you, Mr. Hensley.

• Mr. Hensley's retreat makes room in MOME for T. Edward Bak, who presents the first chapter of a new graphic biography of German naturalist Georg Wilhelm Steller, who traveled with Vitus Bering on what is generally known as the Second Kamchatka Expedition in 1741. We highly recommend you search out Bak's previous book, *Service Industry* (Bodega Publishing, 2007).

• We would also like to welcome up-and-comer Noah Van Sciver to the pages of MOME, and commend him for being the most tenacious cartoonist to have ever pursued MOME's ranks. Aspiring cartoonists take note: Patience and perseverance will be rewarded.

• We have wanted to publish the great Spanish cartoonist Max in our pages for some time. This issue we present "The Confederacy of Villains," translated from Spanish by MOME's ambassador to the outside world, Kim Thompson. We are proud to present it in book form, for the first time, in its intended format; previous foreign editions of this work featured four pages per page due to the small size of the original films. Thanks to our excellent printer, TWP of Singapore, for working with us to accommodate this unusual presentation. This story was originally published in the late, great Spanish comics anthology *El Víbora* #93 (Ediciones La Cúpula, 1987).

• "Life with Mr. Dangerous" by Paul Hornschemeier will conclude next issue, contrary to prior estimates.

• We enjoy your letters of comment. Please write us at fbicomix@fantagraphics.com and include "MOME MAIL" in the subject line.

• While we welcome submissions, we have very little room for them, so please don't hate us if we don't accept them.

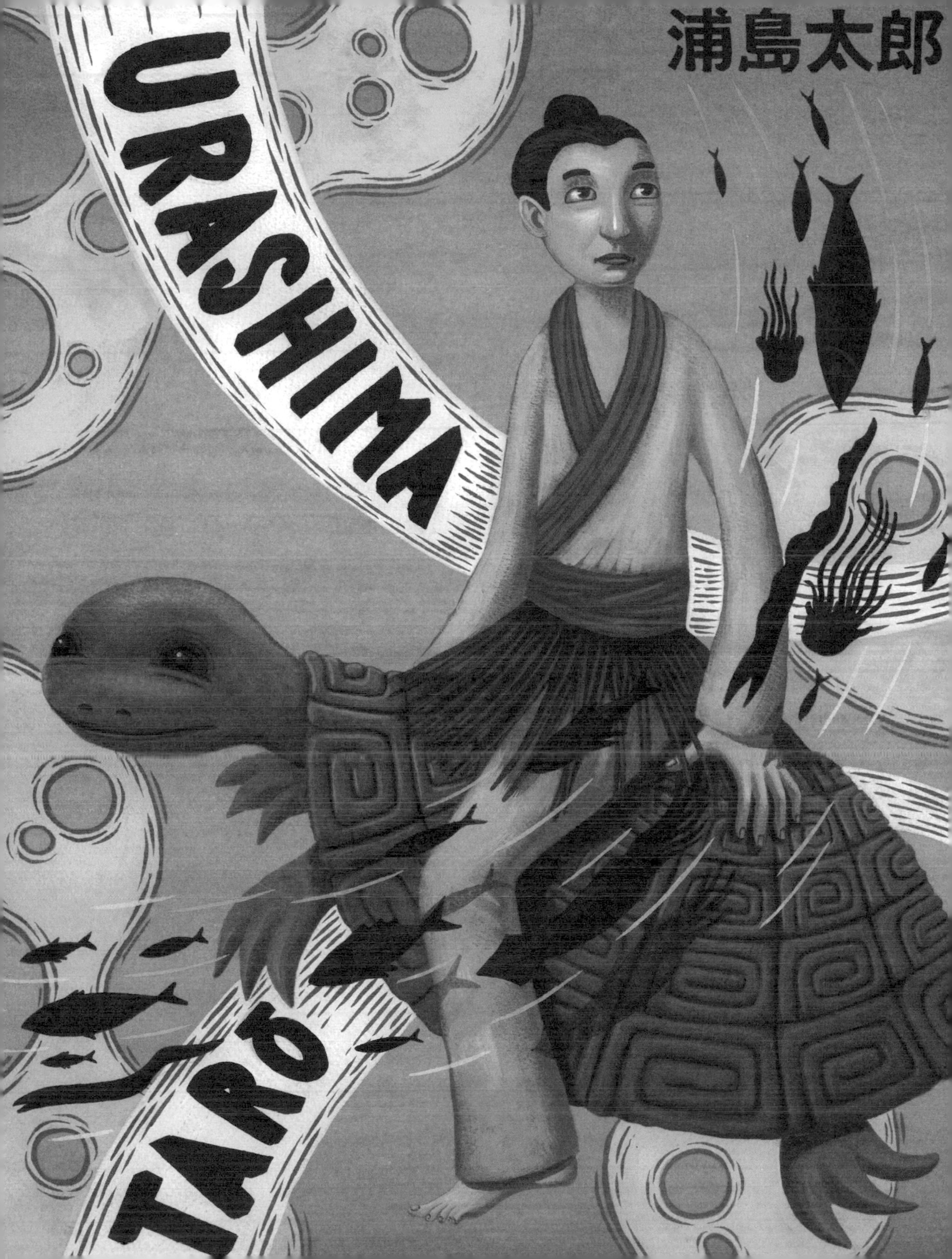
浦島太郎
URASHIMA
TARO

more MOME

$14.95 ea. Available in bookstores or at Fantagraphics.com.

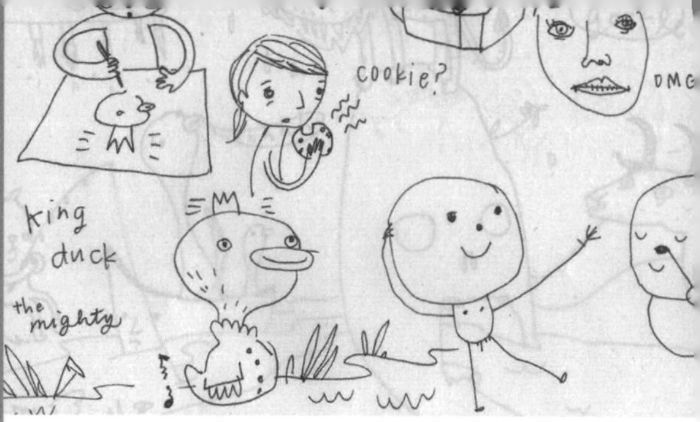

cookie?
OMG
king
duck
the mighty

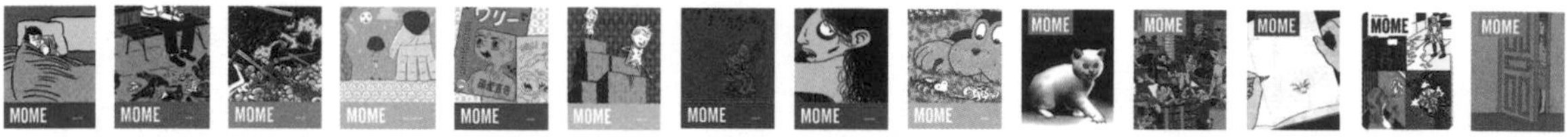

BACK ISSUES:

MOME SUMMER 2005 (VOL. 1): The debut issue, featuring Gabrielle Bell, Kurt Wolfgang, Martin Cendreda, Jeffrey Brown, Paul Hornschemeier, John Pham, David Heatley, Anders Nilsen, Jonathan Bennett, Sophie Crumb and Andrice Arp. Includes an interview with Paul Hornschemeier and covers by Gabrielle Bell.

MOME FALL 2005 (VOL. 2): Tim Hensley makes his Mome debut. Also included: Nilsen, Bennett, Wolfgang, Cendreda, Hornschemeier, Crumb, Bell, Heatley, Pham, Brown and Arp. Plus: A Gabrielle Bell interview and covers by Jonathan Bennett.

MOME WINTER 2006 (VOL. 3): Featuring Cendreda, Nilsen, Bennett, Heatley, Arp, Bell and Brown. Plus an interview with Kurt Wolfgang, as well as the debuts of David B. (contributing the 36-page "Armed Garden") and R. Kikuo Johnson. Covers by David B.

MOME SPRING/SUMMER 2006 (VOL. 4): Featuring Heatley, Nilsen, Crumb, Cendreda, Bennett, Hornschemeier, Pham, Bell and Brown. Includes an interview with Jonathan Bennett, David B.'s 33-page "The Veiled Prophet," and R. Kikuo Johnson's "John James Audubon." Covers by John Pham.

MOME FALL 2006 (VOL. 5): Featuring Arp, Nilsen, Crumb, Brown, Hornschemeier, Bell and Wolfgang. Hensley returns with his first "Wally Gropius" strips, Andrice Arp is interviewed, and Zak Sally and Robert Goodin make their MOME debuts. Covers by Tim Hensley.

MOME WINTER 2007 (VOL. 6): Featuring Johnson, Hensley, Cendreda, Nilsen, Heatley, Brown, Hornschemeier, Crumb, Bennett, Bell and Wolfgang. Tim Hensley is interviewed, while French cartoonists Émile Bravo and Lewis Trondheim make their first appearances. Covers by Martin Cendreda.

MOME SPRING 2007 (VOL. 7): Featuring the MOME debuts of Al Columbia, Eleanor Davis, and Tom Kaczynski, as well as returning artists Heatley, Hornschemeier, Bell, Crumb, Wolfgang, Trondheim, Arp, and Nilsen. Anders Nilsen is interviewed, under covers by Lewis Trondheim.

MOME SUMMER 2007 (VOL. 8): Featuring the MOME debuts of Ray Fenwick and Joe Kimball, and sophomore stories by Kaczynski, Davis (who is cover-featured and interviewed), Columbia, and Émile Bravo, whose "Young Americans" in this issue is a 2008 Eisner Award Nominee for "Best Short Story." Plus regulars Crumb, Bennett, Hornschemeier, and the final chapter of Trondheim's "At Loose Ends," also nominated for said Eisner Award.

MOME FALL 2007 (VOL. 9): Featuring return favorites Fenwick, Hensley, Columbia, Davis, Bell, Arp, Kimball, Kaczynski, Wolfgang, Hornschemeier, and Crumb. Also: a collaboration between O. Henry Prize-winning author Brian Evenson and Zak Sally; a ballpoint gallery from frequent Built to Spill album artist, Mike Scheer; the first part (of two) of a 45-page "Frank" story by Jim Woodring, "The Lute String," previously published only in Japan. Our fattest issue yet.

MOME WINTER/SPRING 2008 (VOL. 10): Featuring original covers by Al Columbia, as well as returning favorites Crumb, Fenwick, Bravo, Goodin, Kaczynski, Wolfgang, Hornschemeier and Hensley. Also: the second and final chapter of Woodring's "The Lute String," as well as the debuts of Dash Shaw, John Hankiewicz, and Jeremy Eaton, and an interview with Tom Kaczynski conducted by Gary Groth.

MOME SUMMER 2008 (VOL. 11): Featuring covers by and the Mome debut of French great Killoffer, as well as Mome familiars Columbia, Wolfgang, Fenwick, Davis, Shaw, Hankiewicz, Bravo, Arp, Kaczynski and Hornschemeier. Also: an interview with Ray Fenwick by Gary Groth, and the debuts of Nate Neal and Conor O'Keefe.

MOME FALL 2008 (VOL. 12): Featuring covers by and the Mome debut of Olivier Schrauwen, as well as the debuts of Jon Vermilyea, Derek Van Gieson, and Sara Edward-Corbett. Also, returning regulars Crumb, Neal, Fenwick, Shaw, Kaczynski, Columbia, Killoffer, David B., and Hornschemeier.

MOME WINTER 2009 (VOL. 13): Original covers by Dash Shaw and the story "Satellite CMYK," as well as the first chapter (of three) of Gilbert Shelton & Pic's "Last Gig in Shnagrlig", and the debuts of T. Ott, Josh Simmons, Laura Park, and David Greenberger. Also, returning regulars Hensley, O'Keefe, Wolfgang, Neal, Edward-Corbett and Van Gieson.

MOME SPRING 2009 (VOL. 14): Covers by Lilli Carré, spotlighting her 32-page graphic novella, "The Carnival." Also: Shelton & Pic, Van Gieson, Park, Shaw, Fenwick, Edward-Corbett, O'Keefe, Bravo, Vermilyea, and Simmons. Plus: A special "Cold Heat story by Frank Santoro, Ben Jones and Jon Vermilyea, and a Spanish treat from Hernámn Migoya and Juaco Vizuete.

SUBSCRIBE TO MOME:

Save 10 dollars per year off the cover price. Rates for a four-issue subscription are as follows:

$49.95 U.S. & Canada only
$54.95 for global surface mail
$69.95 for global air mail

Each issue is carefully boxed prior to being shipped. To subscribe using your Visa or MasterCard, call us toll-free at 1-800-657-1100 or visit our website: www.fantagraphics.com. Otherwise, send U.S. check or money order to: MOME SUBSCRIPTIONS, c/o Fantagraphics Books, 7563 Lake City Way NE, Seattle, WA 98115 USA.

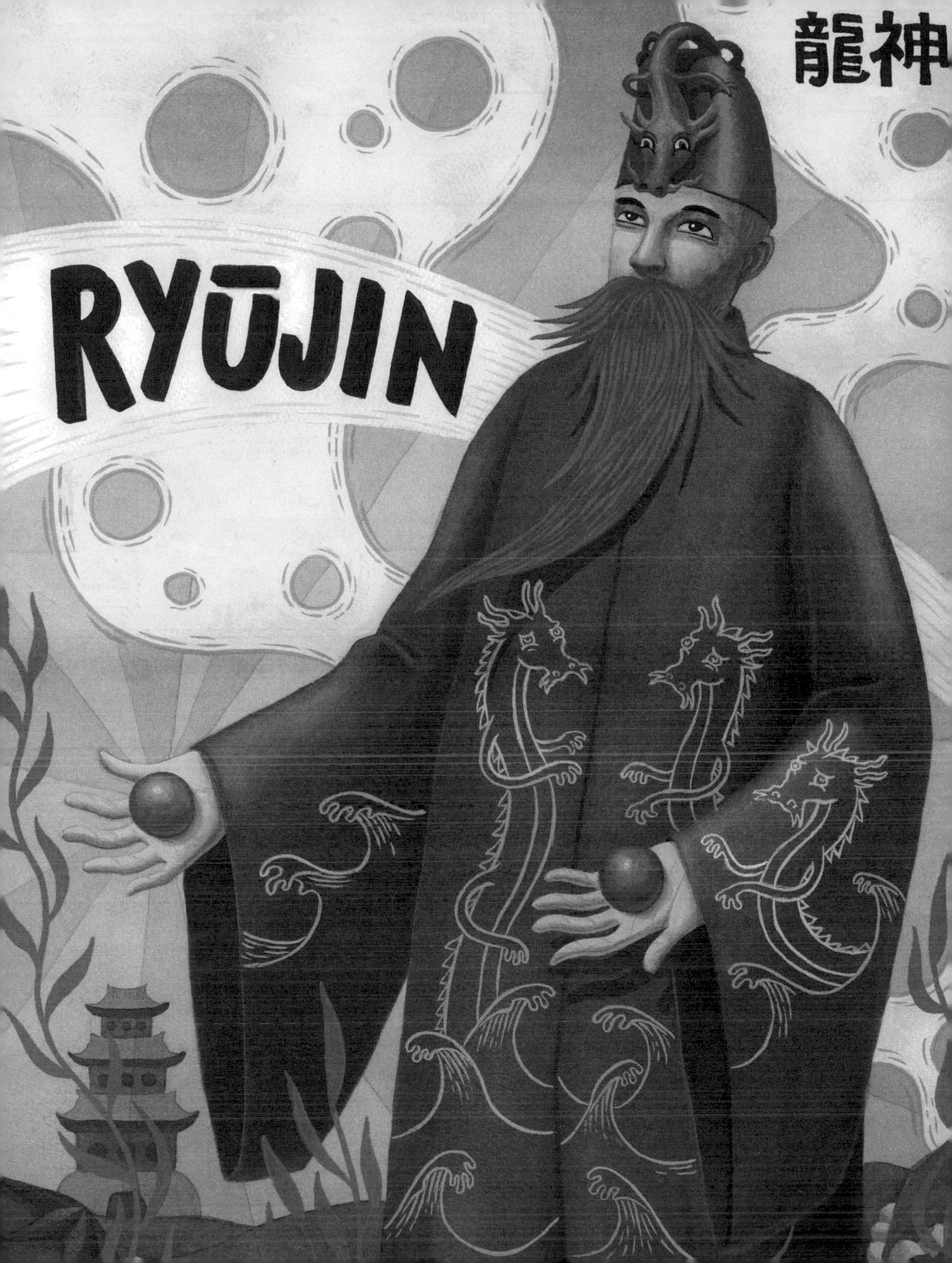
龍神
RYŪJIN

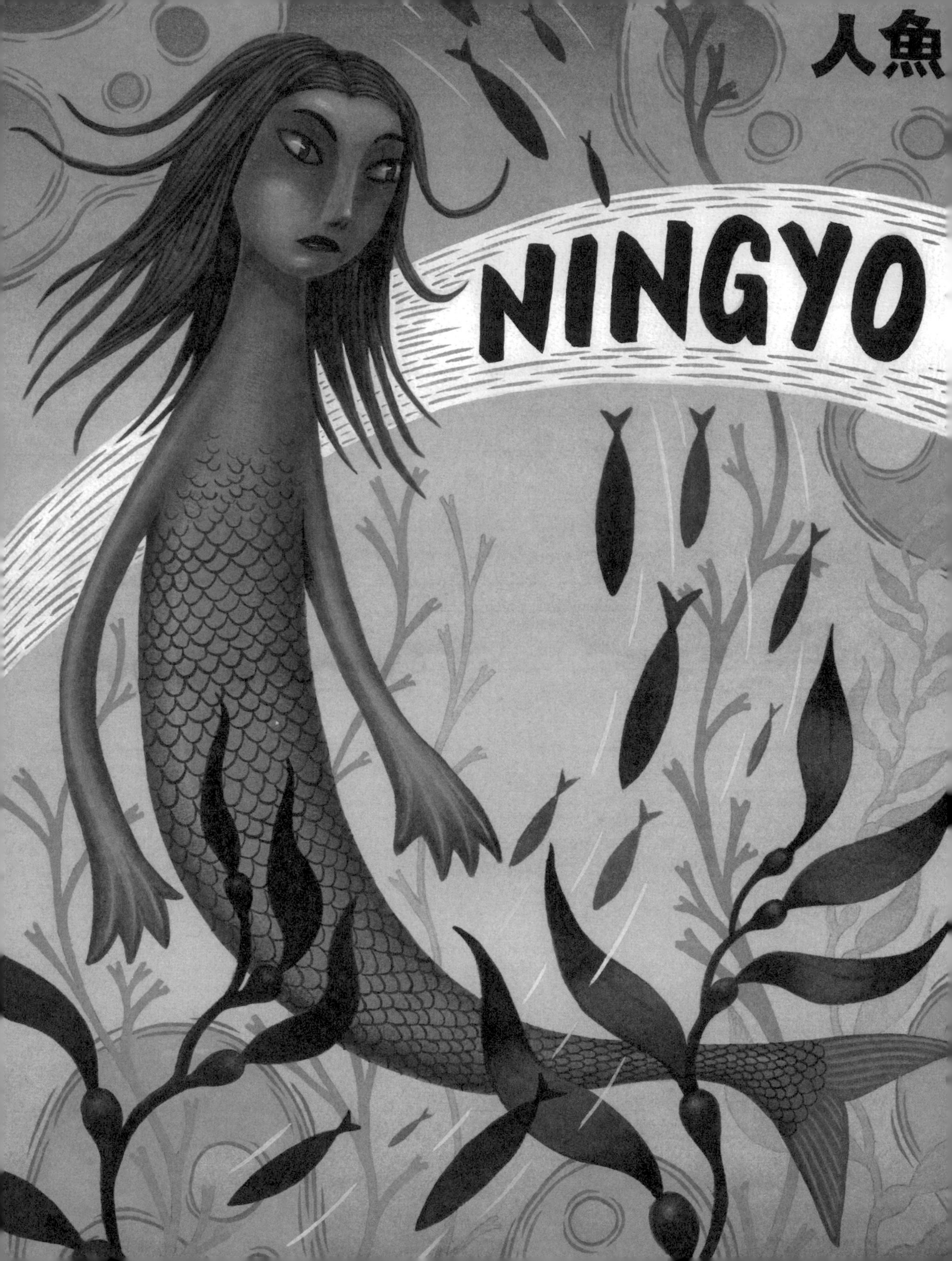
人魚
NINGYO

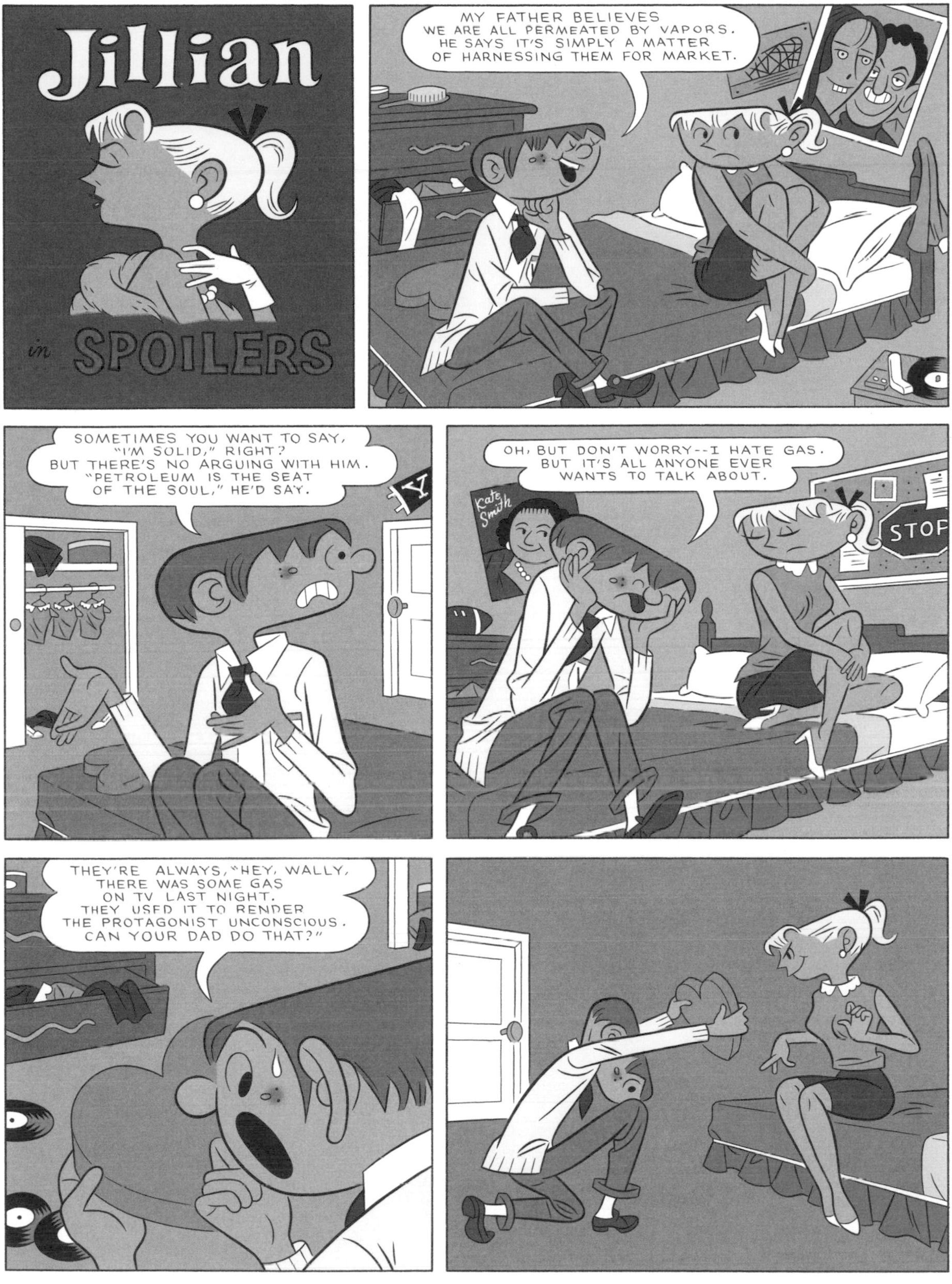
Jillian
in SPOILERS
MY FATHER BELIEVES WE ARE ALL PERMEATED BY VAPORS. HE SAYS IT'S SIMPLY A MATTER OF HARNESSING THEM FOR MARKET.
SOMETIMES YOU WANT TO SAY, "I'M SOLID," RIGHT? BUT THERE'S NO ARGUING WITH HIM. "PETROLEUM IS THE SEAT OF THE SOUL," HE'D SAY.
Y
OH, BUT DON'T WORRY--I HATE GAS. BUT IT'S ALL ANYONE EVER WANTS TO TALK ABOUT.
Kate Smith
STOP
THEY'RE ALWAYS, "HEY, WALLY, THERE WAS SOME GAS ON TV LAST NIGHT. THEY USED IT TO RENDER THE PROTAGONIST UNCONSCIOUS. CAN YOUR DAD DO THAT?"

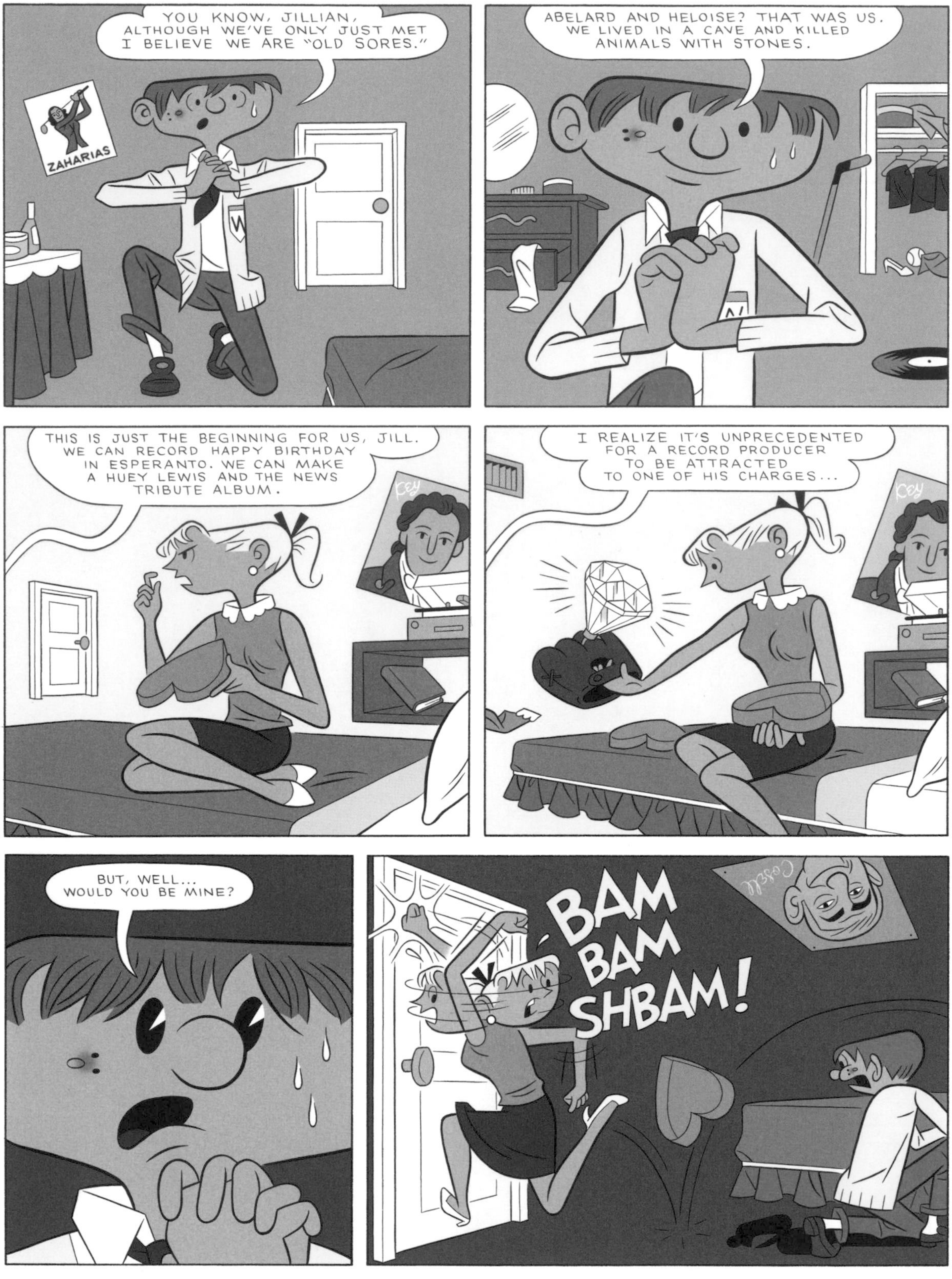

YOU KNOW, JILLIAN, ALTHOUGH WE'VE ONLY JUST MET I BELIEVE WE ARE "OLD SORES."
ZAHARIAS
ABELARD AND HELOISE? THAT WAS US. WE LIVED IN A CAVE AND KILLED ANIMALS WITH STONES.
THIS IS JUST THE BEGINNING FOR US, JILL. WE CAN RECORD HAPPY BIRTHDAY IN ESPERANTO. WE CAN MAKE A HUEY LEWIS AND THE NEWS TRIBUTE ALBUM.
I REALIZE IT'S UNPRECEDENTED FOR A RECORD PRODUCER TO BE ATTRACTED TO ONE OF HIS CHARGES...
BUT, WELL... WOULD YOU BE MINE?
BAM BAM SHBAM!

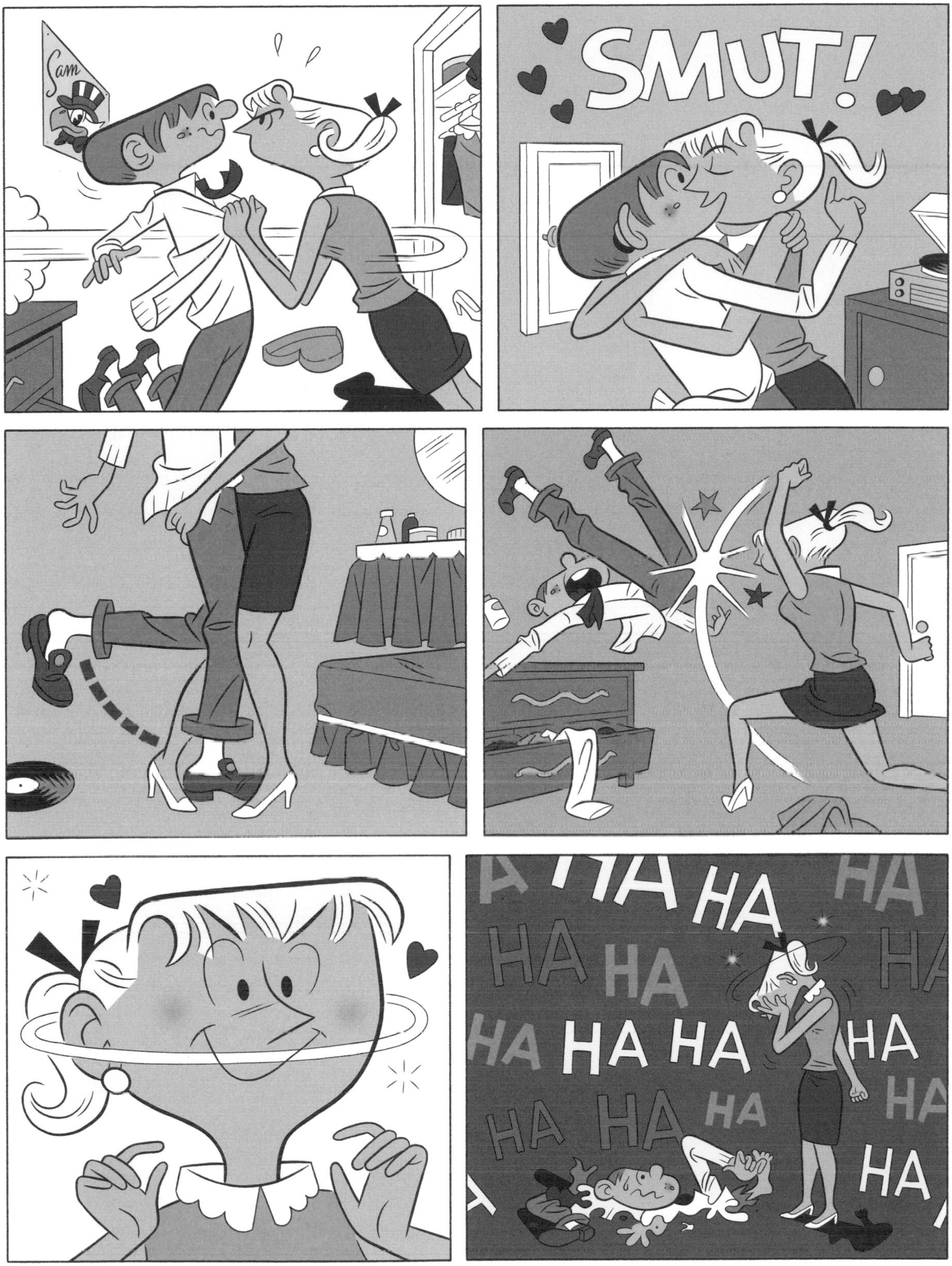

Sam
SMUT!
HA HA HA HA HA HA HA HA HA HA HA HA HA HA HA HA HA

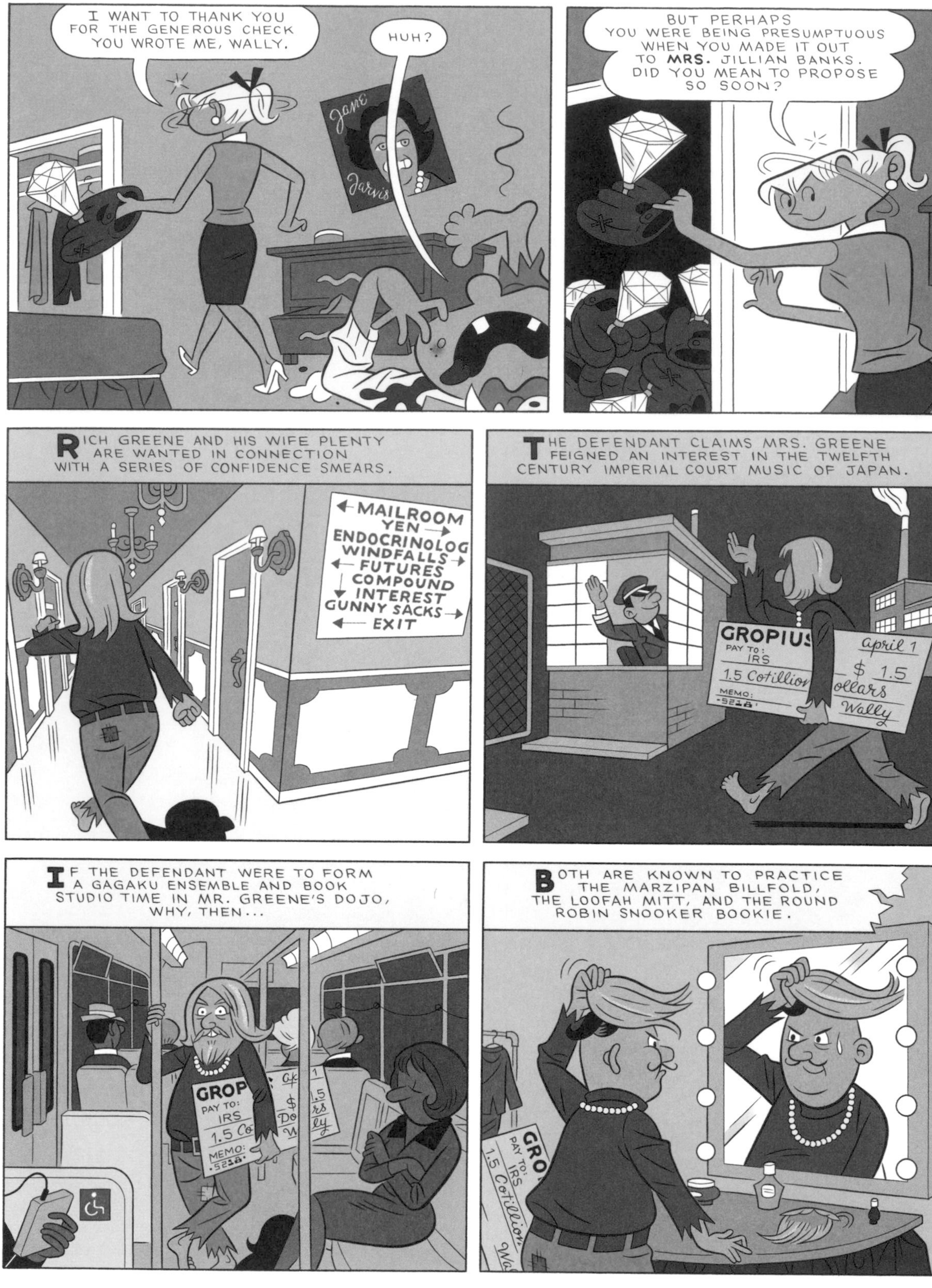
I WANT TO THANK YOU FOR THE GENEROUS CHECK YOU WROTE ME, WALLY.
HUH?
Jane Jarvis
BUT PERHAPS YOU WERE BEING PRESUMPTUOUS WHEN YOU MADE IT OUT TO **MRS.** JILLIAN BANKS. DID YOU MEAN TO PROPOSE SO SOON?
RICH GREENE AND HIS WIFE PLENTY ARE WANTED IN CONNECTION WITH A SERIES OF CONFIDENCE SMEARS.
← MAILROOM
YEN →
ENDOCRINOLOG
← WINDFALLS →
← FUTURES
COMPOUND
INTEREST
GUNNY SACKS →
← EXIT
THE DEFENDANT CLAIMS MRS. GREENE FEIGNED AN INTEREST IN THE TWELFTH CENTURY IMPERIAL COURT MUSIC OF JAPAN.
GROPIUS
PAY TO: IRS
1.5 Cotillion Dollars
MEMO: 5218
April 1
$ 1.5
Wally
IF THE DEFENDANT WERE TO FORM A GAGAKU ENSEMBLE AND BOOK STUDIO TIME IN MR. GREENE'S DOJO, WHY, THEN...
BOTH ARE KNOWN TO PRACTICE THE MARZIPAN BILLFOLD, THE LOOFAH MITT, AND THE ROUND ROBIN SNOOKER BOOKIE.

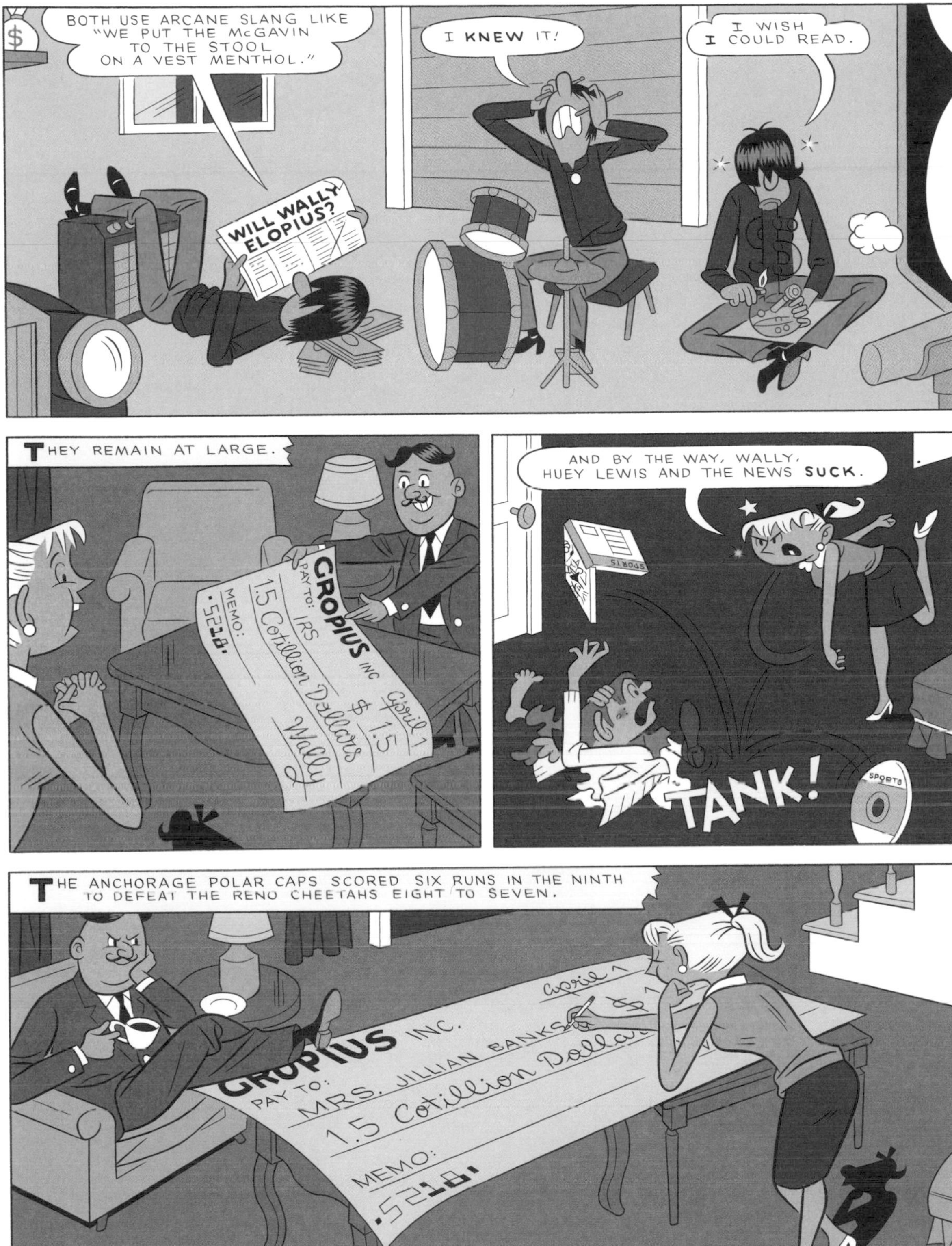
BOTH USE ARCANE SLANG LIKE "WE PUT THE McGAVIN TO THE STOOL ON A VEST MENTHOL."
WILL WALLY ELOPIUS?
I KNEW IT!
I WISH I COULD READ.
THEY REMAIN AT LARGE.
GROPIUS INC
PAY TO: IRS
April 1
$ 1.5
1.5 Cotillion Dollars
MEMO: .5218.
Wally
AND BY THE WAY, WALLY, HUEY LEWIS AND THE NEWS SUCK.
SPORTS
TANK!
THE ANCHORAGE POLAR CAPS SCORED SIX RUNS IN THE NINTH TO DEFEAT THE RENO CHEETAHS EIGHT TO SEVEN.
GROPIUS INC.
PAY TO: MRS. JILLIAN BANKS
April 1
1.5 Cotillion Dollar
MEMO: .5218.

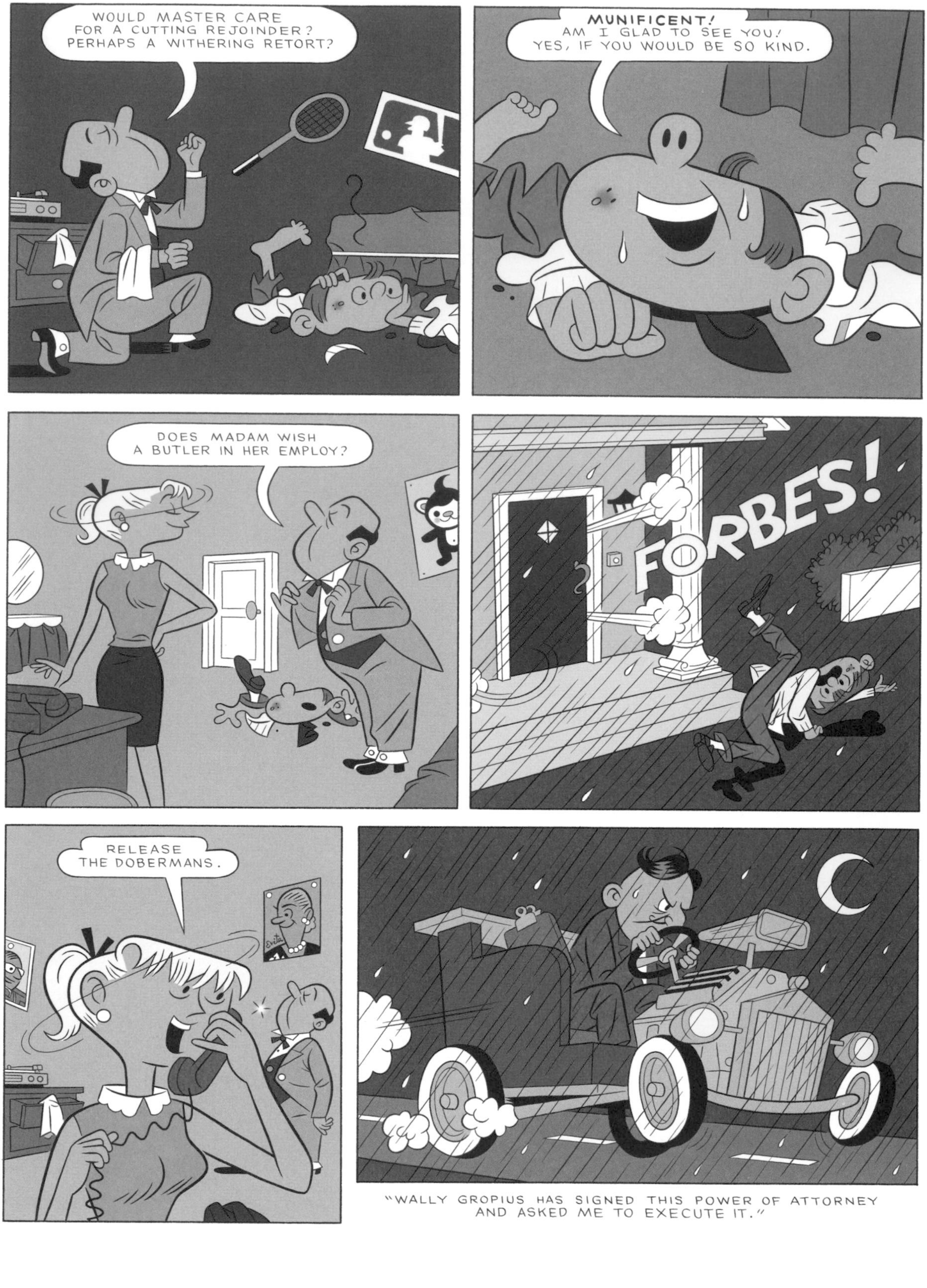
WOULD MASTER CARE FOR A CUTTING REJOINDER? PERHAPS A WITHERING RETORT?
MUNIFICENT! AM I GLAD TO SEE YOU! YES, IF YOU WOULD BE SO KIND.
DOES MADAM WISH A BUTLER IN HER EMPLOY?
FORBES!
RELEASE THE DOBERMANS.
Evita
"WALLY GROPIUS HAS SIGNED THIS POWER OF ATTORNEY AND ASKED ME TO EXECUTE IT."

"GROPIUS BESIEGED"

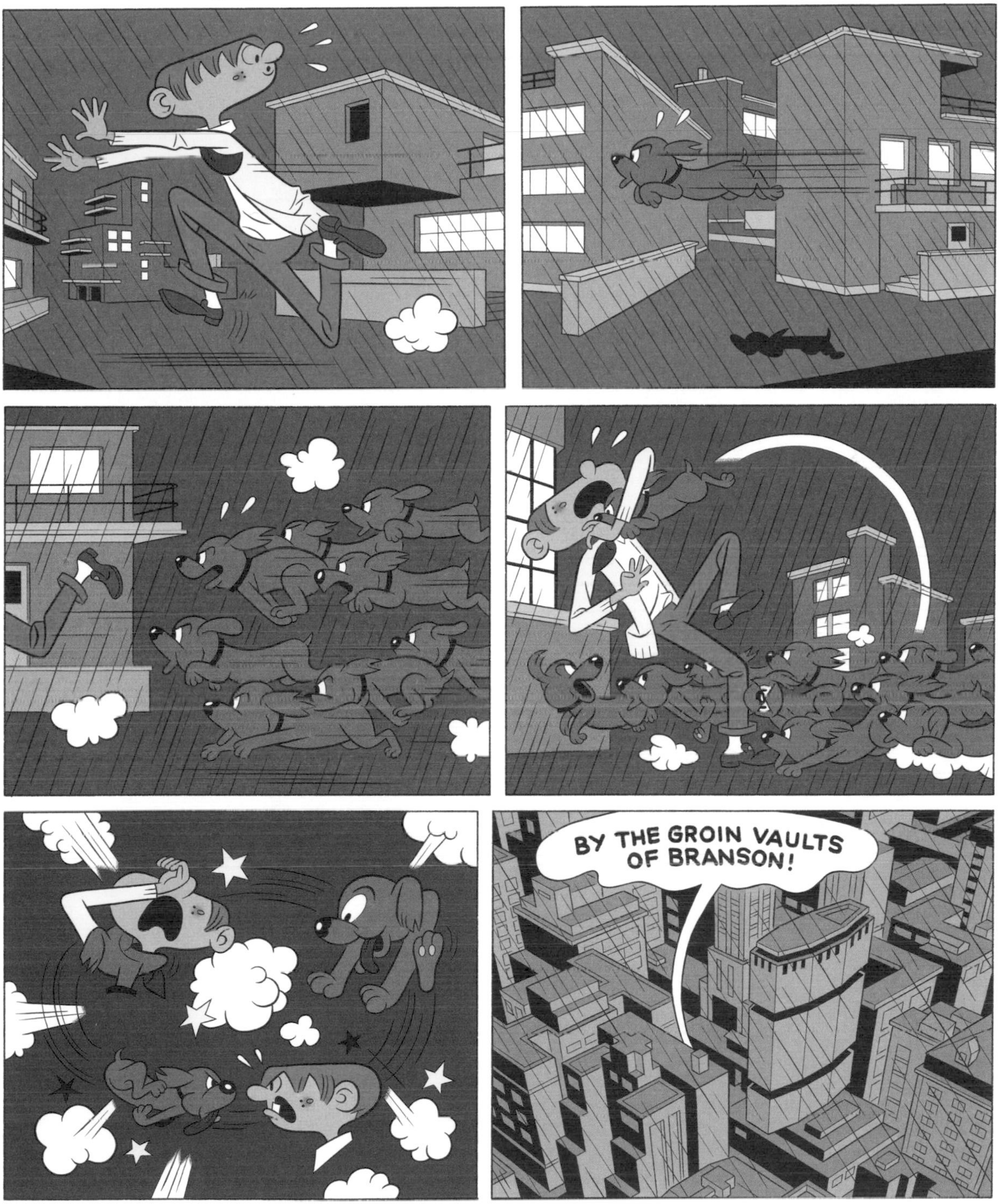
BY THE GROIN VAULTS OF BRANSON!

Nondenominational

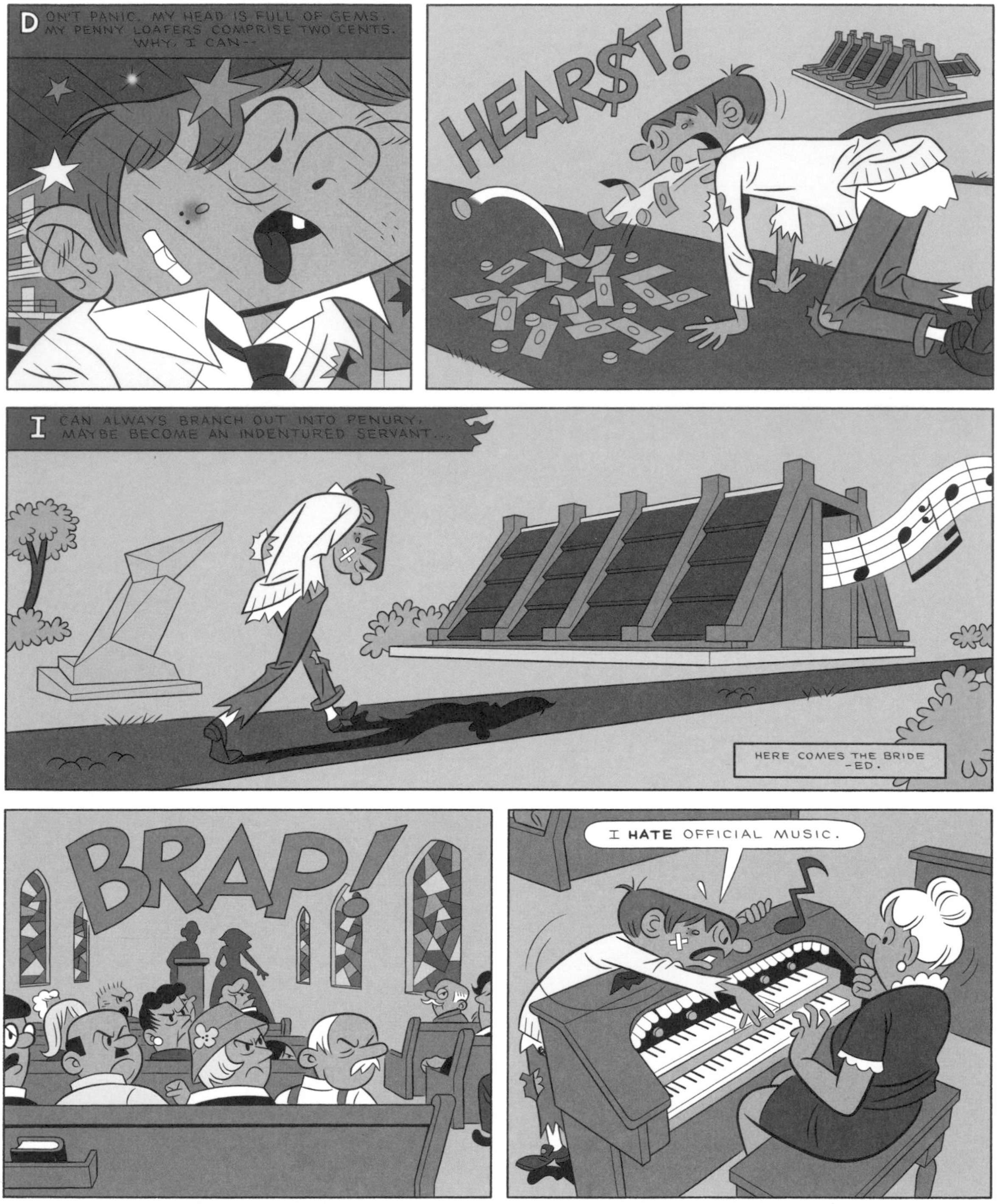

DON'T PANIC. MY HEAD IS FULL OF GEMS. MY PENNY LOAFERS COMPRISE TWO CENTS. WHY, I CAN--
HEAR$T!
I CAN ALWAYS BRANCH OUT INTO PENURY, MAYBE BECOME AN INDENTURED SERVANT...
HERE COMES THE BRIDE -ED.
BRAP!
I HATE OFFICIAL MUSIC.

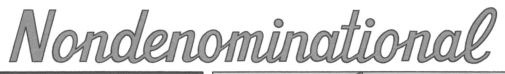

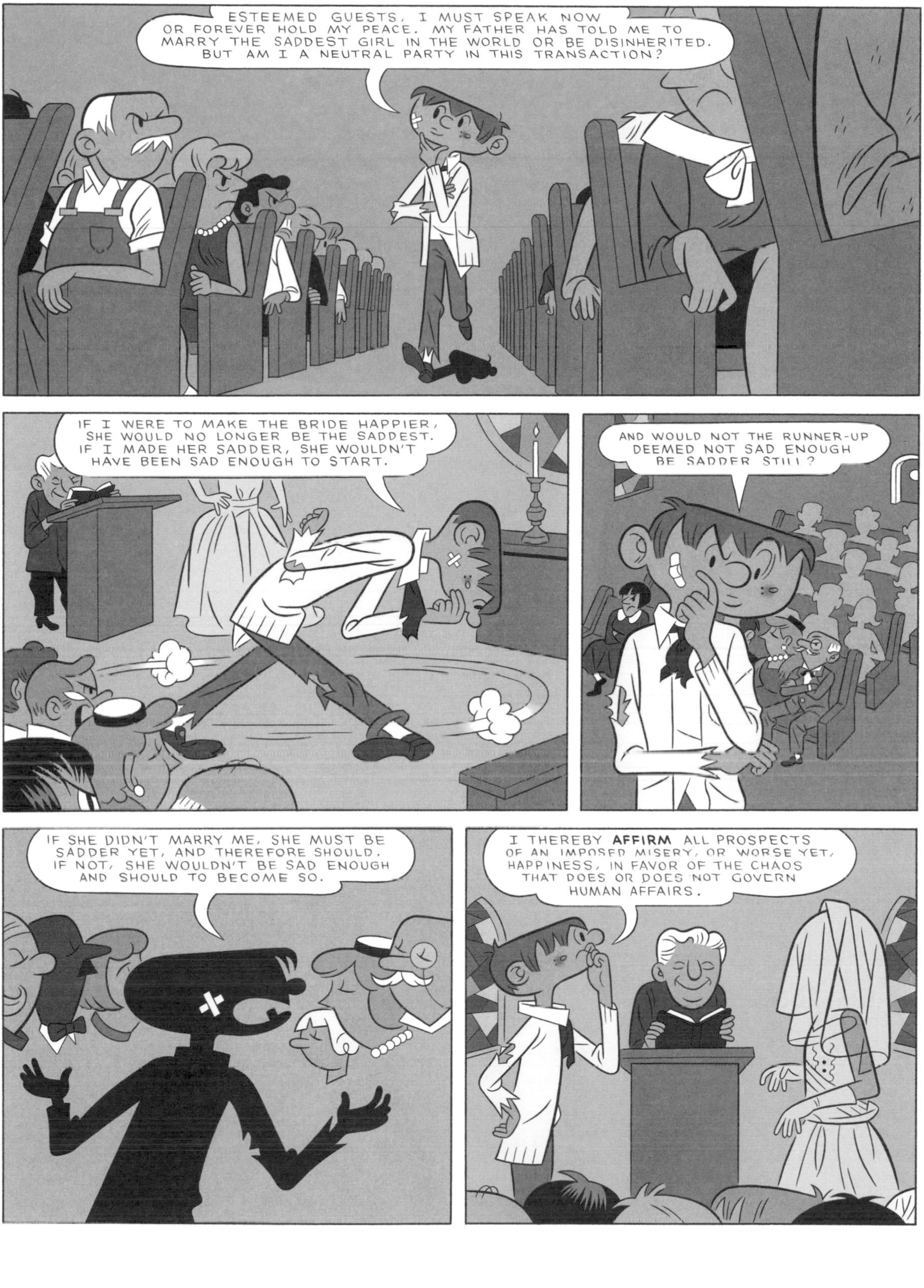
ESTEEMED GUESTS, I MUST SPEAK NOW OR FOREVER HOLD MY PEACE. MY FATHER HAS TOLD ME TO MARRY THE SADDEST GIRL IN THE WORLD OR BE DISINHERITED. BUT AM I A NEUTRAL PARTY IN THIS TRANSACTION?
IF I WERE TO MAKE THE BRIDE HAPPIER, SHE WOULD NO LONGER BE THE SADDEST. IF I MADE HER SADDER, SHE WOULDN'T HAVE BEEN SAD ENOUGH TO START.
AND WOULD NOT THE RUNNER-UP DEEMED NOT SAD ENOUGH BE SADDER STILL?
IF SHE DIDN'T MARRY ME, SHE MUST BE SADDER YET, AND THEREFORE SHOULD. IF NOT, SHE WOULDN'T BE SAD ENOUGH AND SHOULD TO BECOME SO.
I THEREBY **AFFIRM** ALL PROSPECTS OF AN IMPOSED MISERY, OR WORSE YET, HAPPINESS, IN FAVOR OF THE CHAOS THAT DOES OR DOES NOT GOVERN HUMAN AFFAIRS.

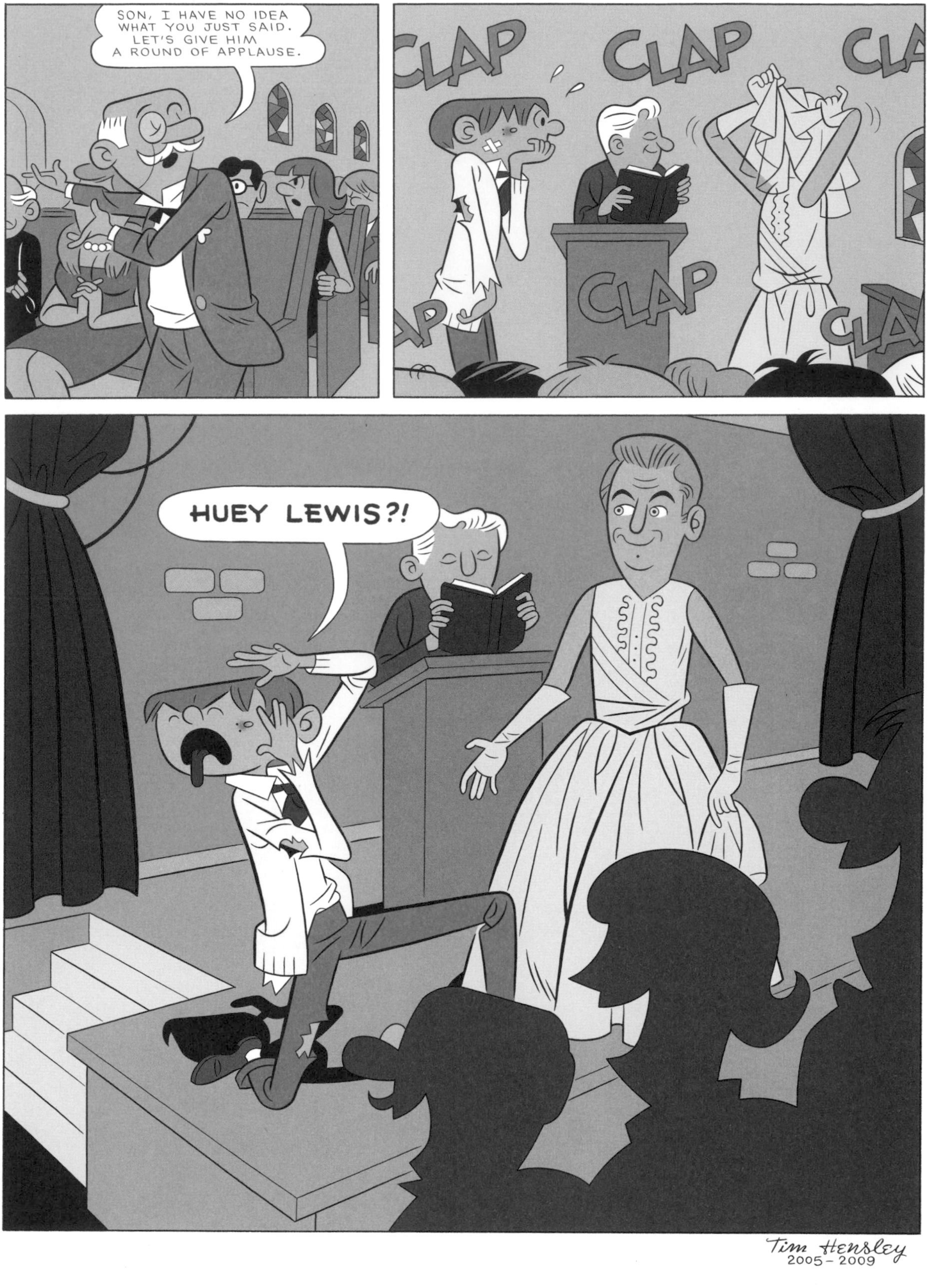
SON, I HAVE NO IDEA WHAT YOU JUST SAID. LET'S GIVE HIM A ROUND OF APPLAUSE.
CLAP
CLAP
CLA
CLAP
CLAP
CLA
HUEY LEWIS?!

Tim Hensley
2005–2009

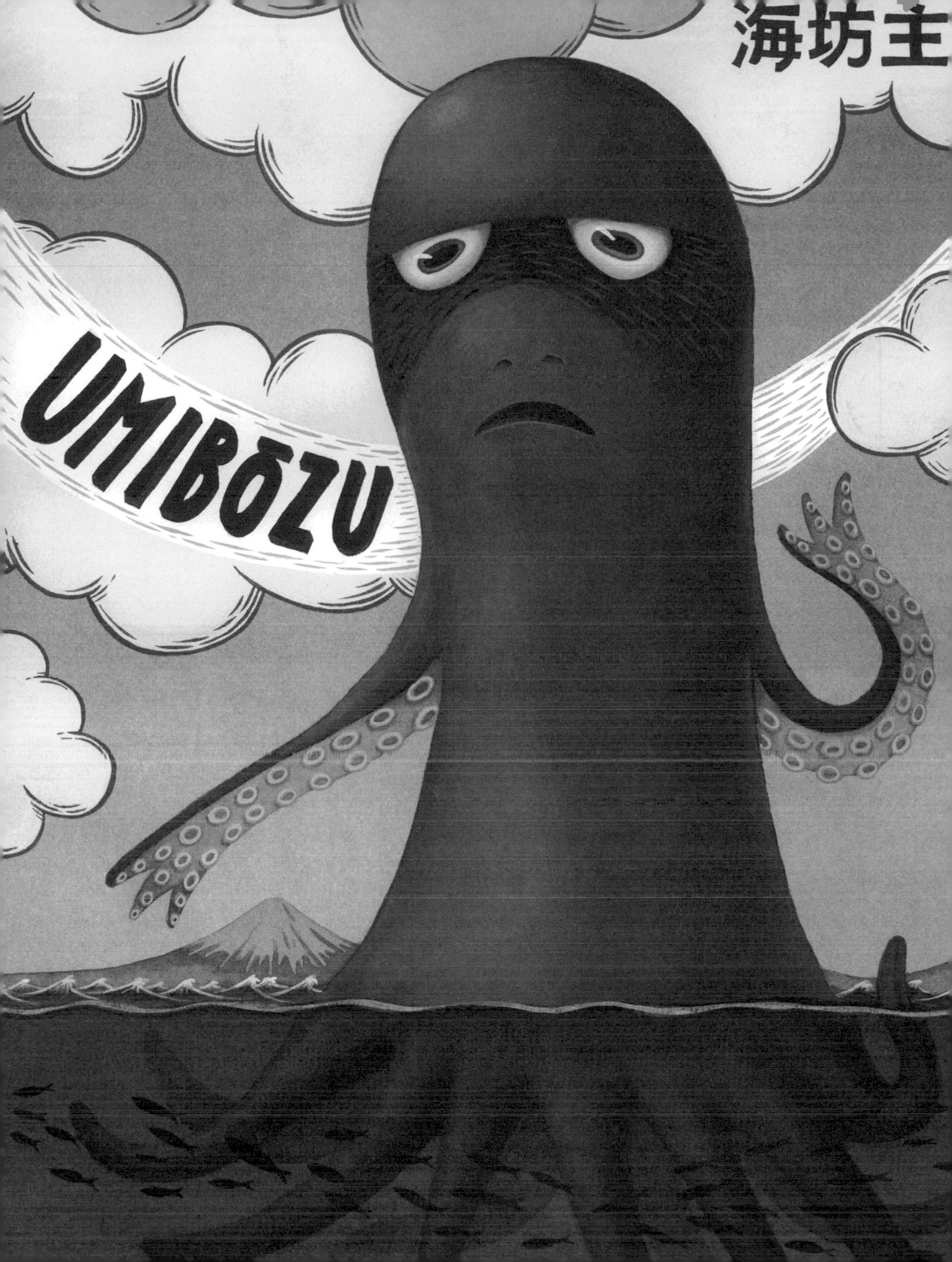
海坊主
UMIBŌZU

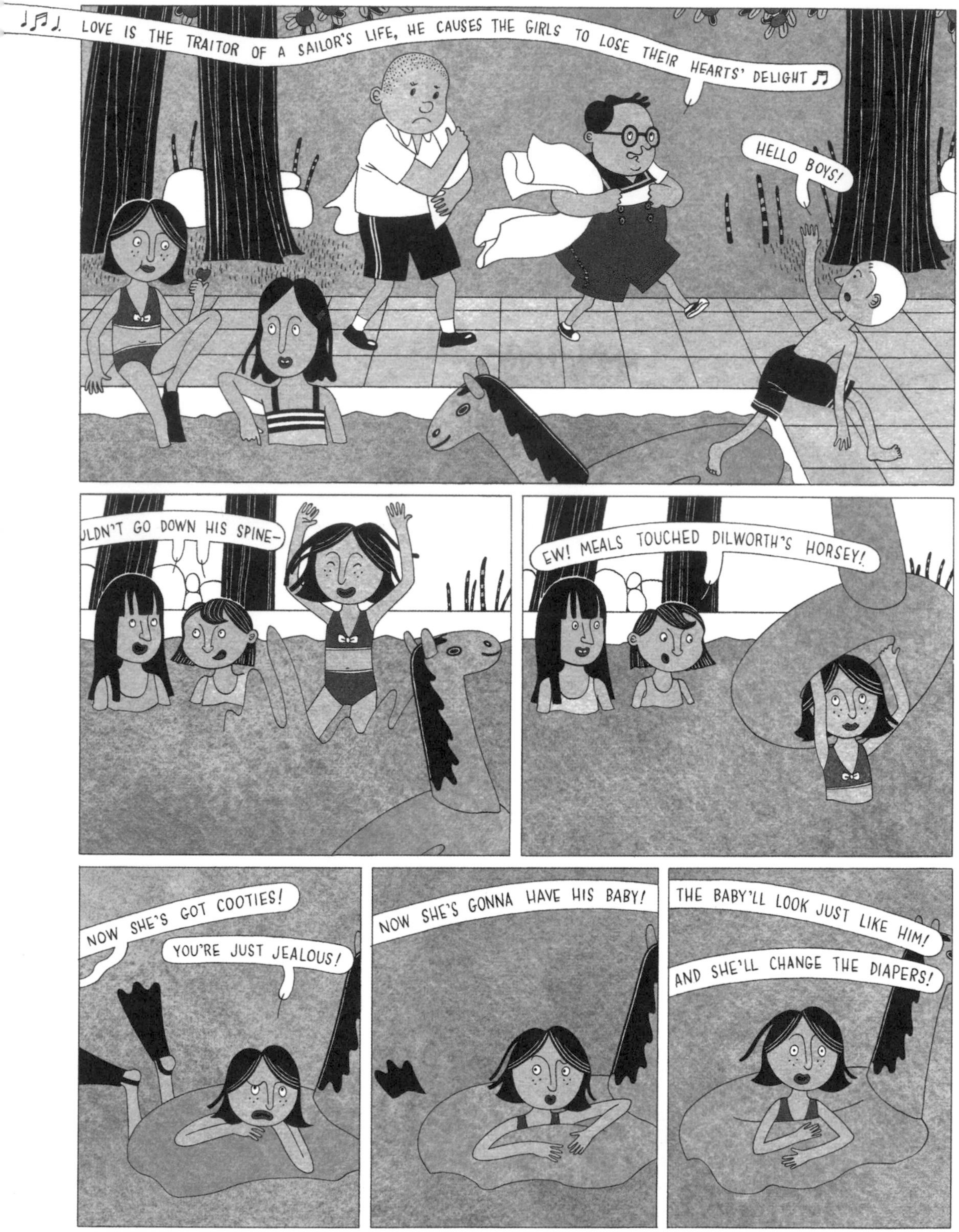
♩♬♩. LOVE IS THE TRAITOR OF A SAILOR'S LIFE, HE CAUSES THE GIRLS TO LOSE THEIR HEARTS' DELIGHT ♬
HELLO BOYS!
ULDN'T GO DOWN HIS SPINE-
EW! MEALS TOUCHED DILWORTH'S HORSEY!
NOW SHE'S GOT COOTIES!
YOU'RE JUST JEALOUS!
NOW SHE'S GONNA HAVE HIS BABY!
THE BABY'LL LOOK JUST LIKE HIM!
AND SHE'LL CHANGE THE DIAPERS!

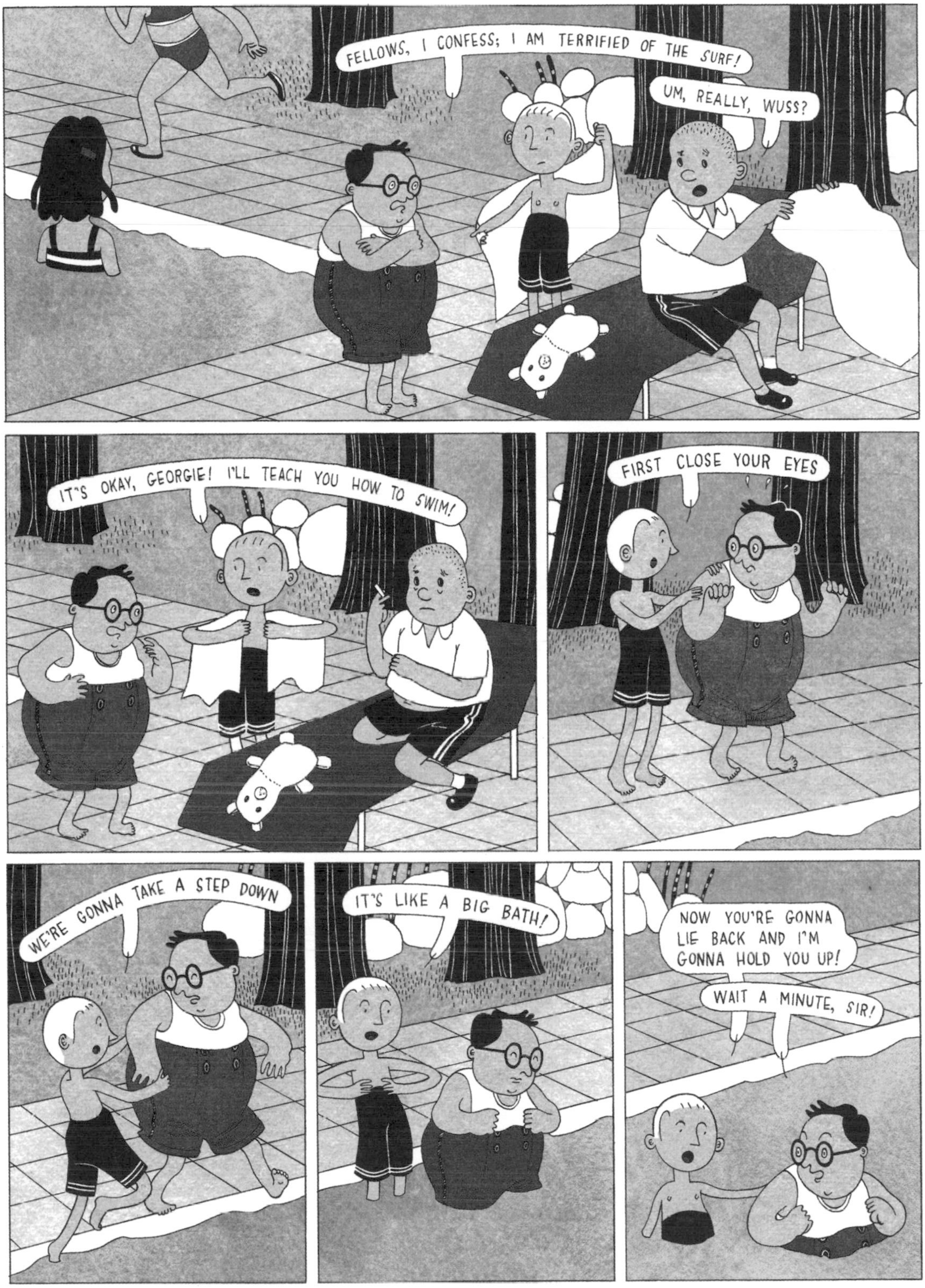
FELLOWS, I CONFESS; I AM TERRIFIED OF THE SURF!
UM, REALLY, WUSS?
IT'S OKAY, GEORGIE! I'LL TEACH YOU HOW TO SWIM!
FIRST CLOSE YOUR EYES
WE'RE GONNA TAKE A STEP DOWN
IT'S LIKE A BIG BATH!
NOW YOU'RE GONNA LIE BACK AND I'M GONNA HOLD YOU UP!
WAIT A MINUTE, SIR!

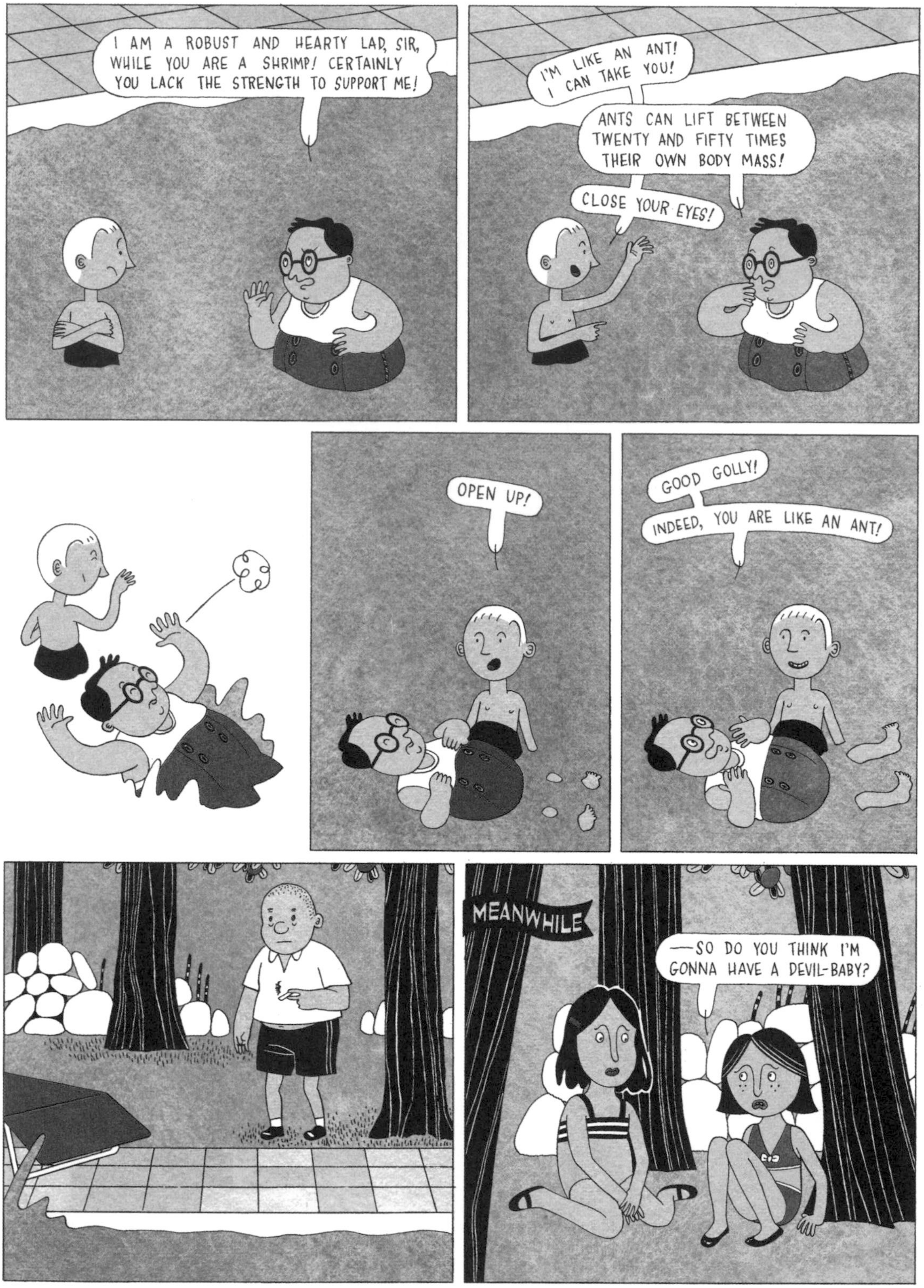
I AM A ROBUST AND HEARTY LAD, SIR, WHILE YOU ARE A SHRIMP! CERTAINLY YOU LACK THE STRENGTH TO SUPPORT ME!
I'M LIKE AN ANT! I CAN TAKE YOU!
ANTS CAN LIFT BETWEEN TWENTY AND FIFTY TIMES THEIR OWN BODY MASS!
CLOSE YOUR EYES!
OPEN UP!
GOOD GOLLY!
INDEED, YOU ARE LIKE AN ANT!
MEANWHILE
—SO DO YOU THINK I'M GONNA HAVE A DEVIL-BABY?

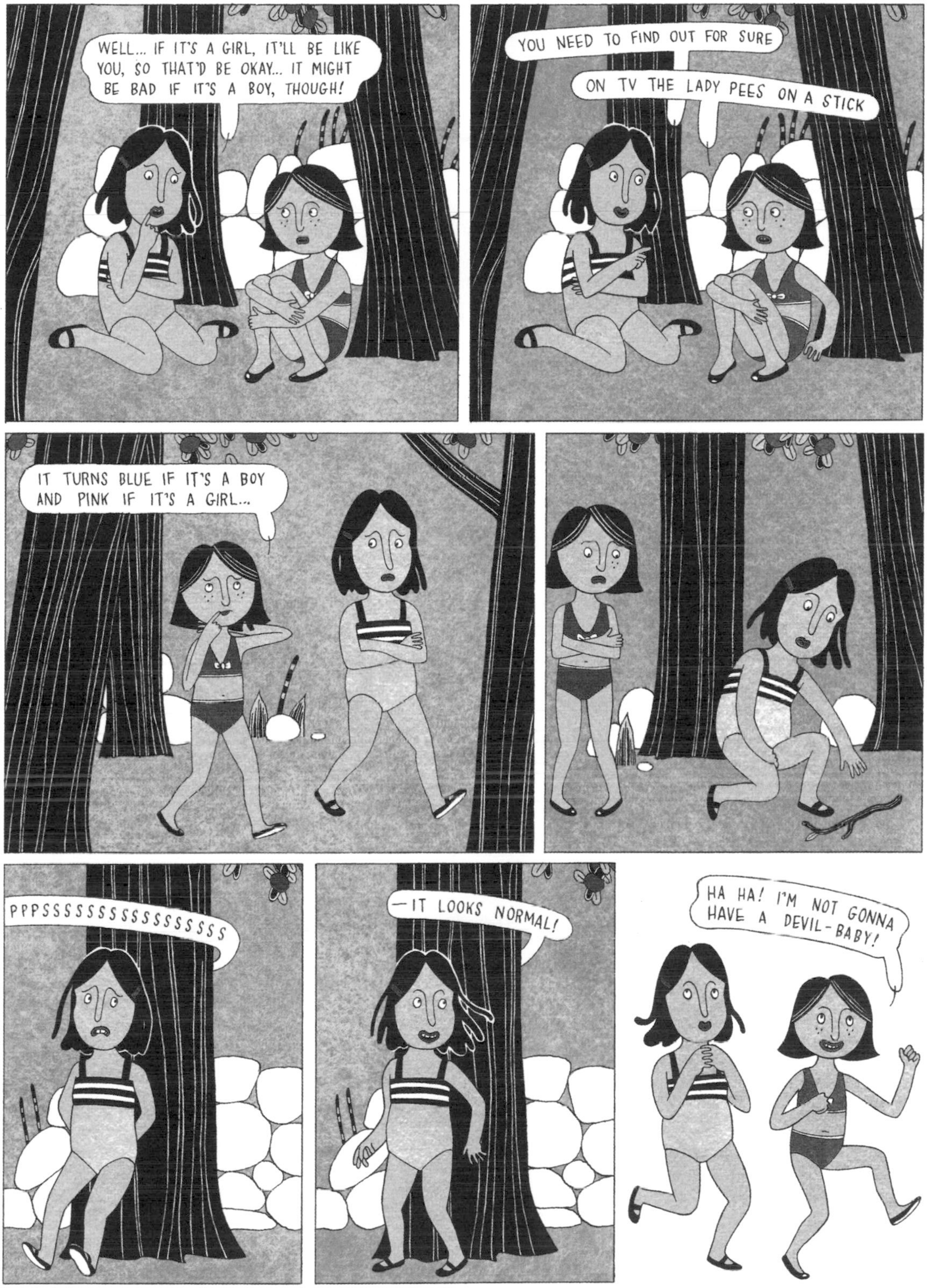
WELL... IF IT'S A GIRL, IT'LL BE LIKE YOU, SO THAT'D BE OKAY... IT MIGHT BE BAD IF IT'S A BOY, THOUGH!
YOU NEED TO FIND OUT FOR SURE
ON TV THE LADY PEES ON A STICK
IT TURNS BLUE IF IT'S A BOY AND PINK IF IT'S A GIRL...
PPPSSSSSSSSSSSSSSSSSS
—IT LOOKS NORMAL!
HA HA! I'M NOT GONNA HAVE A DEVIL-BABY!

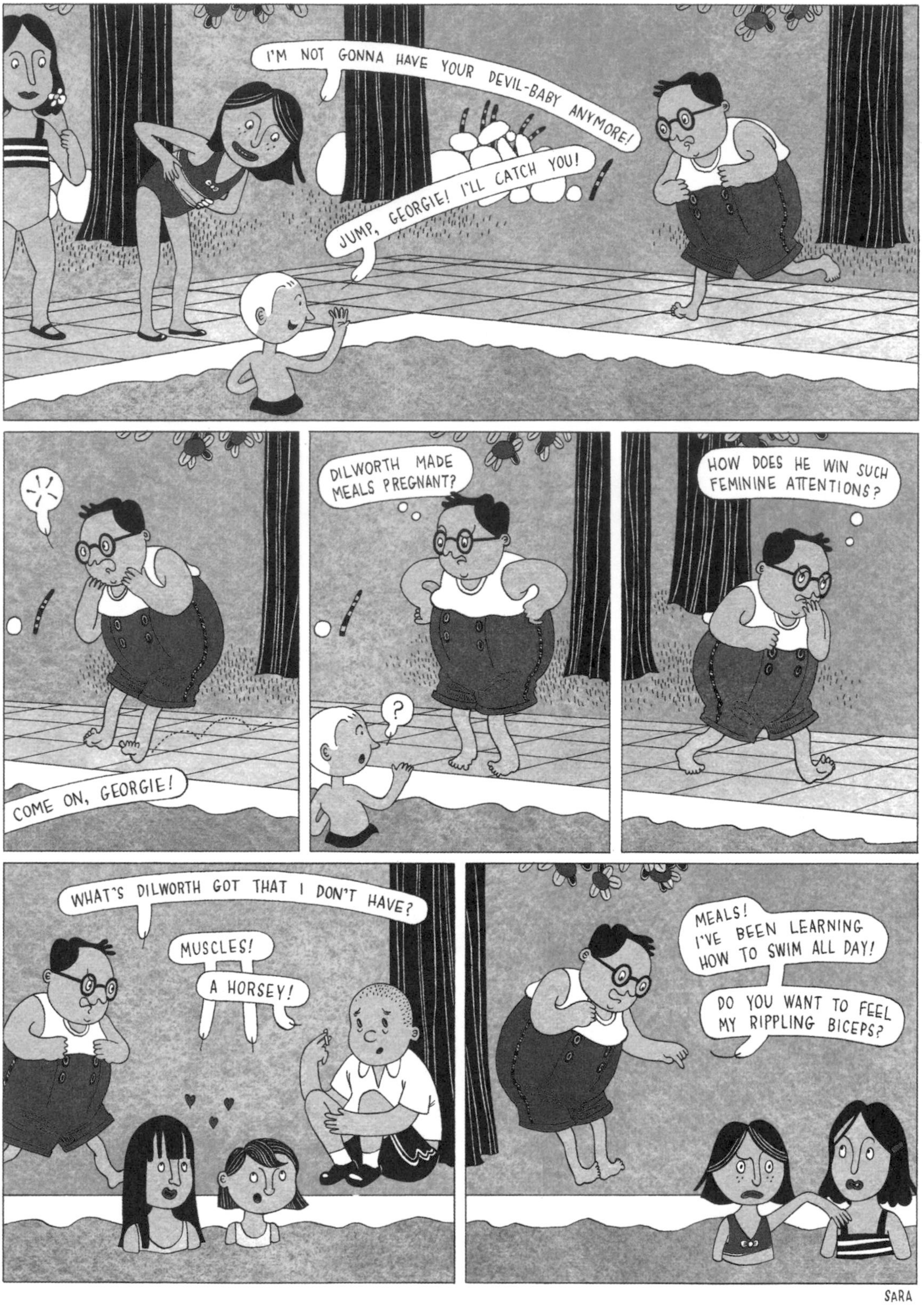
I'M NOT GONNA HAVE YOUR DEVIL-BABY ANYMORE!
JUMP, GEORGIE! I'LL CATCH YOU!
!
COME ON, GEORGIE!
DILWORTH MADE MEALS PREGNANT?
?
HOW DOES HE WIN SUCH FEMININE ATTENTIONS?
WHAT'S DILWORTH GOT THAT I DON'T HAVE?
MUSCLES!
A HORSEY!
MEALS! I'VE BEEN LEARNING HOW TO SWIM ALL DAY!
DO YOU WANT TO FEEL MY RIPPLING BICEPS?

SARA

How
I Do
It

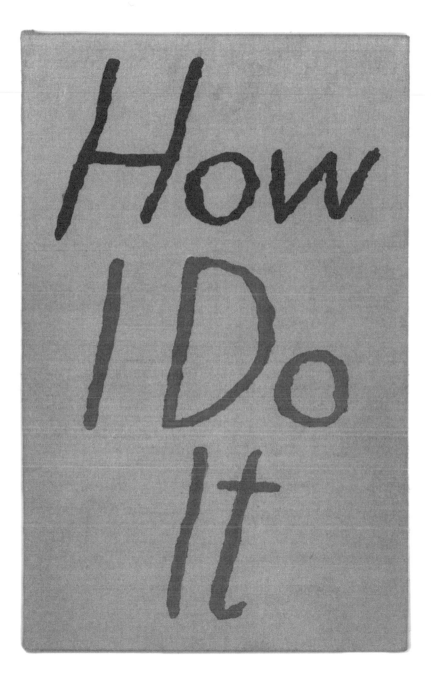

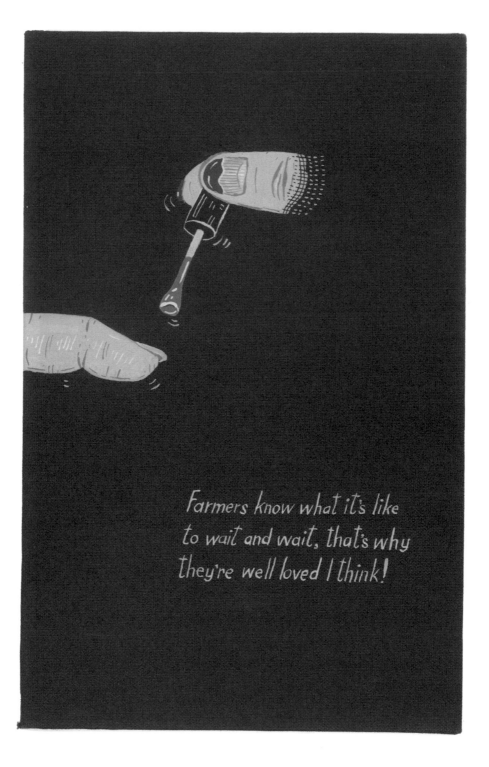

Farmers know what it's like
to wait and wait, that's why
they're well loved I think!

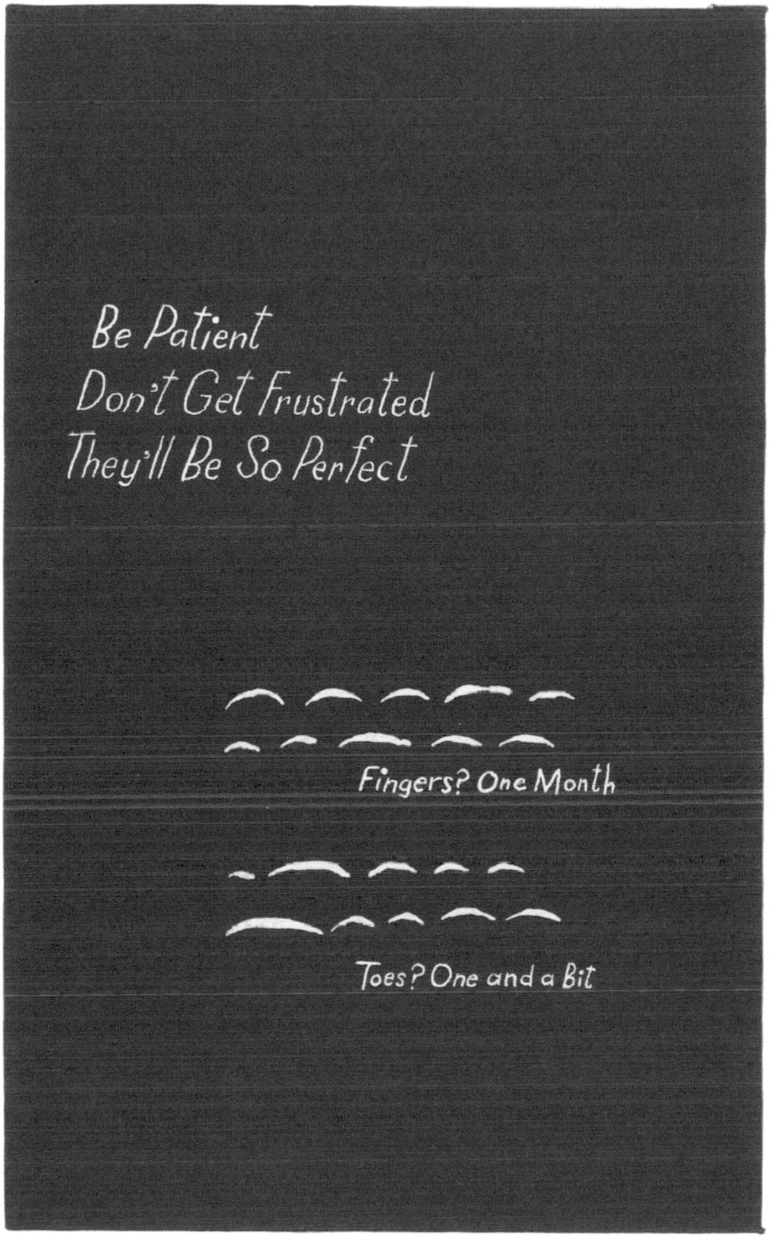
Be Patient
Don't Get Frustrated
They'll Be So Perfect
Fingers? One Month
Toes? One and a Bit

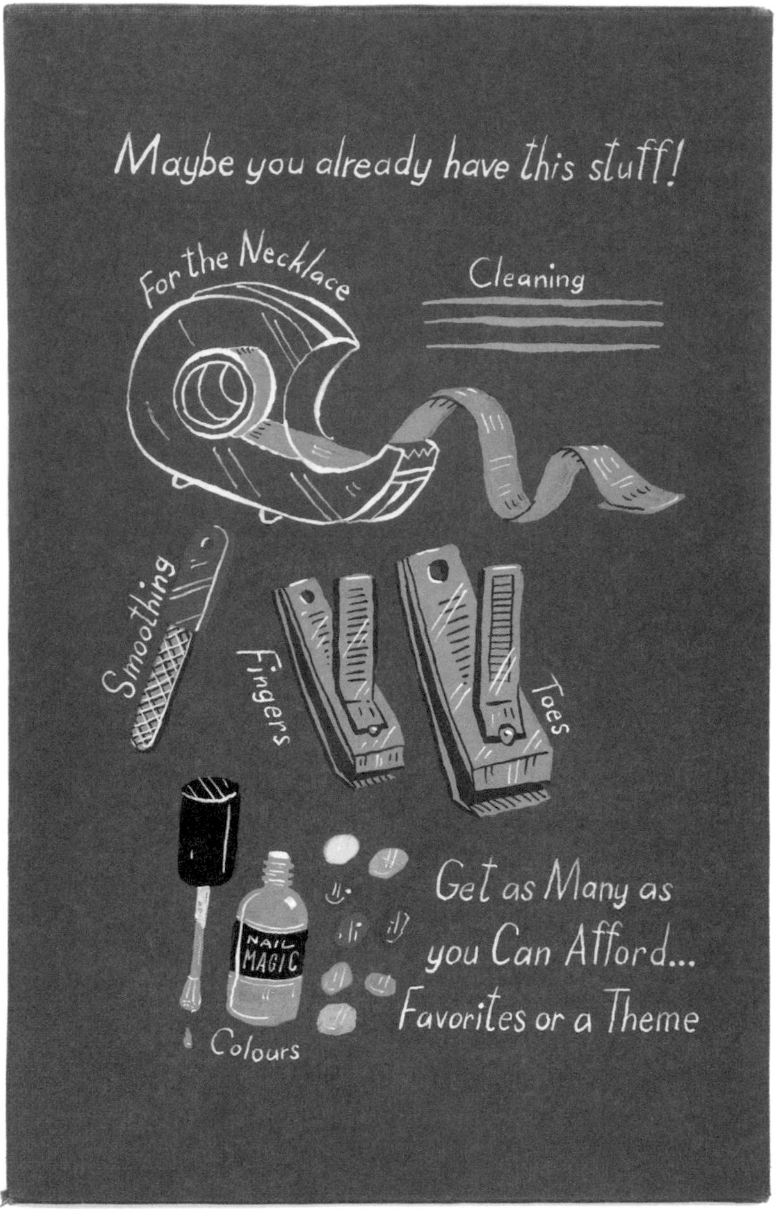
Maybe you already have this stuff!
For the Necklace
Cleaning
Smoothing
Fingers
Toes
NAIL MAGIC
Colours
Get as Many as
you Can Afford...
Favorites or a Theme

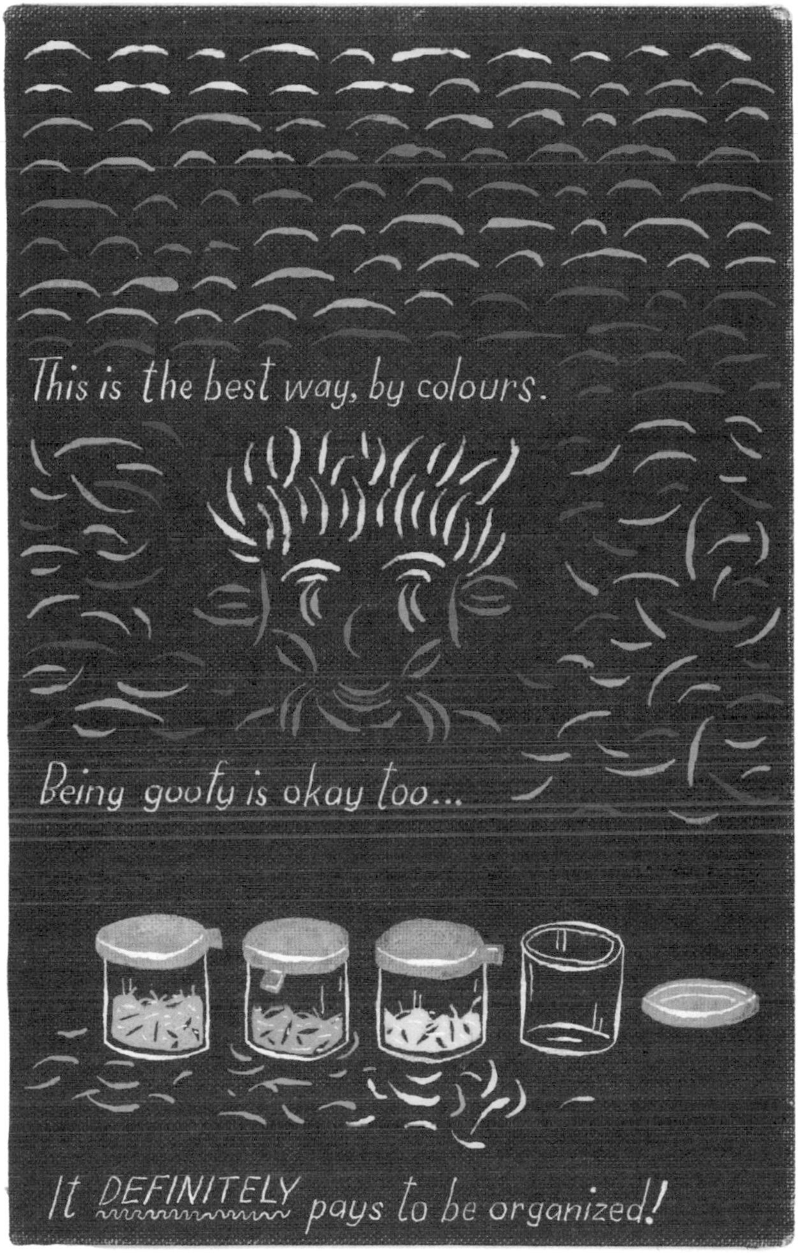
This is the best way, by colours.
Being goofy is okay too...
It DEFINITELY pays to be organized!

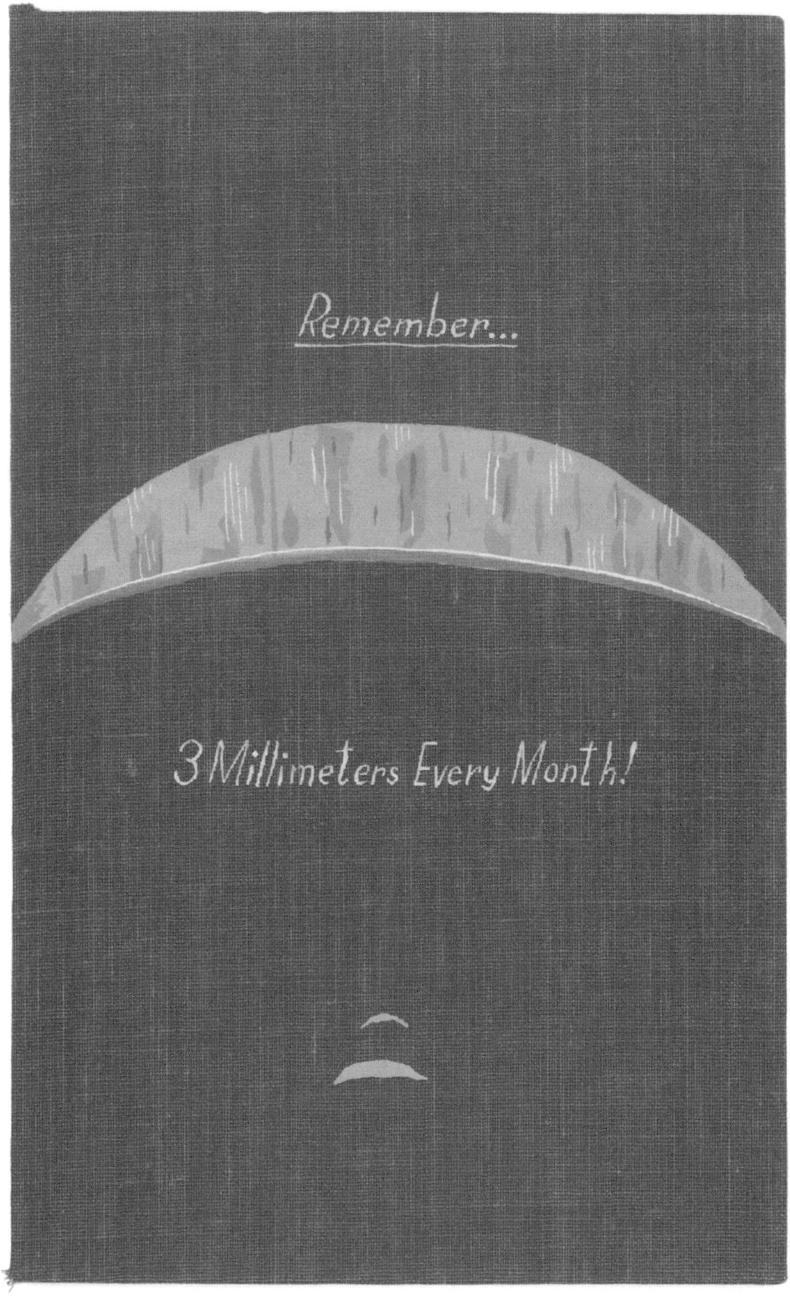
Remember...
3 Millimeters Every Month!

When you are Ready...

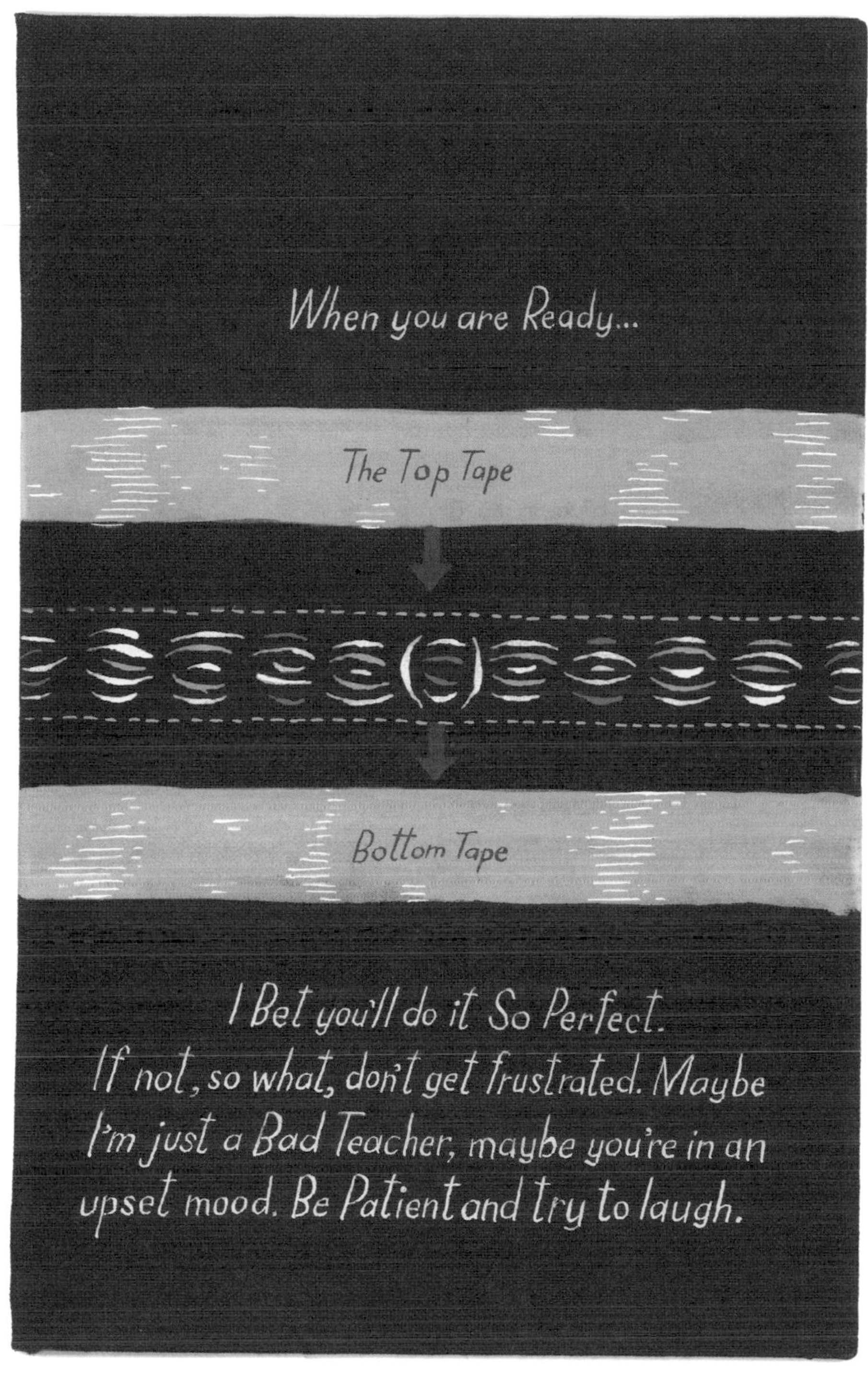
The Top Tape
Bottom Tape

I Bet you'll do it So Perfect.
If not, so what, don't get frustrated. Maybe I'm just a Bad Teacher, maybe you're in an upset mood. Be Patient and try to laugh.

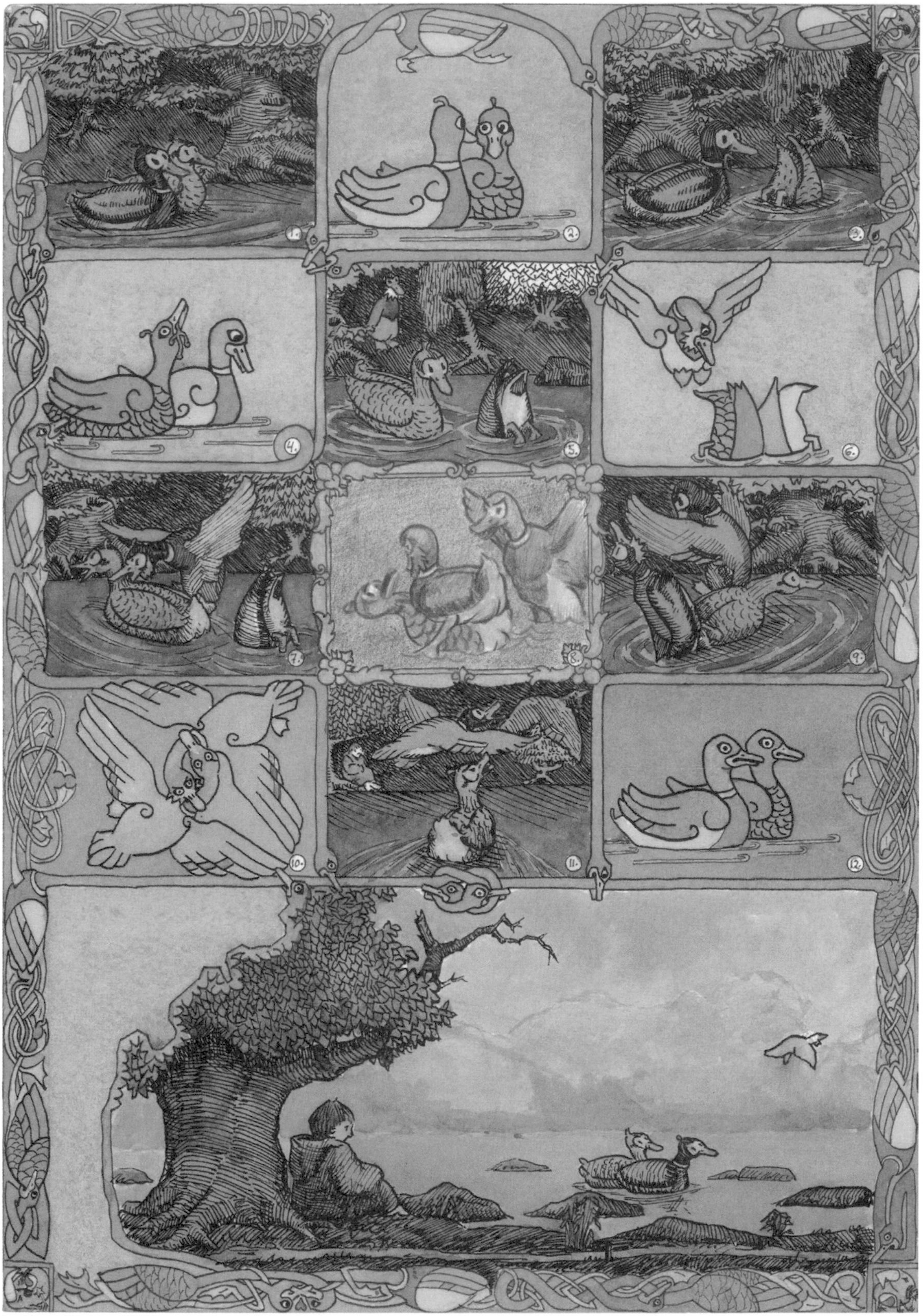

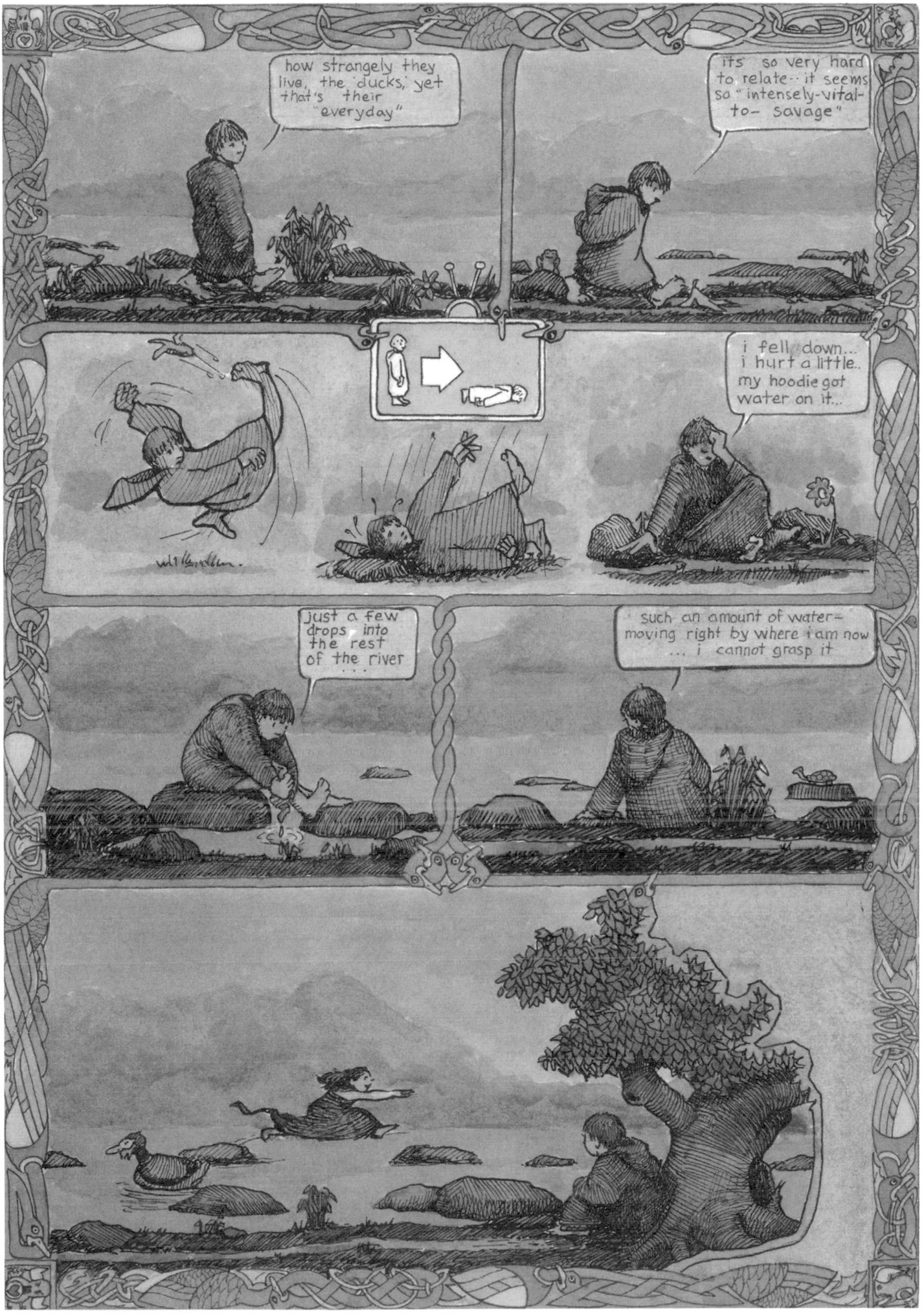

how strangely they live, the "ducks," yet that's their "everyday"
its so very hard to relate -- it seems so "intensely-vital-to- savage"
i fell down... i hurt a little.. my hoodie got water on it...
just a few drops into the rest of the river . . .
such an amount of water= moving right by where i am now ... i cannot grasp it

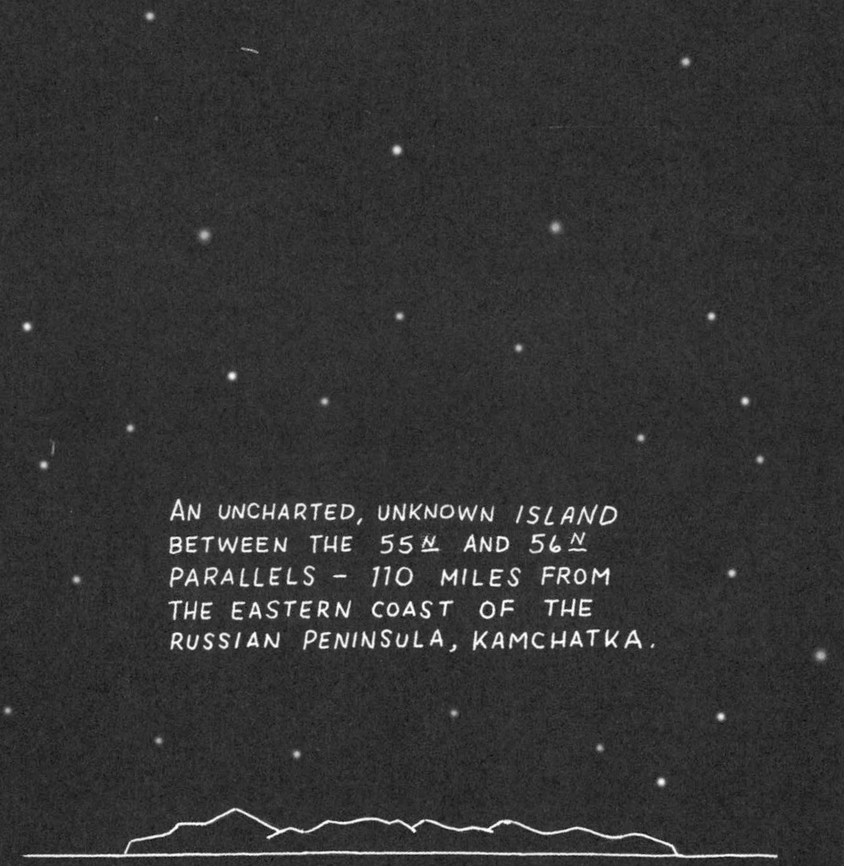
AN UNCHARTED, UNKNOWN ISLAND
BETWEEN THE 55N AND 56N
PARALLELS – 110 MILES FROM
THE EASTERN COAST OF THE
RUSSIAN PENINSULA, KAMCHATKA.

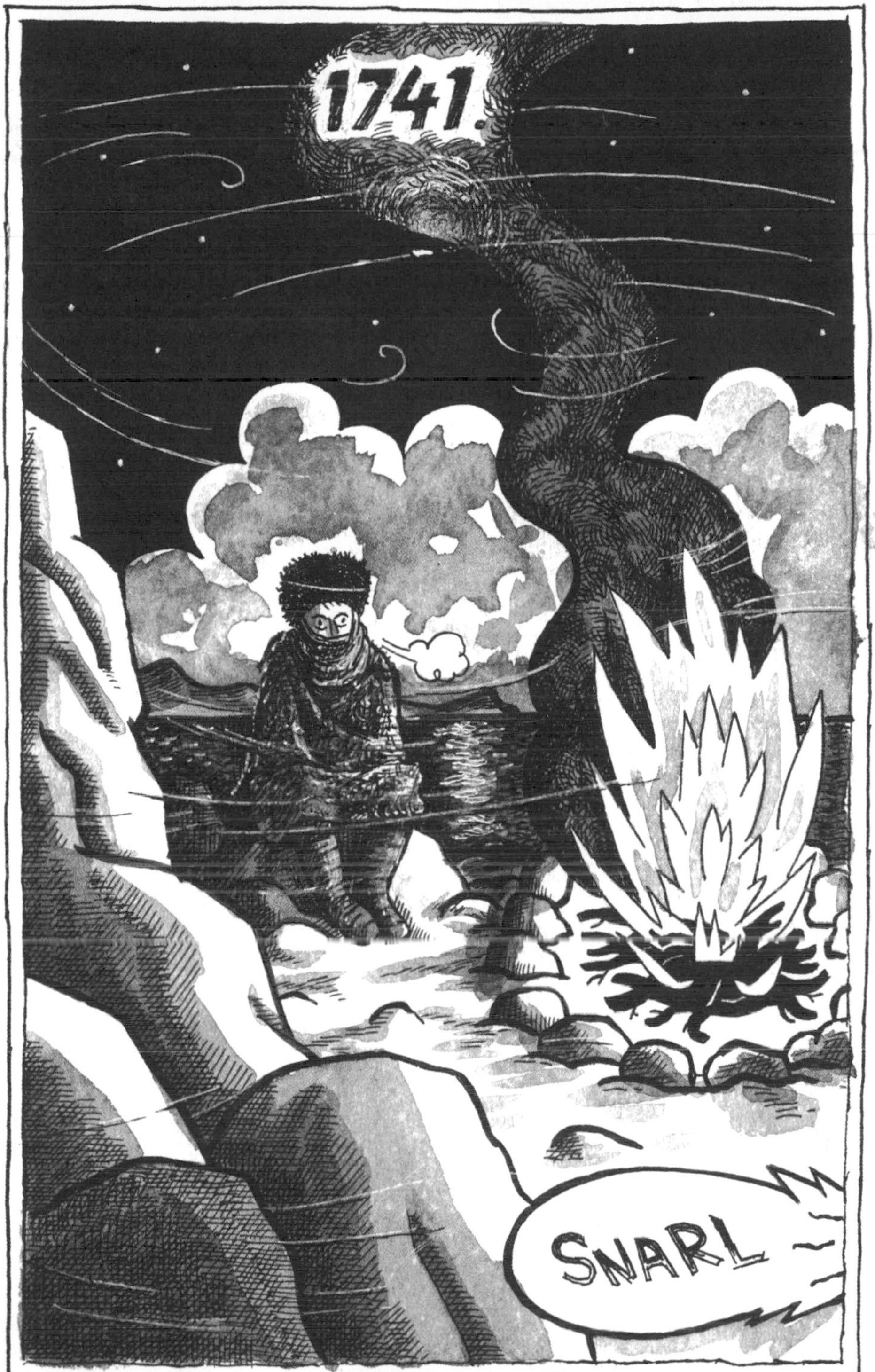
1741.
SNARL

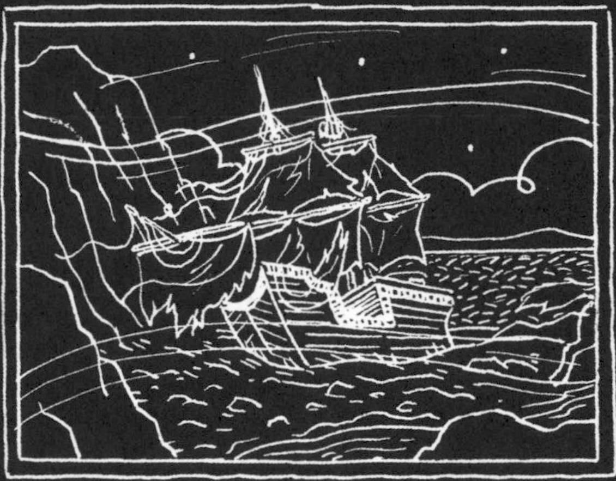

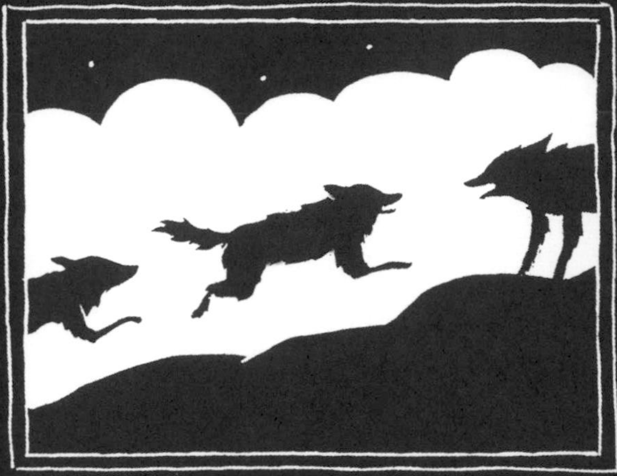

FLOGGED BY DECEMBER'S HOWLING ONSLAUGHT, THE CREW OF THE SHIPWRECKED ST. PETER WATCH HELPLESSLY AS SWARMS OF ARCTIC FOXES BESIEGE THEIR BROKEN, SCURVY-RAVAGED COMPANIONS.

BOOTS, LIMBS AND TONGUES ARE TORN FROM THE BODIES OF THE DEAD AND DYING.

FROZEN CORPSES ARE EXHUMED FROM THE BOSOM OF BURIAL OVERLOOKING THE DESOLATE SHORE.

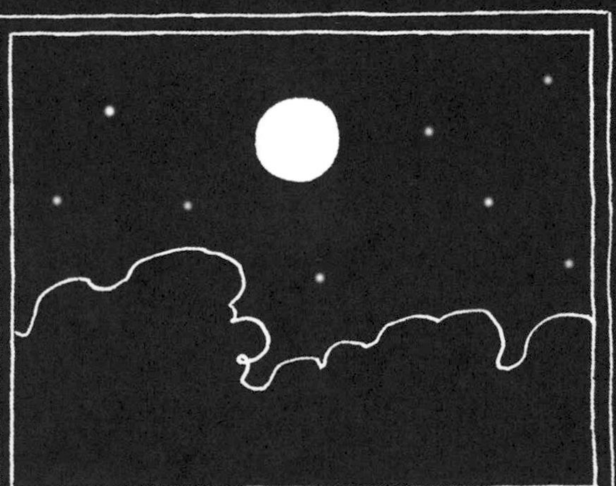

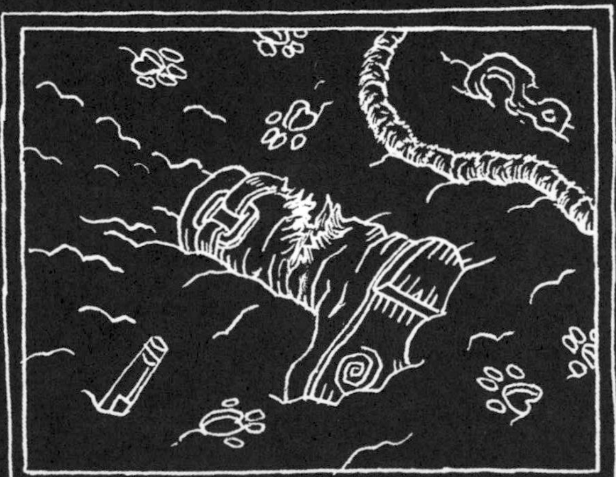

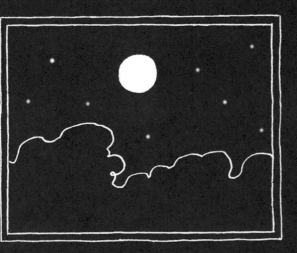

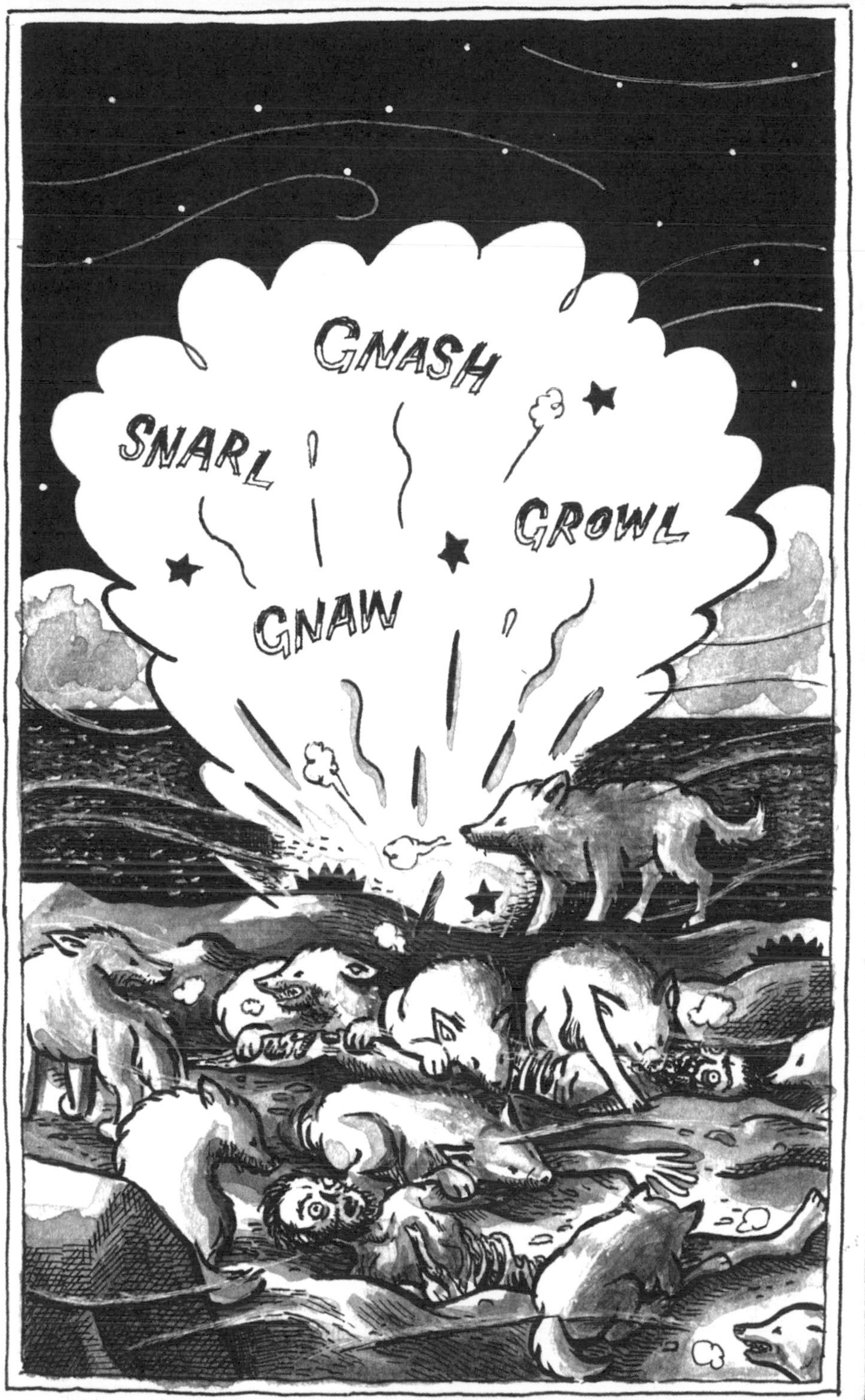
SNARL
GNASH
GROWL
GNAW

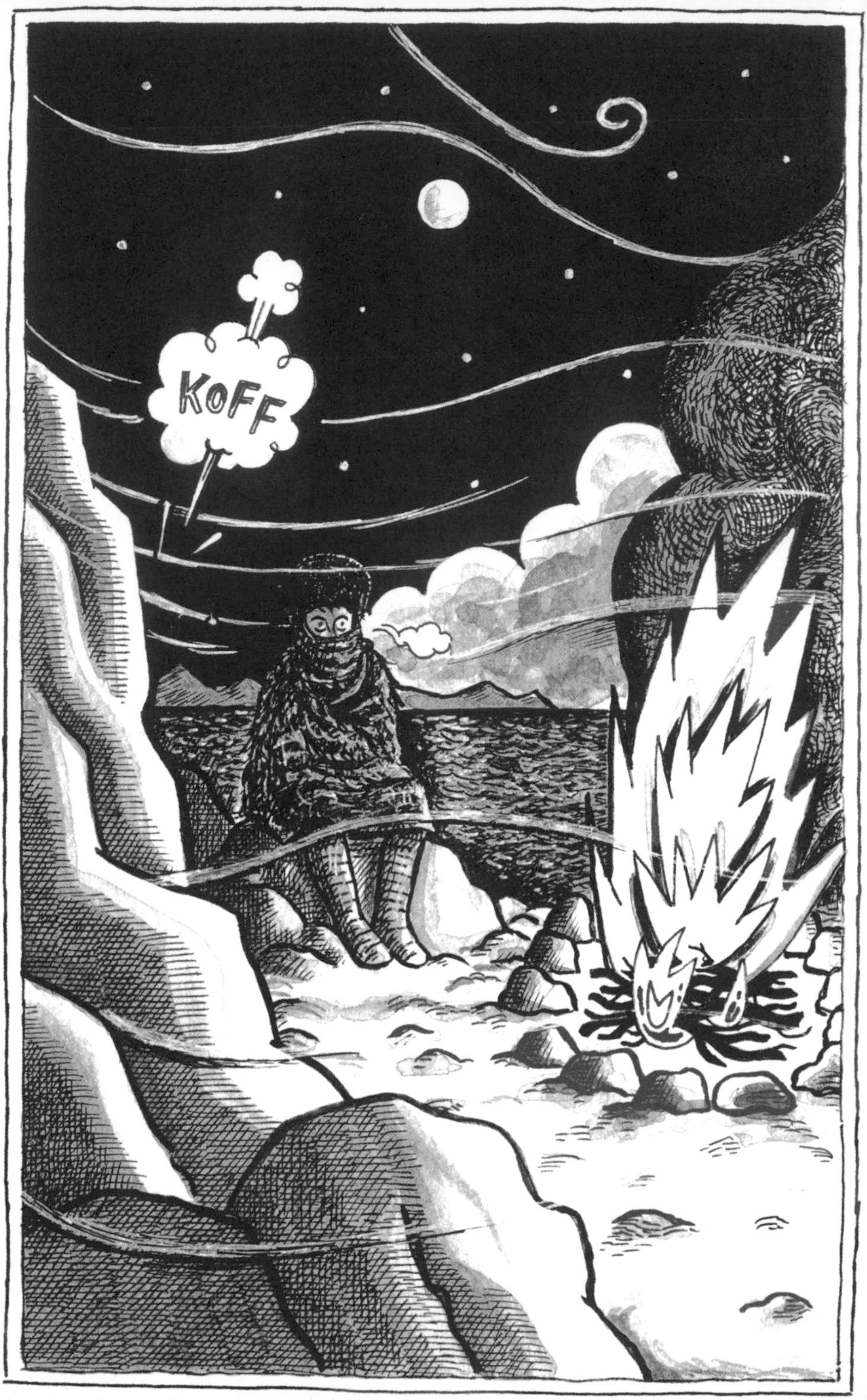
KOFF

GRIPPED BY THE FEVER OF DESPAIR, THE SURVIVORS SURRENDER TO FATE AND SETTLE INTO A MAKESHIFT ENCAMPMENT FOR THE LONG NORTH PACIFIC WINTER.

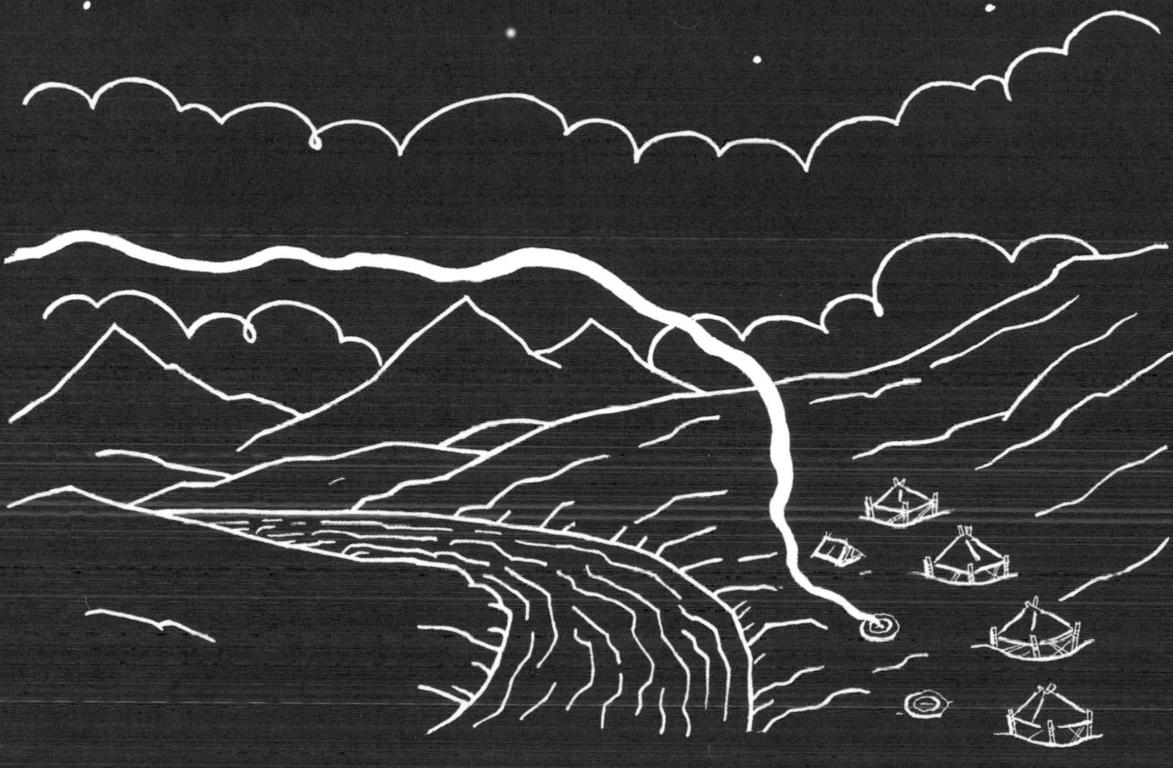

A JOURNAL ENTRY BY THE St. PETER'S MINERALOGIST AND NATURALIST — GEORG WILHELM STELLER — REVEALS THAT THEIR DIRE CIRCUMSTANCE DID NOT SOON IMPROVE:

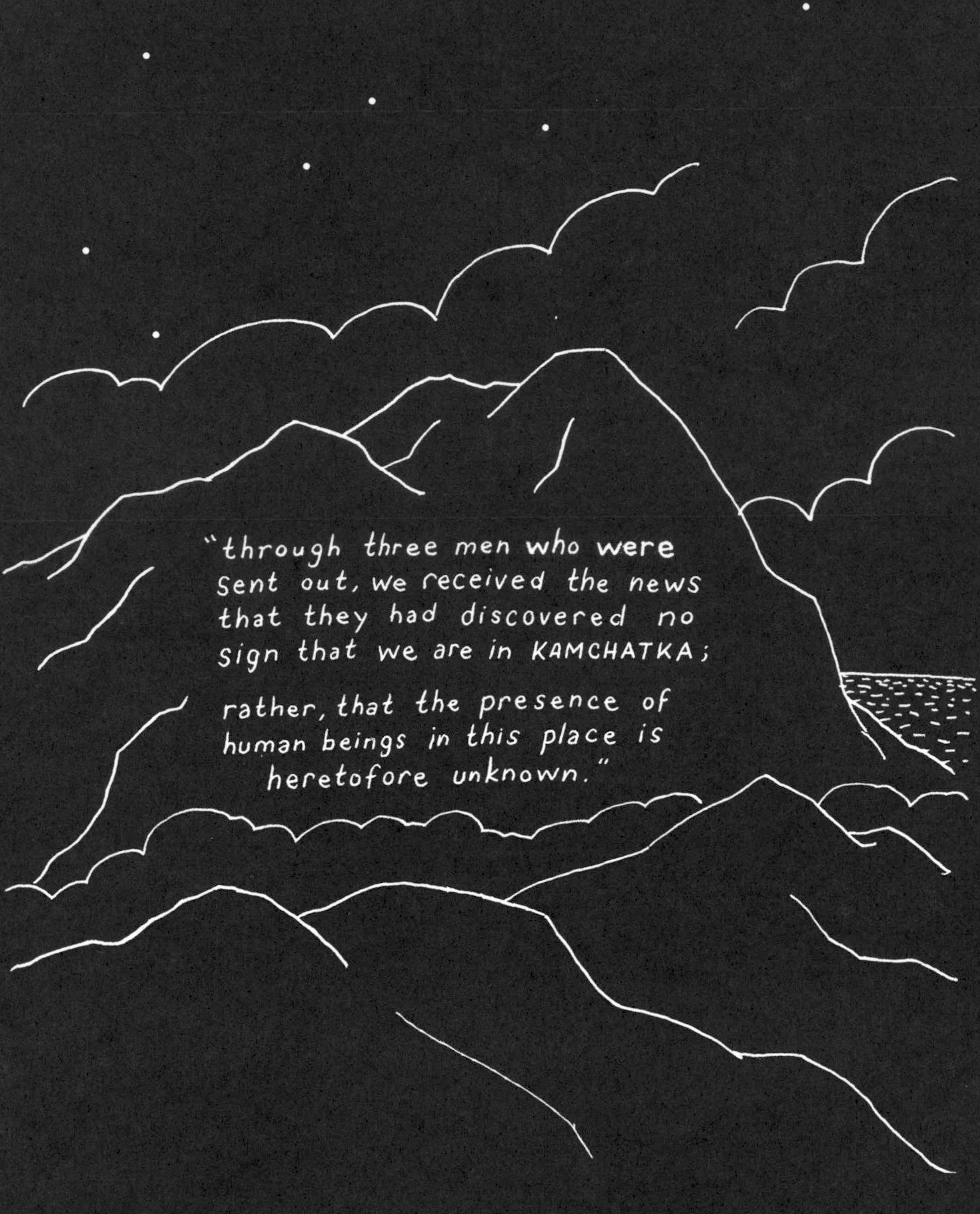
"through three men who were sent out, we received the news that they had discovered no sign that we are in KAMCHATKA;
rather, that the presence of human beings in this place is heretofore unknown."

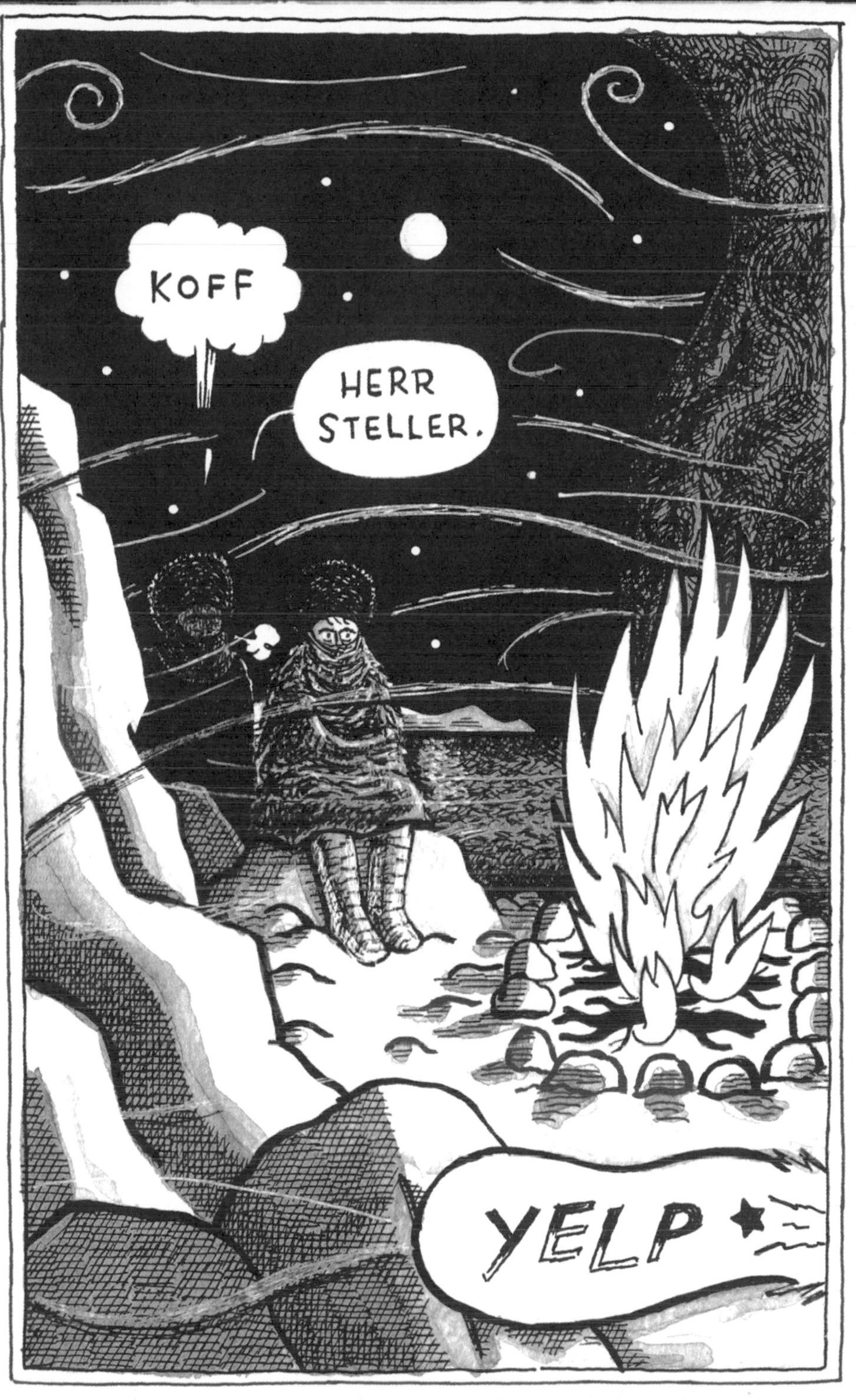
KOFF
HERR STELLER.
YELP

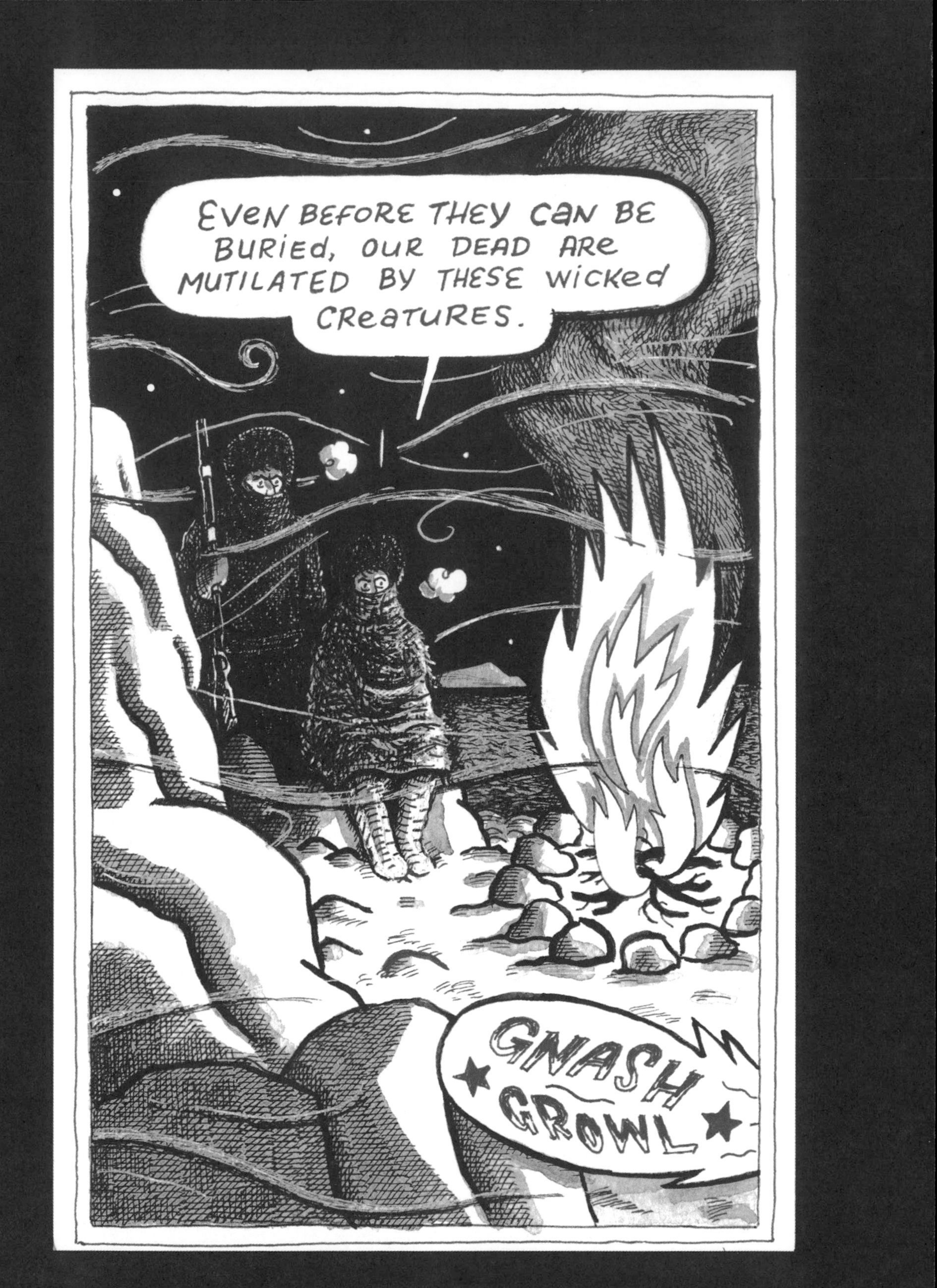
EVEN BEFORE THEY CAN BE BURIED, OUR DEAD ARE MUTILATED BY THESE WICKED CREATURES.
GNASH GROWL

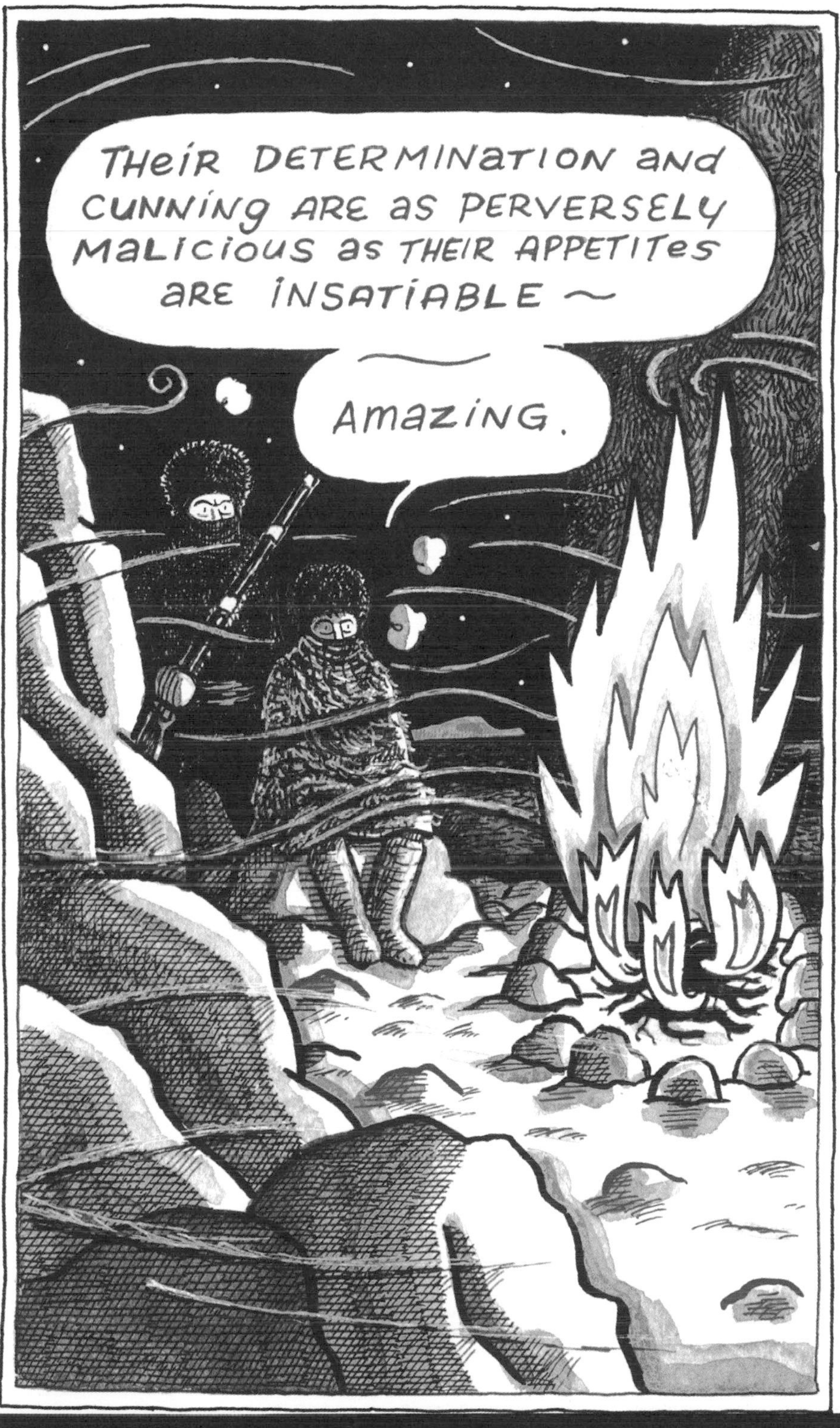
THEIR DETERMINATION AND CUNNING ARE AS PERVERSELY MALICIOUS AS THEIR APPETITES ARE INSATIABLE ~
AMAZING.

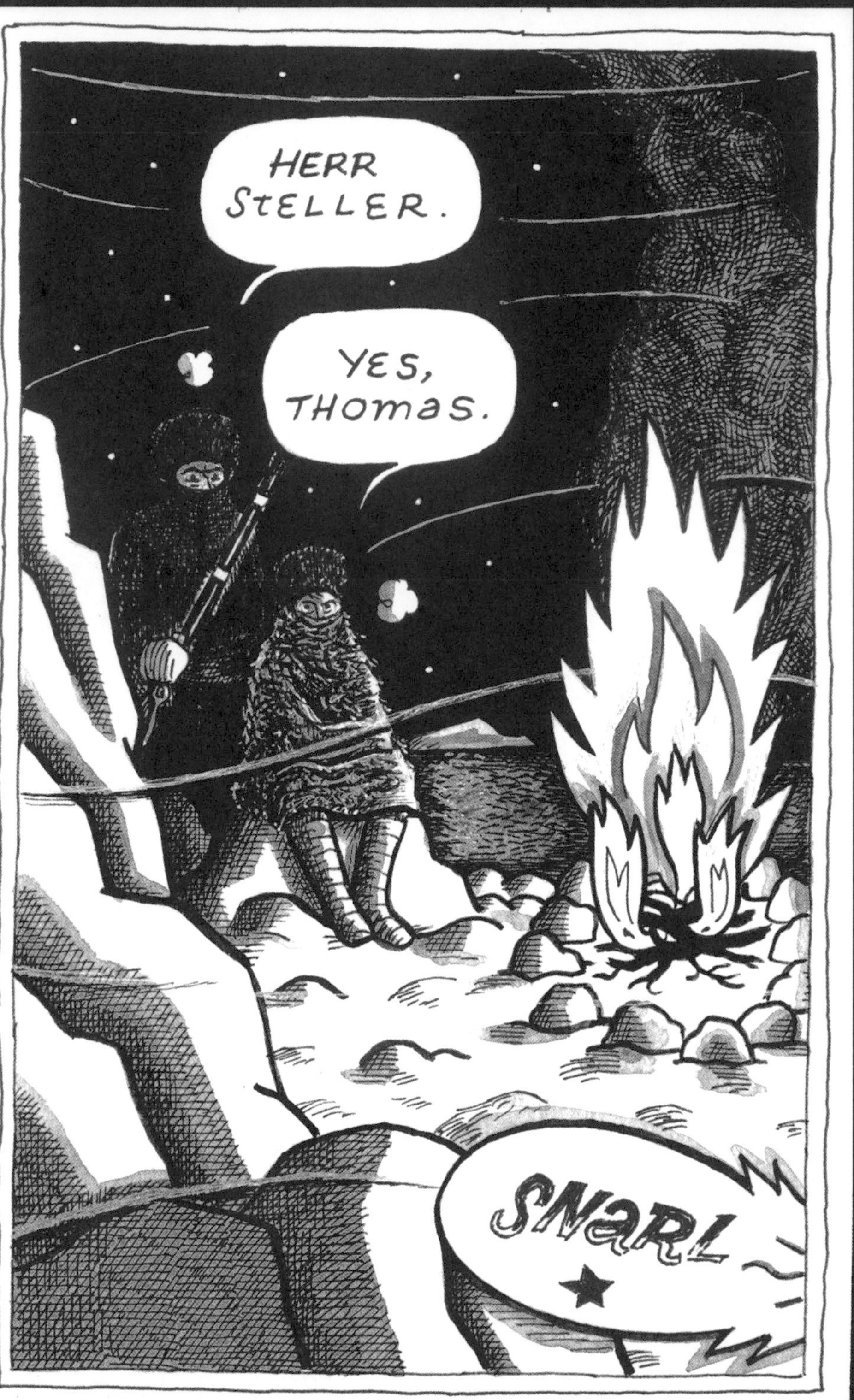
HERR STELLER.
YES, THOMAS.
SNARL

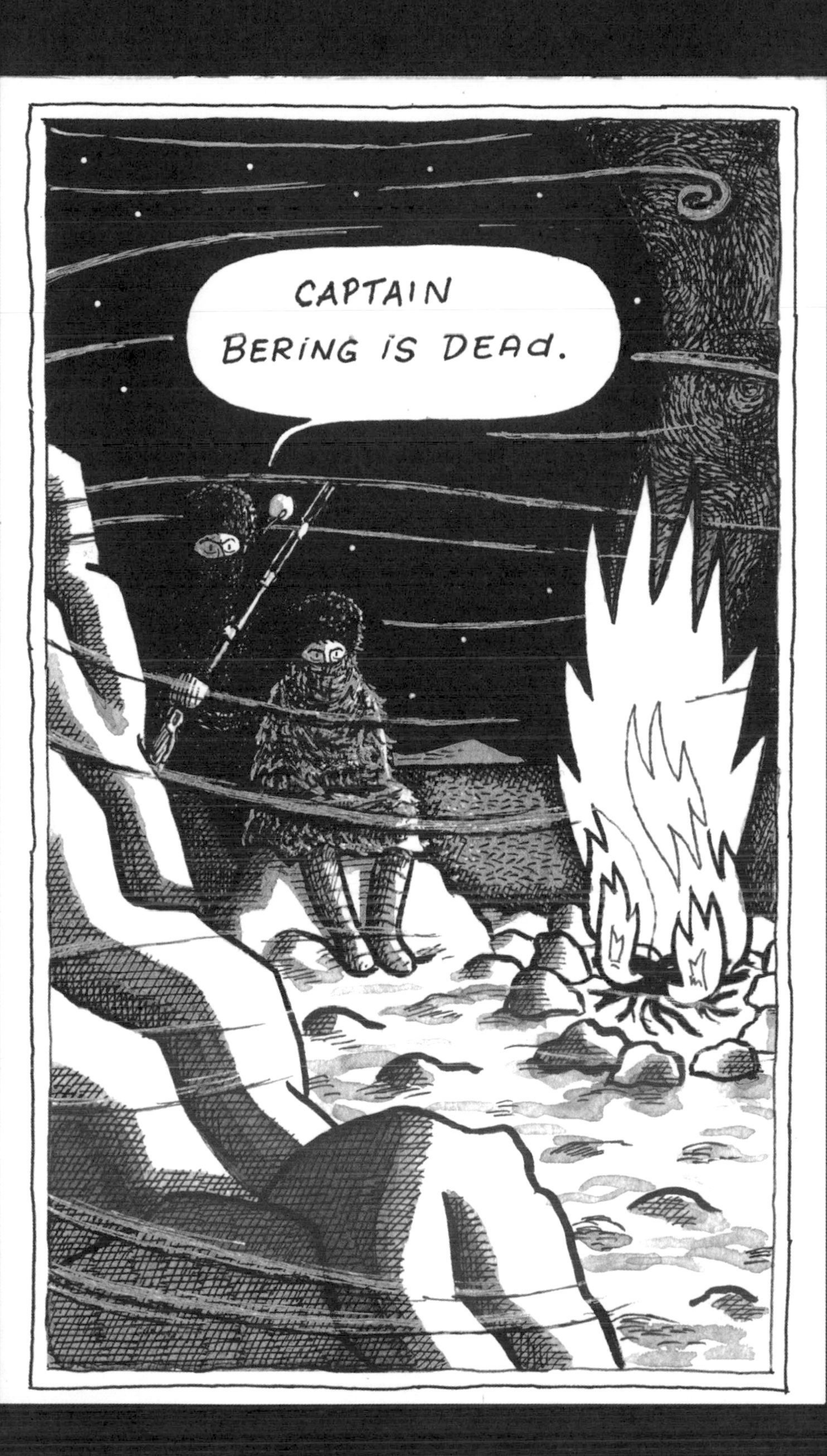
CAPTAIN BERING IS DEAD.

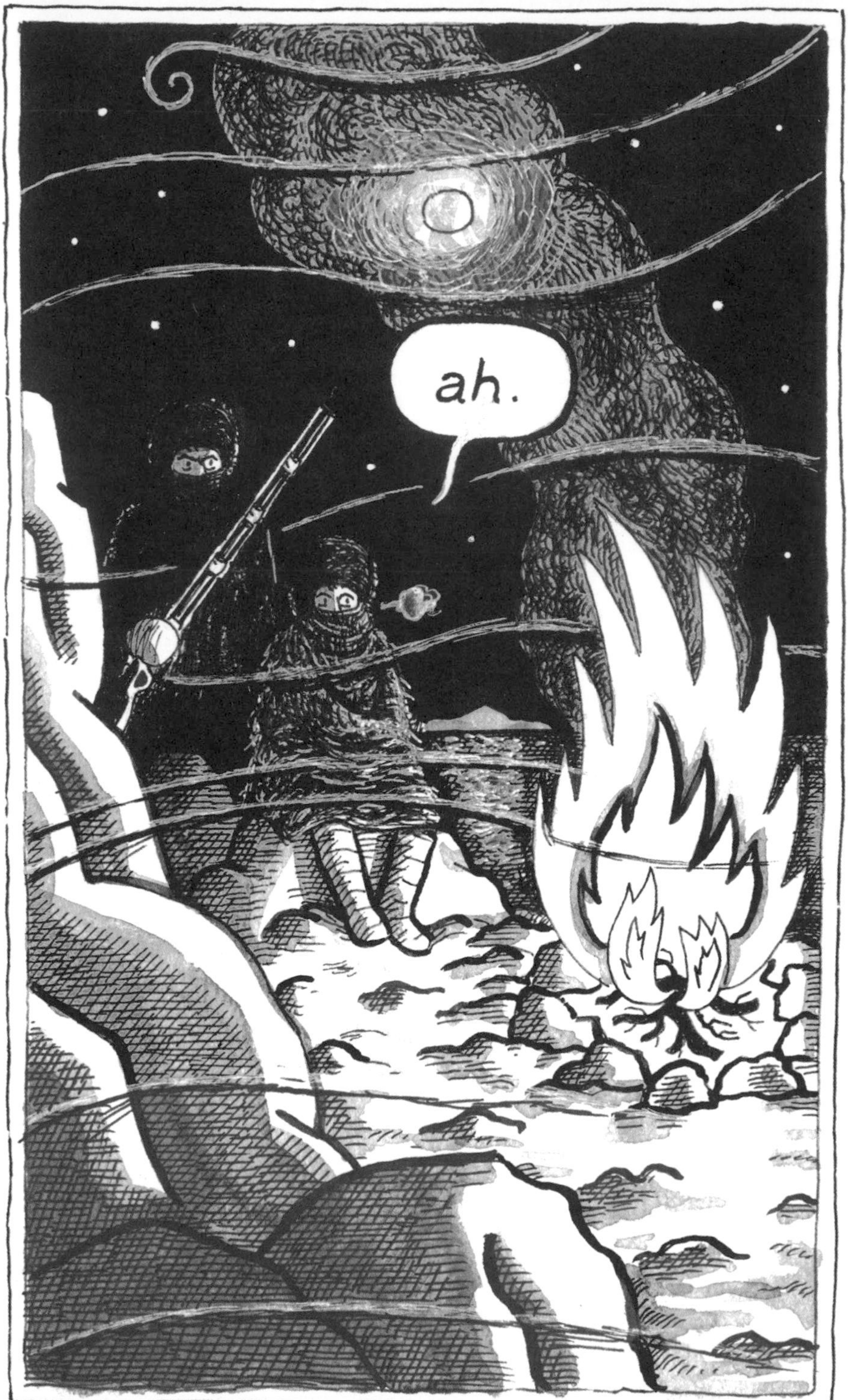
ah.

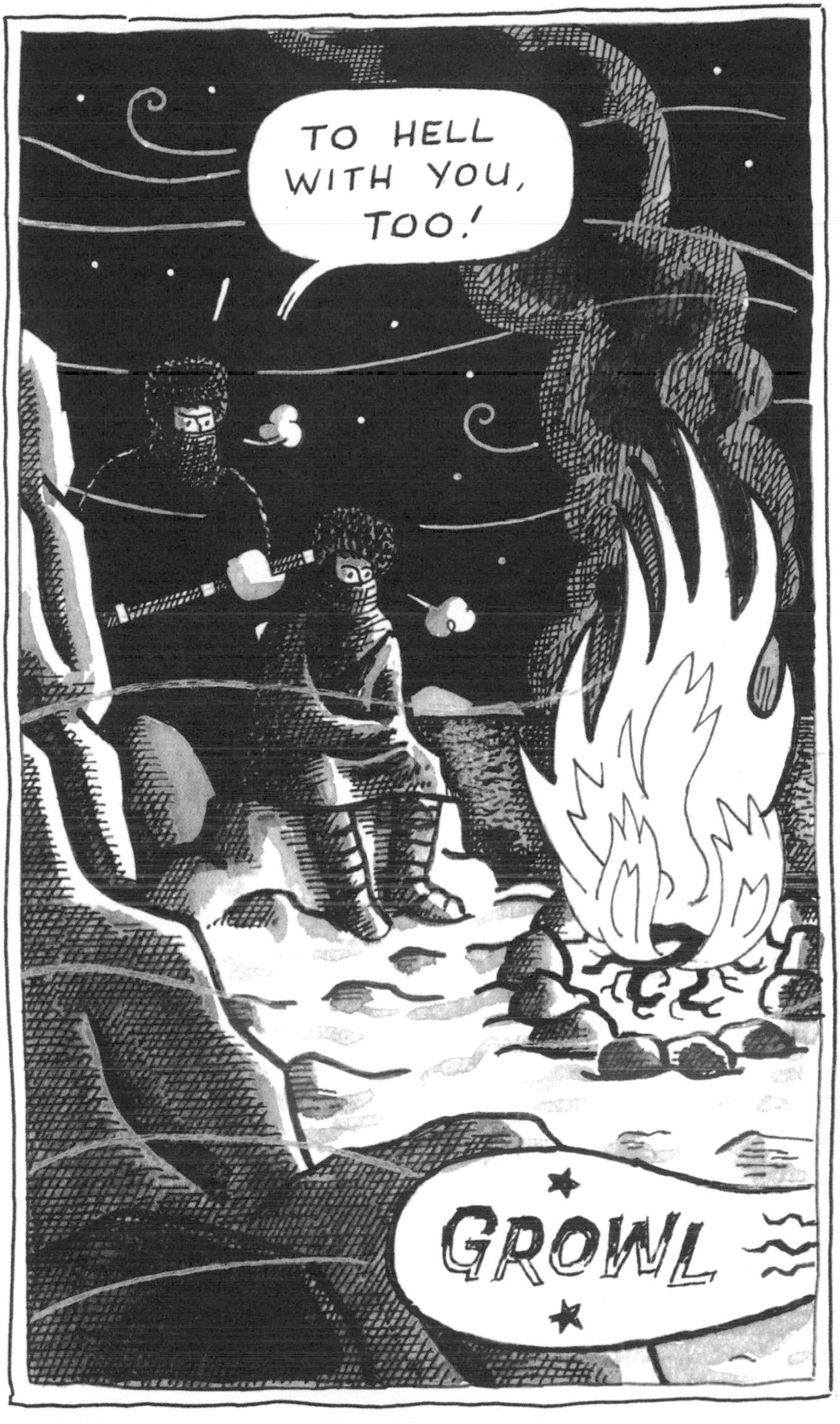
TO HELL WITH YOU, TOO!
GROWL

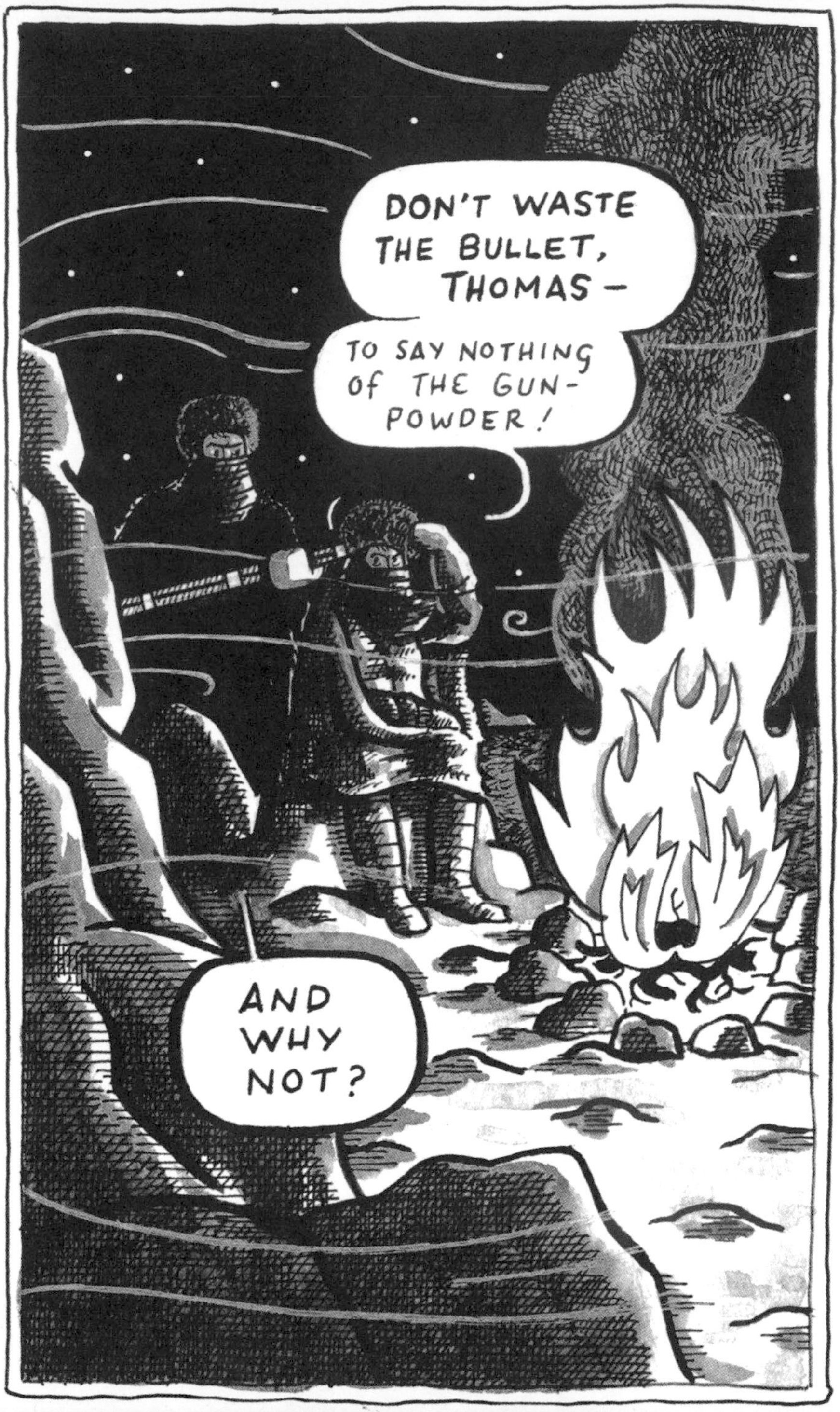
DON'T WASTE THE BULLET, THOMAS –
TO SAY NOTHING OF THE GUN-POWDER!
AND WHY NOT?

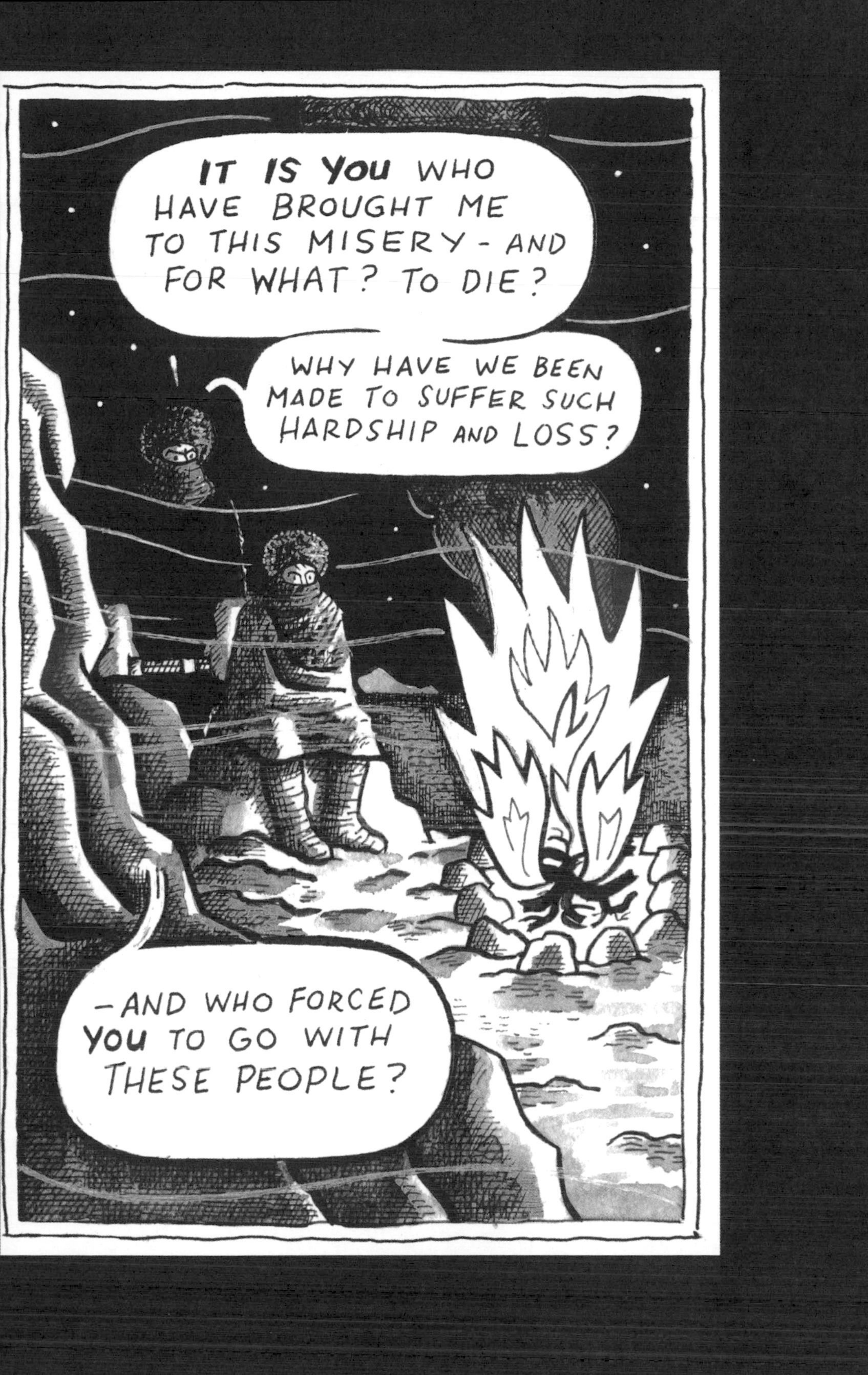
IT IS YOU WHO HAVE BROUGHT ME TO THIS MISERY - AND FOR WHAT? TO DIE?
WHY HAVE WE BEEN MADE TO SUFFER SUCH HARDSHIP AND LOSS?
-AND WHO FORCED YOU TO GO WITH THESE PEOPLE?

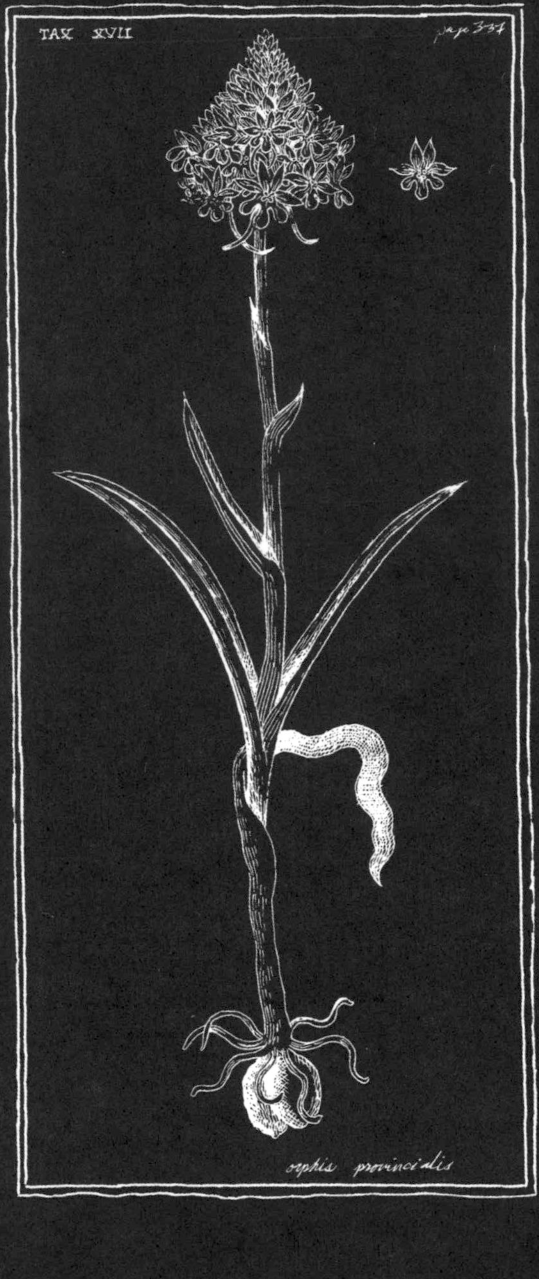
TAX XVII
page 337
orphis provincialis

SIX YEARS EARLIER, THE BAVARIAN-BORN STELLER ARRIVED IN ST PETERSBURG AFTER STUDYING THEOLOGY AND MEDICINE AT THE UNIVERSITIES OF WITTENBERG AND HALLE.

HE RECEIVED HIS BOTANY CERTIFICATION AT THE ROYAL ACADEMY OF SCIENCE IN BERLIN.

IN ST. PETERSBURG'S APOTHECARY GARDEN, STELLER CONSULTED AND BEGAN WORKING WITH DR JOHANN AMMAN, A RENOWNED BOTANIST THROUGH WHOM STELLER WAS INTRODUCED TO THE PRIMATE OF THE RUSSIAN ORTHODOX CHURCH, THE ARCHBISHOP OF NOVOGOROD, Theophan PROKOPOVITCH.

THE ARCHBISHOP WAS IMPRESSED WITH YOUNG STELLER.

WHEN STELLER ACCEPTED A POSITION AS THEOPHAN'S HOUSE-HOLD PHYSICIAN, HE WAS REWARDED BY THE PRIMATE'S EXCEPTIONAL CHARITY, FRIENDSHIP AND INFLUENCE;

THEOPHAN PROKOPOVITCH

IN 1735, WITH THEOPHAN'S RECOMMENDATION, STELLER WAS APPOINTED TO ADJUNCT PROFESSOR OF NATURAL HISTORY AND MINERALOGY AT THE ST. PETERSBURG ACADEMY OF SCIENCES.

STELLER'S BIOGRAPHER, LEONHARD STEJNEGER, SUGGESTS THAT THE MAN LINNAEUS ACCLAIMED AS "A BORN NATURALIST AND BOTANIST" POSSESSED OTHER GIFTS AS WELL.

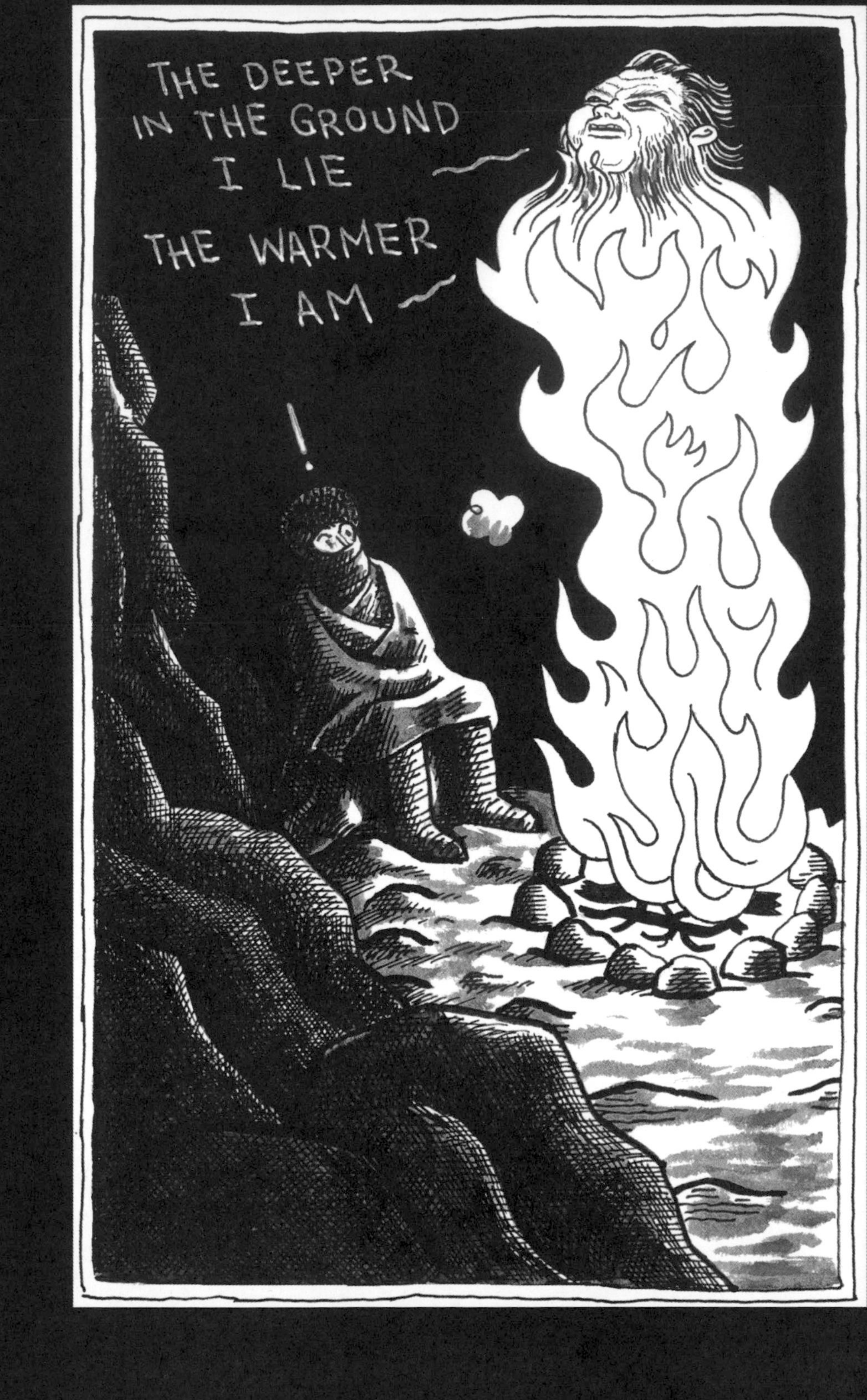
THE DEEPER IN THE GROUND I LIE
THE WARMER I AM
!

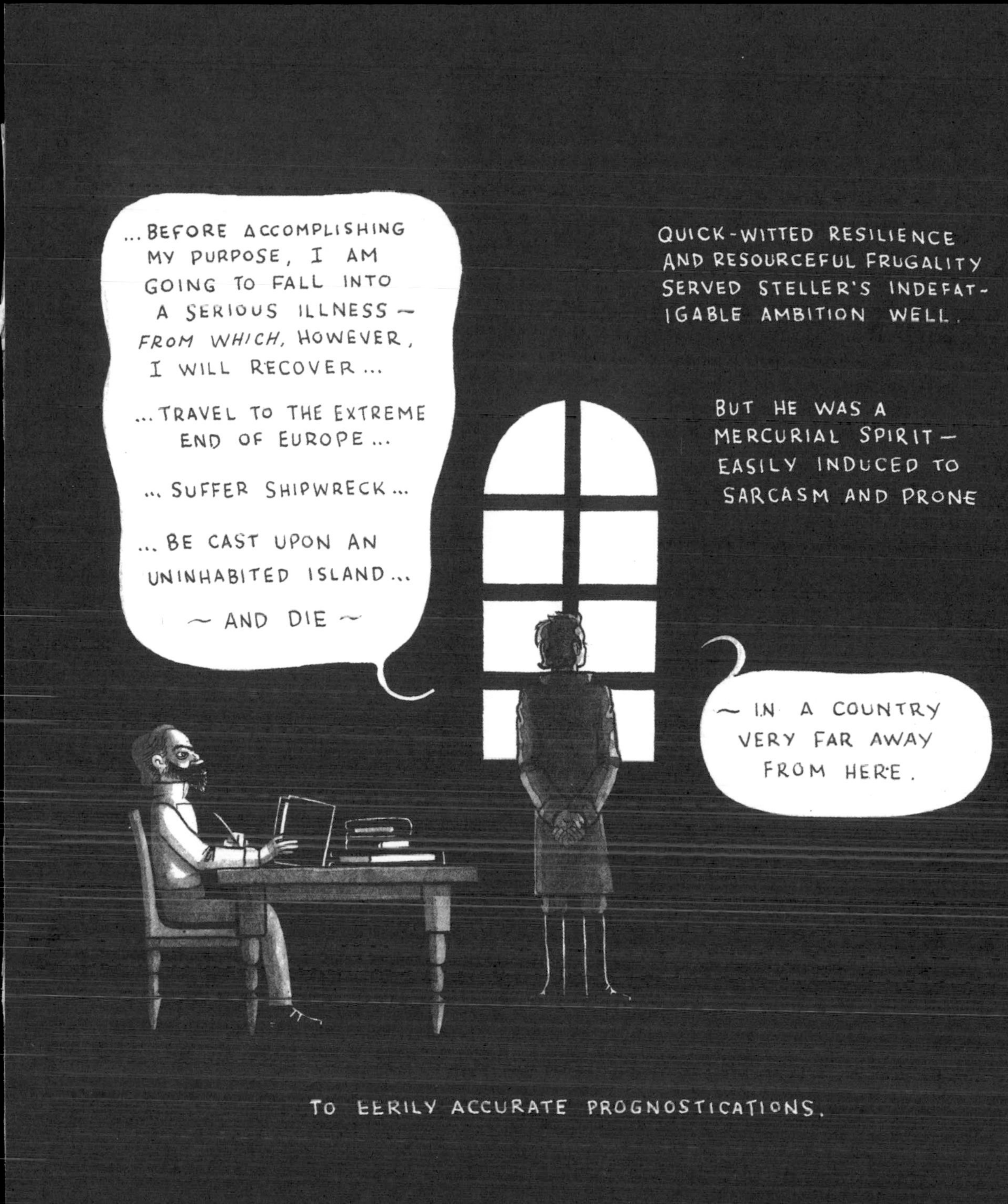
QUICK-WITTED RESILIENCE AND RESOURCEFUL FRUGALITY SERVED STELLER'S INDEFATIGABLE AMBITION WELL.
BUT HE WAS A MERCURIAL SPIRIT— EASILY INDUCED TO SARCASM AND PRONE
...BEFORE ACCOMPLISHING MY PURPOSE, I AM GOING TO FALL INTO A SERIOUS ILLNESS— *FROM WHICH*, HOWEVER, I WILL RECOVER... ...TRAVEL TO THE EXTREME END OF EUROPE... ...SUFFER SHIPWRECK... ...BE CAST UPON AN UNINHABITED ISLAND... ~ AND DIE ~
~ IN A COUNTRY VERY FAR AWAY FROM HERE.
TO EERILY ACCURATE PROGNOSTICATIONS.

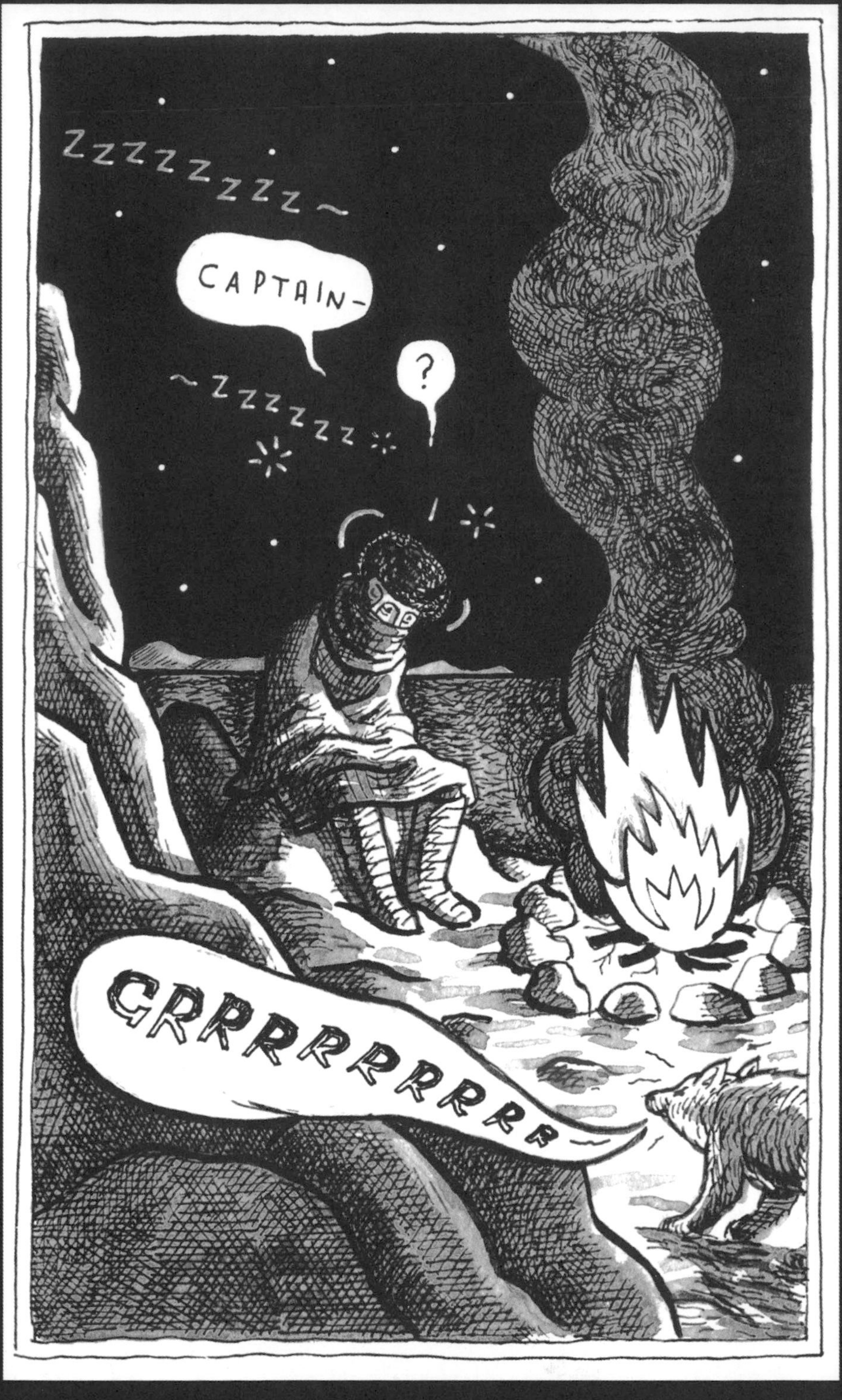
ZZZZZZZZZ~
CAPTAIN-
~ZZZZZZZ
?
GRRRRRRRRRRR~

To be continued…

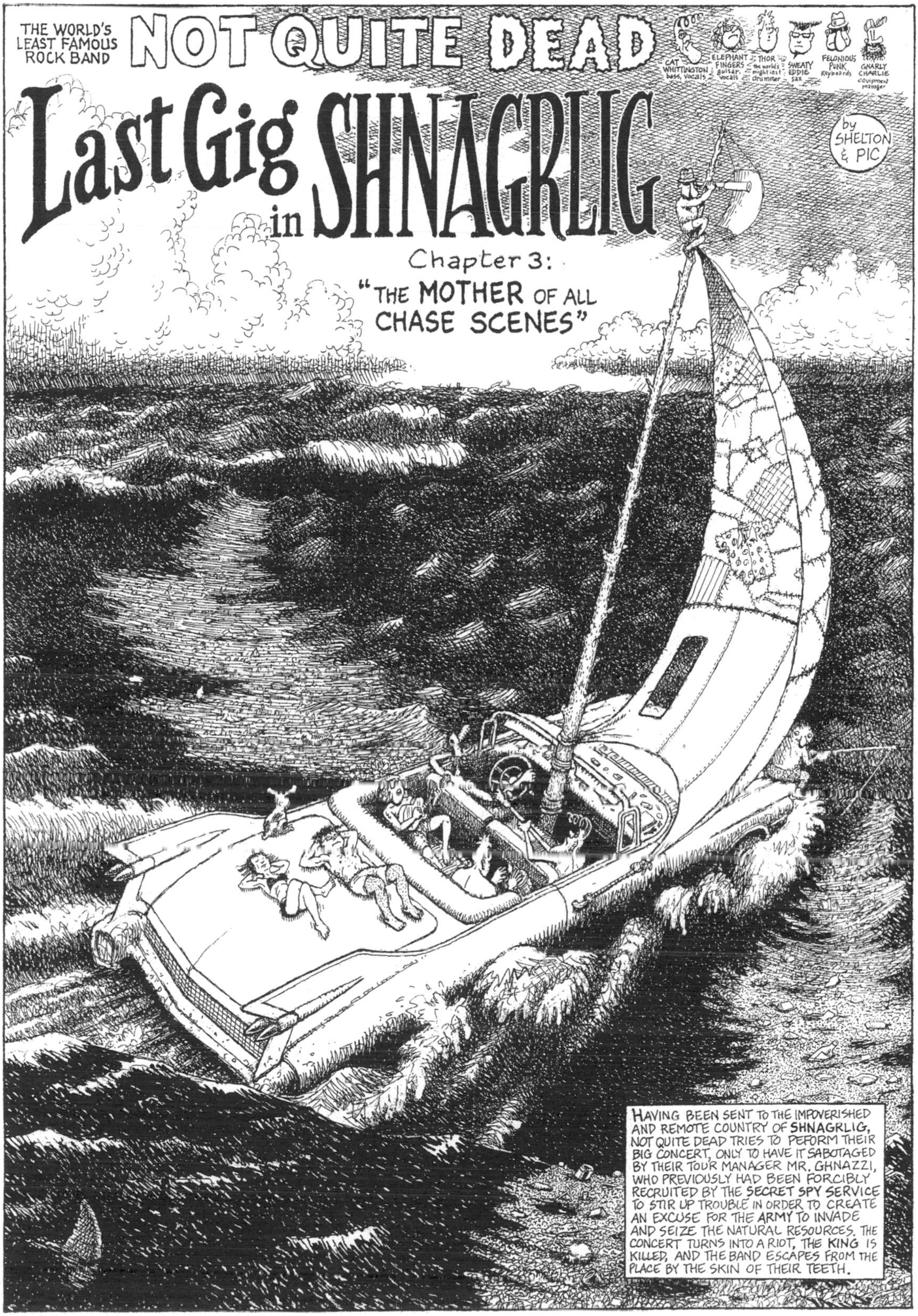
THE WORLD'S LEAST FAMOUS ROCK BAND
NOT QUITE DEAD
CAT WHITTINGTON bass, vocals
ELEPHANT FINGERS guitar, vocals
THOR the world's mightiest drummer
SWEATY EDDIE sax
FELONIOUS PUNK keyboards
GNARLY CHARLIE equipment manager
Last Gig in SHNAGRLIG
by SHELTON & PIC
Chapter 3:
"THE MOTHER OF ALL CHASE SCENES"
HAVING BEEN SENT TO THE IMPOVERISHED AND REMOTE COUNTRY OF SHNAGRLIG, NOT QUITE DEAD TRIES TO PEFORM THEIR BIG CONCERT, ONLY TO HAVE IT SABOTAGED BY THEIR TOUR MANAGER MR. GHNAZZI, WHO PREVIOUSLY HAD BEEN FORCIBLY RECRUITED BY THE SECRET SPY SERVICE TO STIR UP TROUBLE IN ORDER TO CREATE AN EXCUSE FOR THE ARMY TO INVADE AND SEIZE THE NATURAL RESOURCES. THE CONCERT TURNS INTO A RIOT, THE KING IS KILLED, AND THE BAND ESCAPES FROM THE PLACE BY THE SKIN OF THEIR TEETH.

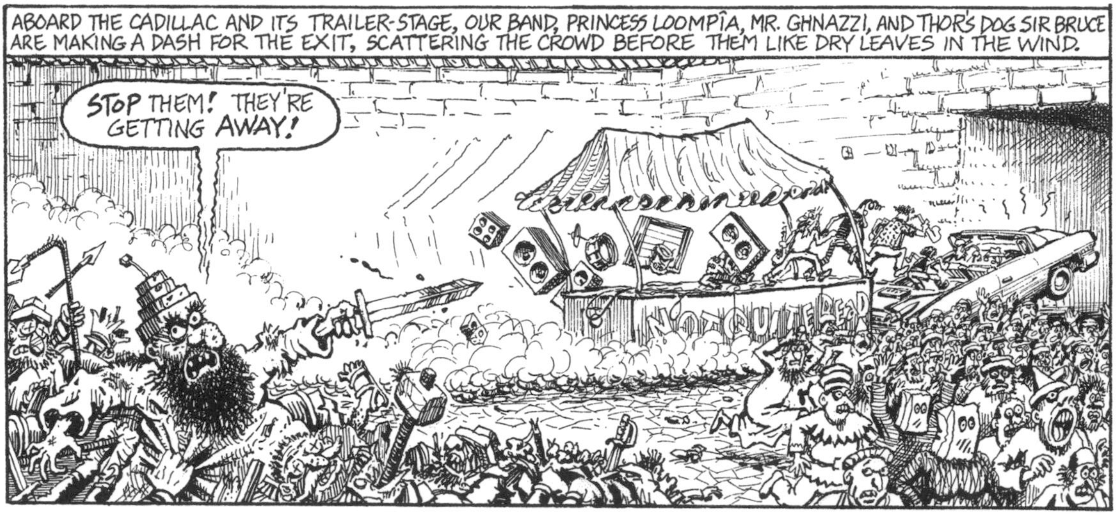

ABOARD THE CADILLAC AND ITS TRAILER-STAGE, OUR BAND, PRINCESS LOOMPÍA, MR. GHNAZZI, AND THOR'S DOG SIR BRUCE ARE MAKING A DASH FOR THE EXIT, SCATTERING THE CROWD BEFORE THEM LIKE DRY LEAVES IN THE WIND.
STOP THEM! THEY'RE GETTING AWAY!
NOT QUITE DEAD

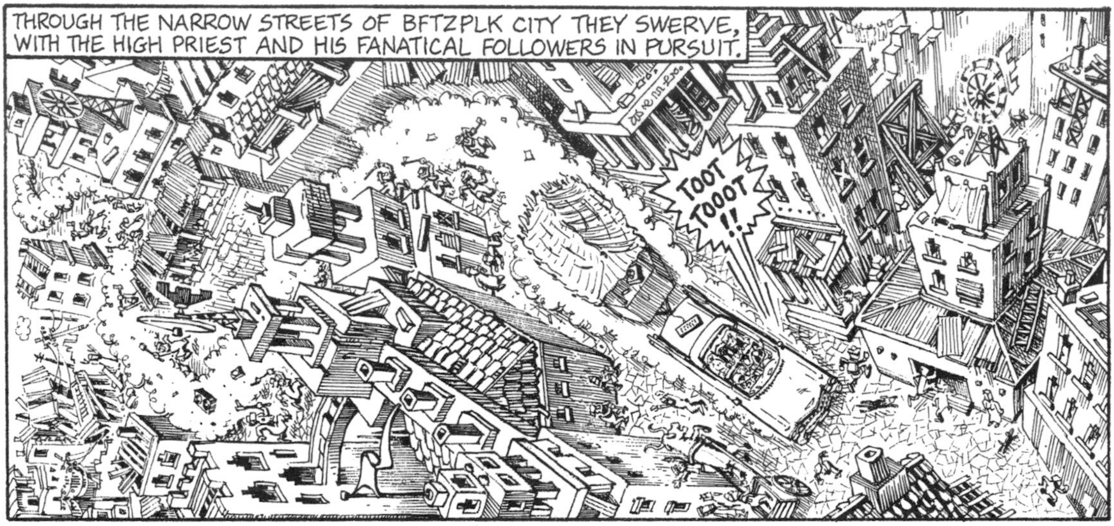

THROUGH THE NARROW STREETS OF BFTZPLK CITY THEY SWERVE, WITH THE HIGH PRIEST AND HIS FANATICAL FOLLOWERS IN PURSUIT.
TOOT TOOOT !!

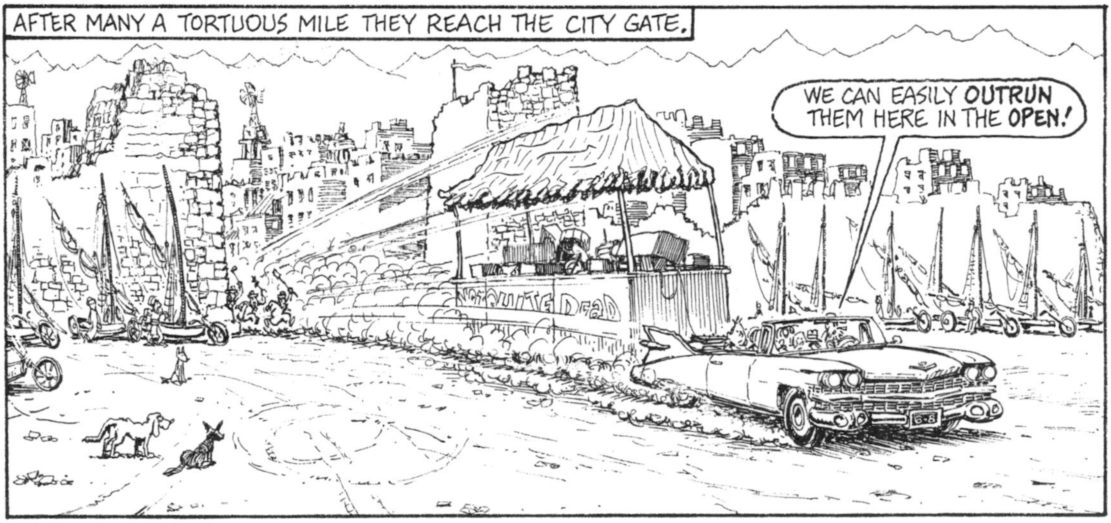

AFTER MANY A TORTUOUS MILE THEY REACH THE CITY GATE.
WE CAN EASILY OUTRUN THEM HERE IN THE OPEN!
NOT QUITE DEAD

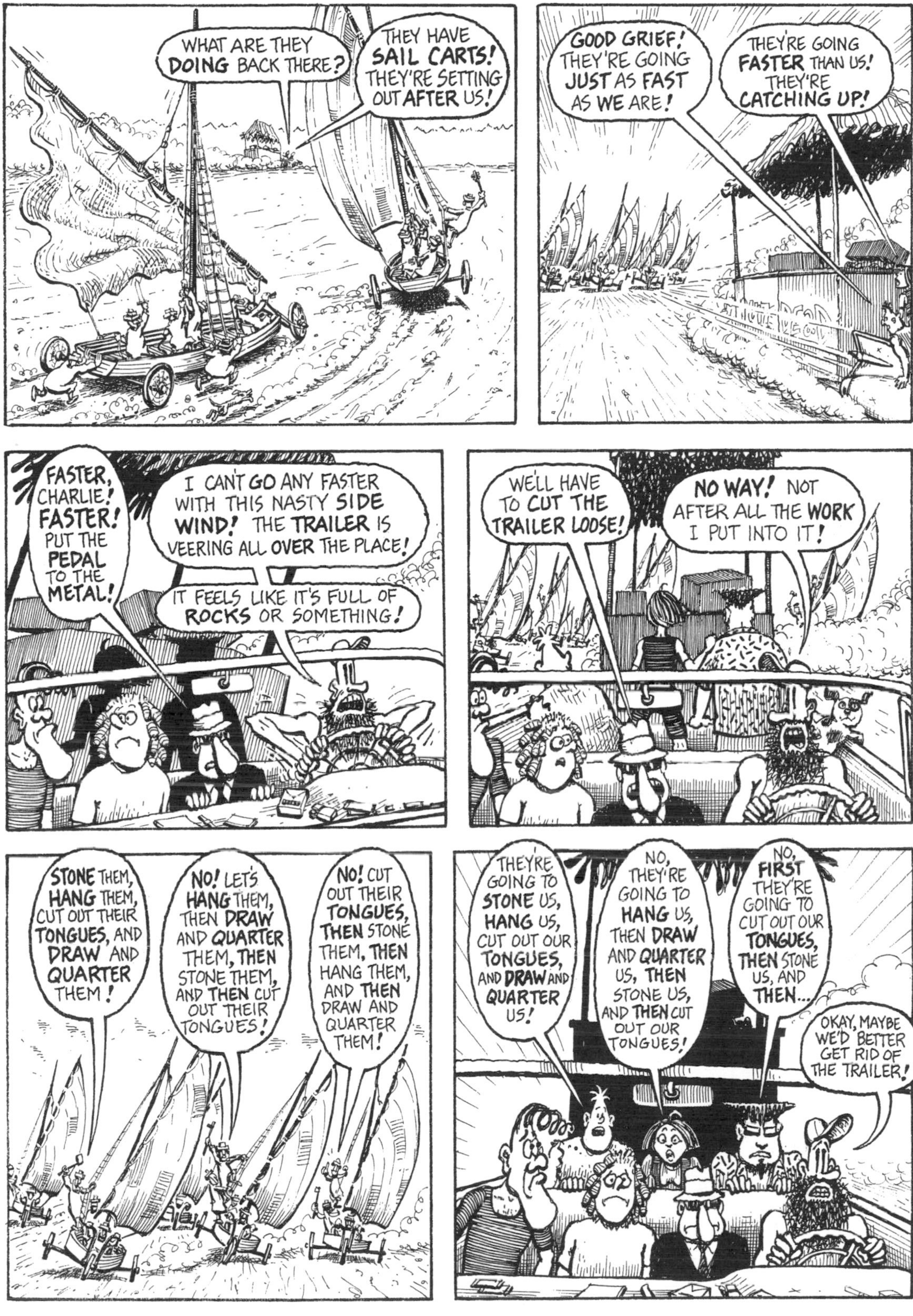
WHAT ARE THEY DOING BACK THERE?
THEY HAVE SAIL CARTS! THEY'RE SETTING OUT AFTER US!
GOOD GRIEF! THEY'RE GOING JUST AS FAST AS WE ARE!
THEY'RE GOING FASTER THAN US! THEY'RE CATCHING UP!
FASTER, CHARLIE! FASTER! PUT THE PEDAL TO THE METAL!
I CAN'T GO ANY FASTER WITH THIS NASTY SIDE WIND! THE TRAILER IS VEERING ALL OVER THE PLACE!
IT FEELS LIKE IT'S FULL OF ROCKS OR SOMETHING!
WE'LL HAVE TO CUT THE TRAILER LOOSE!
NO WAY! NOT AFTER ALL THE WORK I PUT INTO IT!
STONE THEM, HANG THEM, CUT OUT THEIR TONGUES, AND DRAW AND QUARTER THEM!
NO! LET'S HANG THEM, THEN DRAW AND QUARTER THEM, THEN STONE THEM, AND THEN CUT OUT THEIR TONGUES!
NO! CUT OUT THEIR TONGUES, THEN STONE THEM, THEN HANG THEM, AND THEN DRAW AND QUARTER THEM!
THEY'RE GOING TO STONE US, HANG US, CUT OUT OUR TONGUES, AND DRAW AND QUARTER US!
NO, THEY'RE GOING TO HANG US, THEN DRAW AND QUARTER US, THEN STONE US, AND THEN CUT OUT OUR TONGUES!
NO, FIRST THEY'RE GOING TO CUT OUT OUR TONGUES, THEN STONE US, AND THEN...
OKAY, MAYBE WE'D BETTER GET RID OF THE TRAILER!

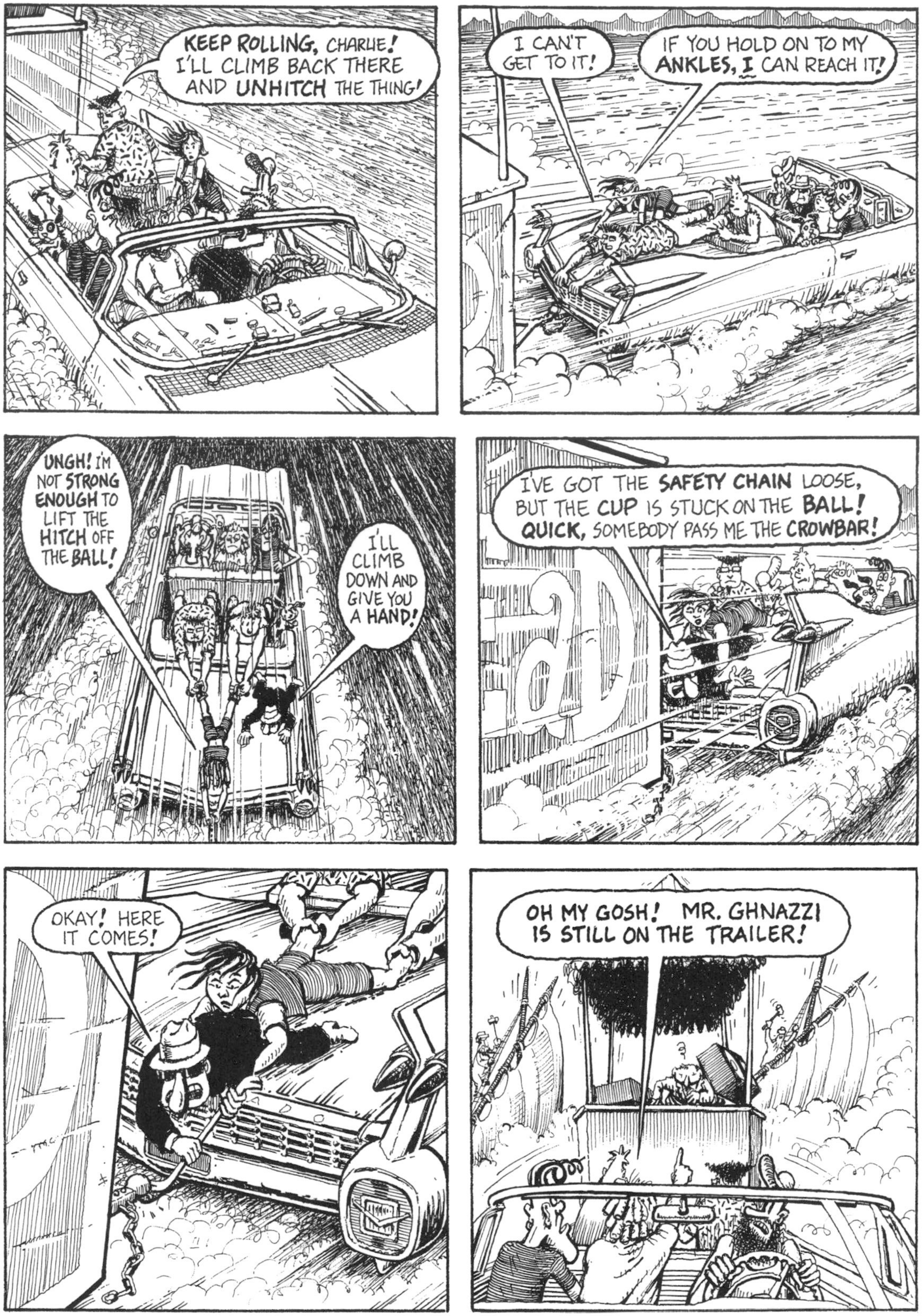
KEEP ROLLING, CHARLIE! I'LL CLIMB BACK THERE AND UNHITCH THE THING!
I CAN'T GET TO IT!
IF YOU HOLD ON TO MY ANKLES, I CAN REACH IT!
UNGH! I'M NOT STRONG ENOUGH TO LIFT THE HITCH OFF THE BALL!
I'LL CLIMB DOWN AND GIVE YOU A HAND!
I'VE GOT THE SAFETY CHAIN LOOSE, BUT THE CUP IS STUCK ON THE BALL! QUICK, SOMEBODY PASS ME THE CROWBAR!
OKAY! HERE IT COMES!
OH MY GOSH! MR. GHNAZZI IS STILL ON THE TRAILER!

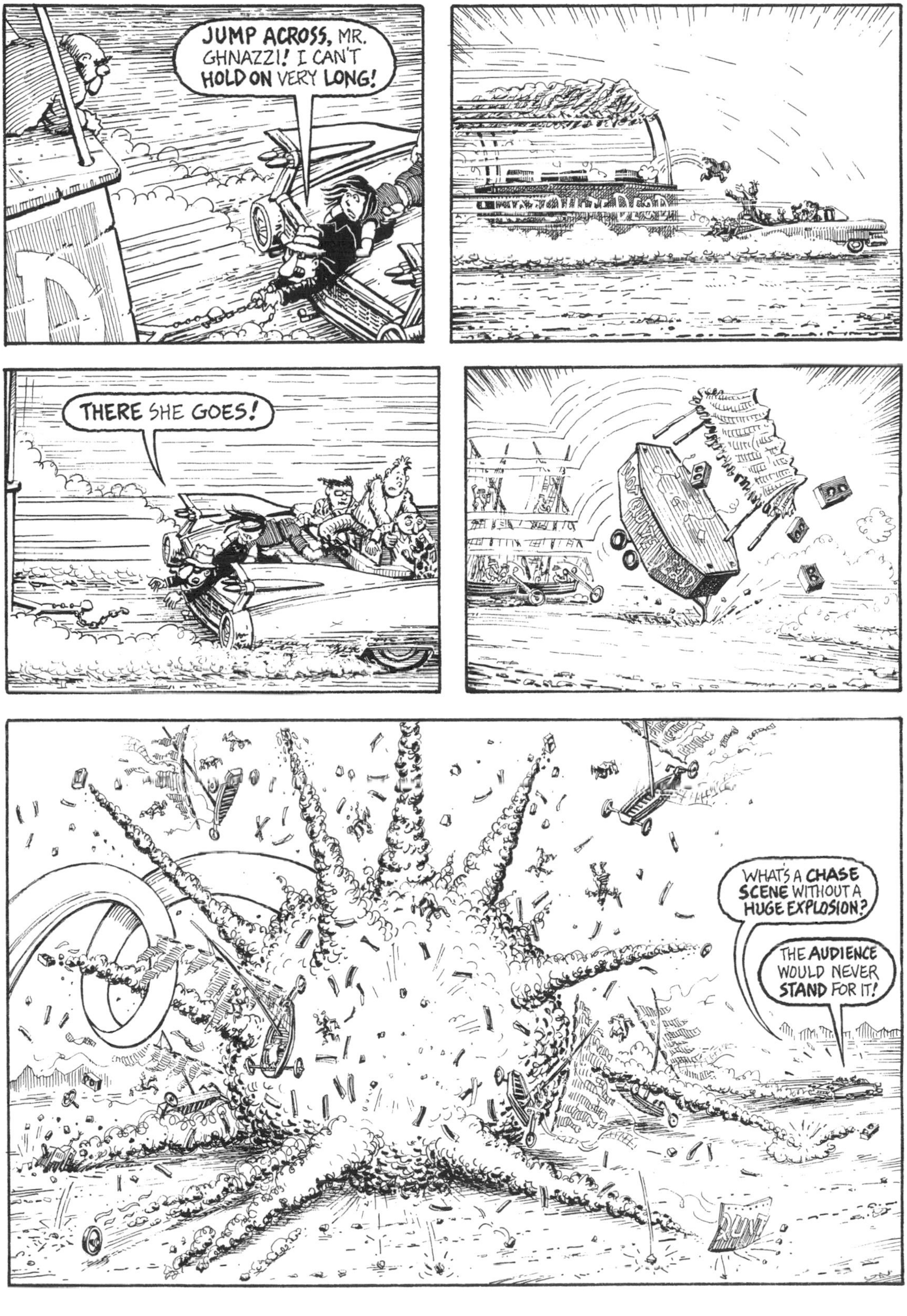
JUMP ACROSS, MR. GHNAZZI! I CAN'T HOLD ON VERY LONG!
THERE SHE GOES!
WHAT'S A CHASE SCENE WITHOUT A HUGE EXPLOSION?
THE AUDIENCE WOULD NEVER STAND FOR IT!
RUN!

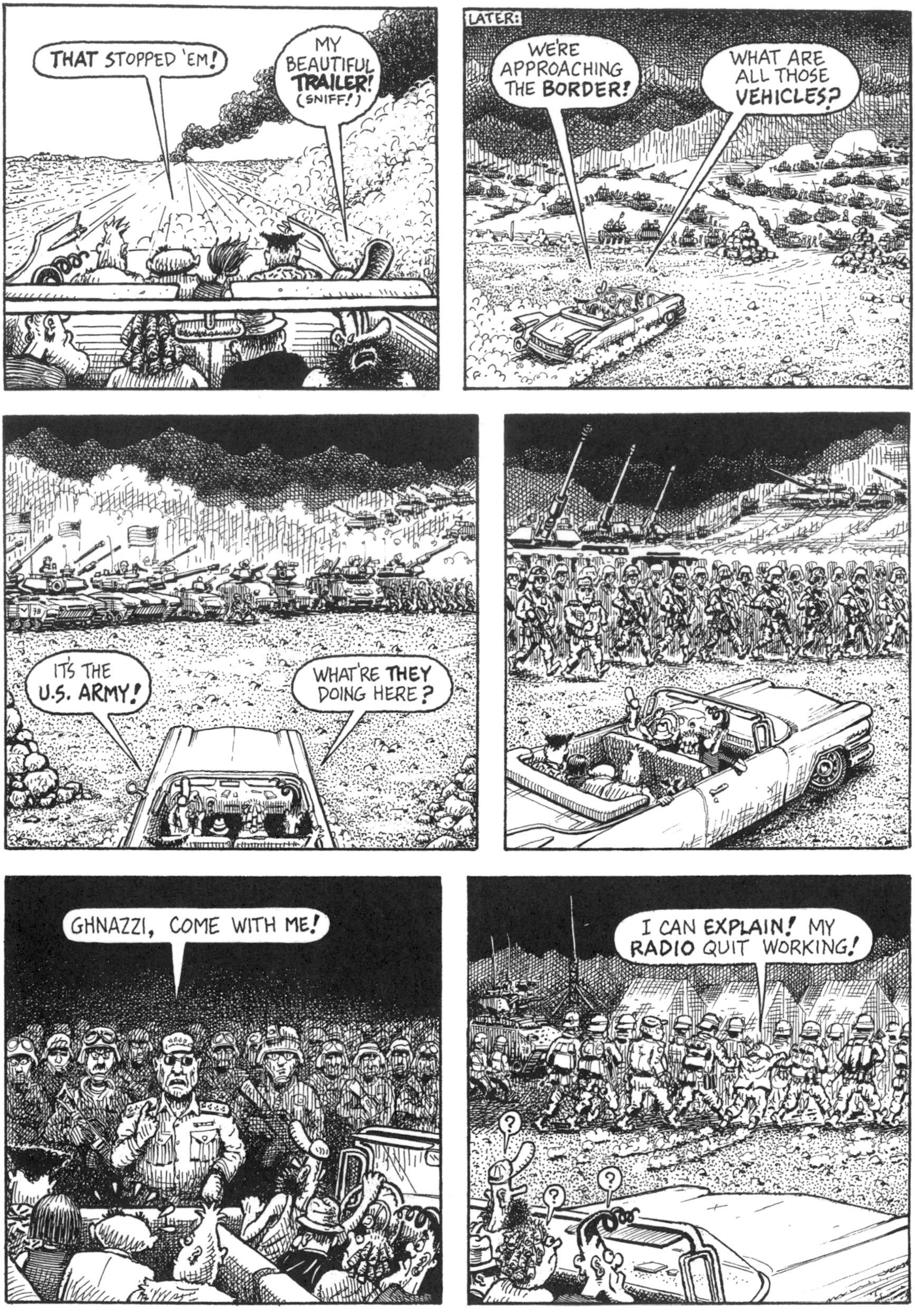
THAT STOPPED 'EM!
MY BEAUTIFUL TRAILER! (SNIFF!)
LATER:
WE'RE APPROACHING THE BORDER!
WHAT ARE ALL THOSE VEHICLES?
IT'S THE U.S. ARMY!
WHAT'RE THEY DOING HERE?
GHNAZZI, COME WITH ME!
I CAN EXPLAIN! MY RADIO QUIT WORKING!
?
?
?

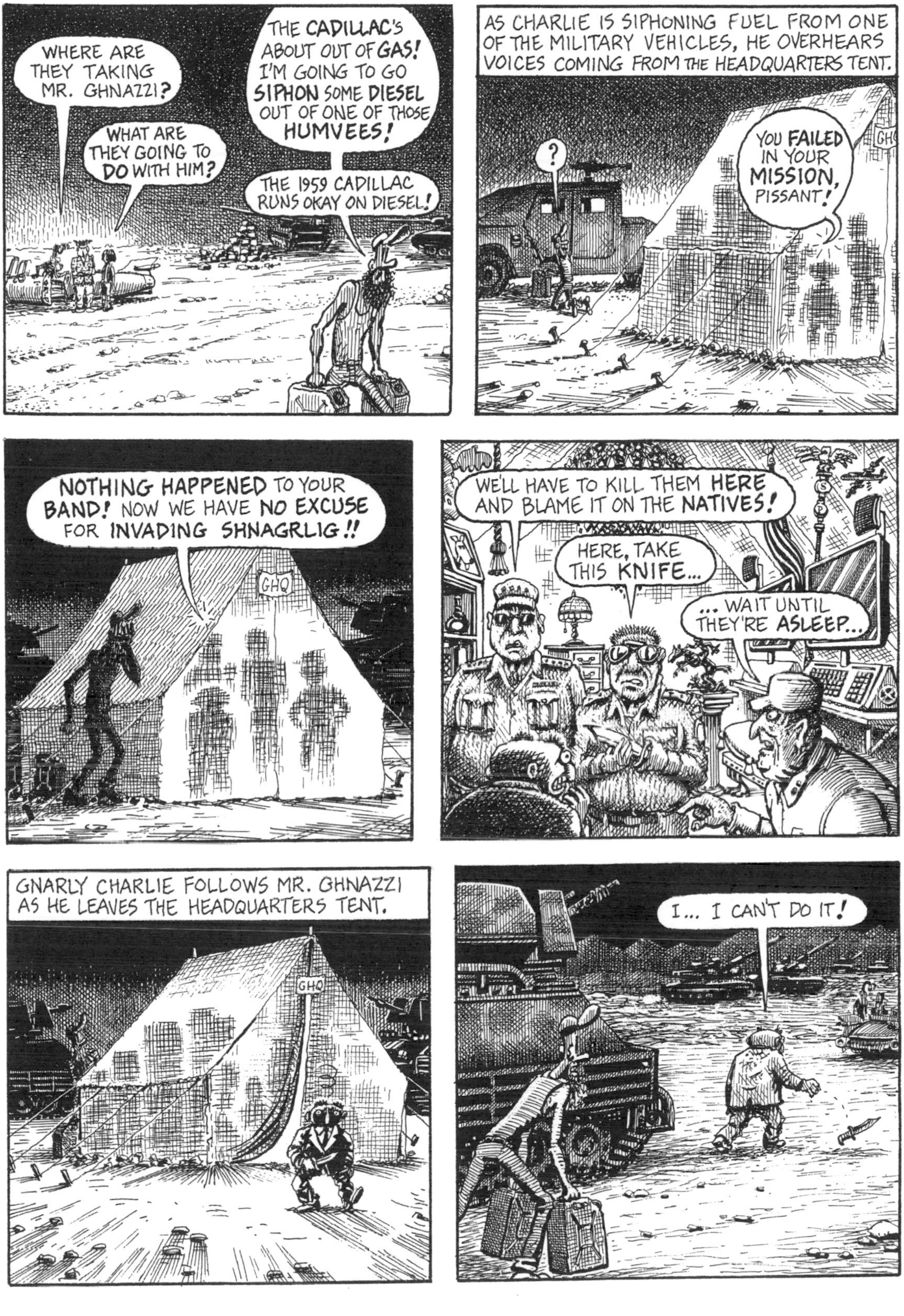
WHERE ARE THEY TAKING MR. GHNAZZI?
WHAT ARE THEY GOING TO DO WITH HIM?
THE CADILLAC'S ABOUT OUT OF GAS! I'M GOING TO GO SIPHON SOME DIESEL OUT OF ONE OF THOSE HUMVEES!
THE 1959 CADILLAC RUNS OKAY ON DIESEL!
AS CHARLIE IS SIPHONING FUEL FROM ONE OF THE MILITARY VEHICLES, HE OVERHEARS VOICES COMING FROM THE HEADQUARTERS TENT.
?
YOU FAILED IN YOUR MISSION, PISSANT!
NOTHING HAPPENED TO YOUR BAND! NOW WE HAVE NO EXCUSE FOR INVADING SHNAGRLIG!!
GHQ
WE'LL HAVE TO KILL THEM HERE AND BLAME IT ON THE NATIVES!
HERE, TAKE THIS KNIFE...
... WAIT UNTIL THEY'RE ASLEEP...
GNARLY CHARLIE FOLLOWS MR. GHNAZZI AS HE LEAVES THE HEADQUARTERS TENT.
GHQ
I... I CAN'T DO IT!

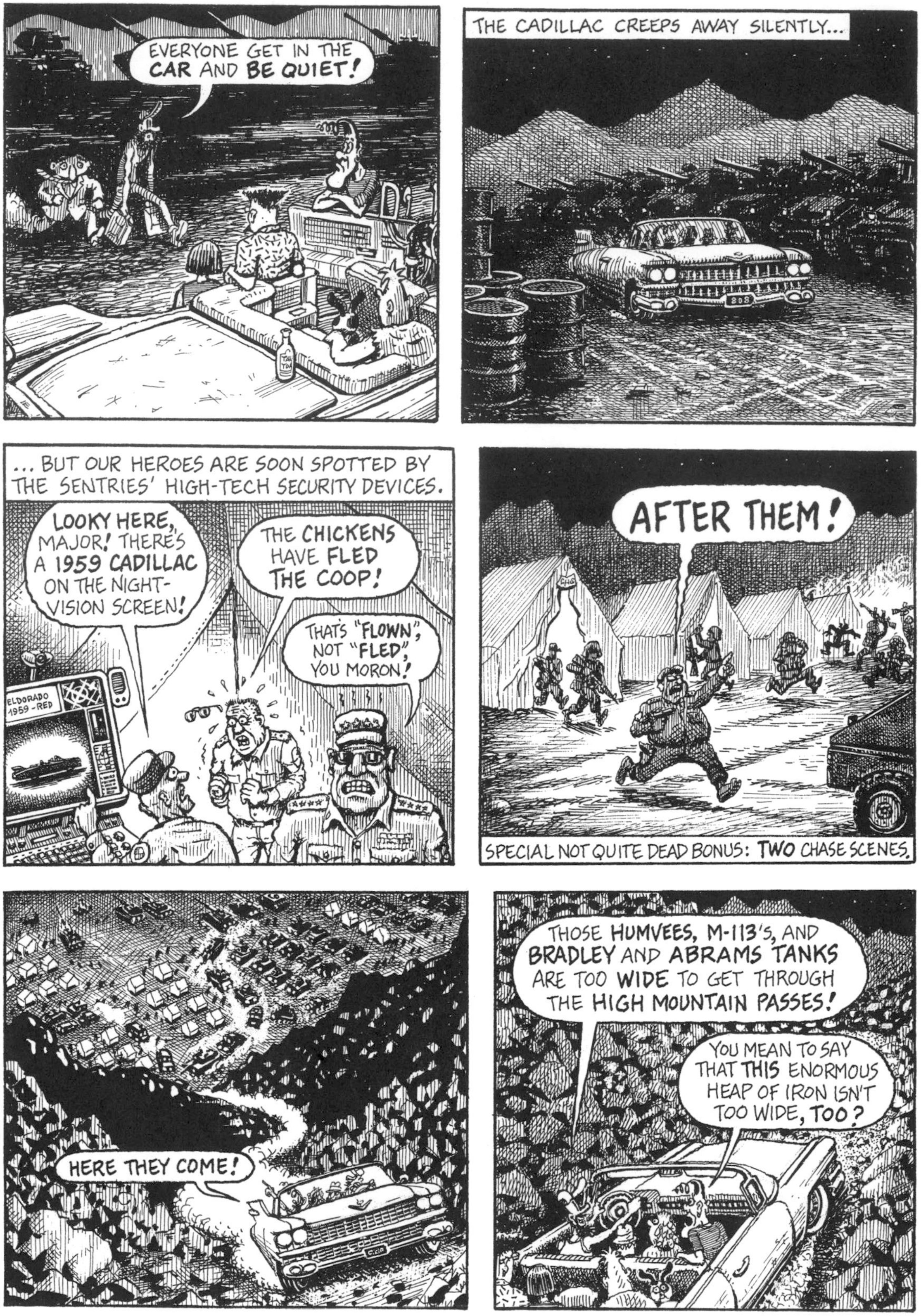
EVERYONE GET IN THE CAR AND BE QUIET!
THE CADILLAC CREEPS AWAY SILENTLY...
... BUT OUR HEROES ARE SOON SPOTTED BY THE SENTRIES' HIGH-TECH SECURITY DEVICES.
LOOKY HERE, MAJOR! THERE'S A 1959 CADILLAC ON THE NIGHT-VISION SCREEN!
THE CHICKENS HAVE FLED THE COOP!
THAT'S "FLOWN", NOT "FLED", YOU MORON!
ELDORADO 1959 - RED
AFTER THEM!
SPECIAL NOT QUITE DEAD BONUS: TWO CHASE SCENES.
HERE THEY COME!
THOSE HUMVEES, M-113'S, AND BRADLEY AND ABRAMS TANKS ARE TOO WIDE TO GET THROUGH THE HIGH MOUNTAIN PASSES!
YOU MEAN TO SAY THAT THIS ENORMOUS HEAP OF IRON ISN'T TOO WIDE, TOO?

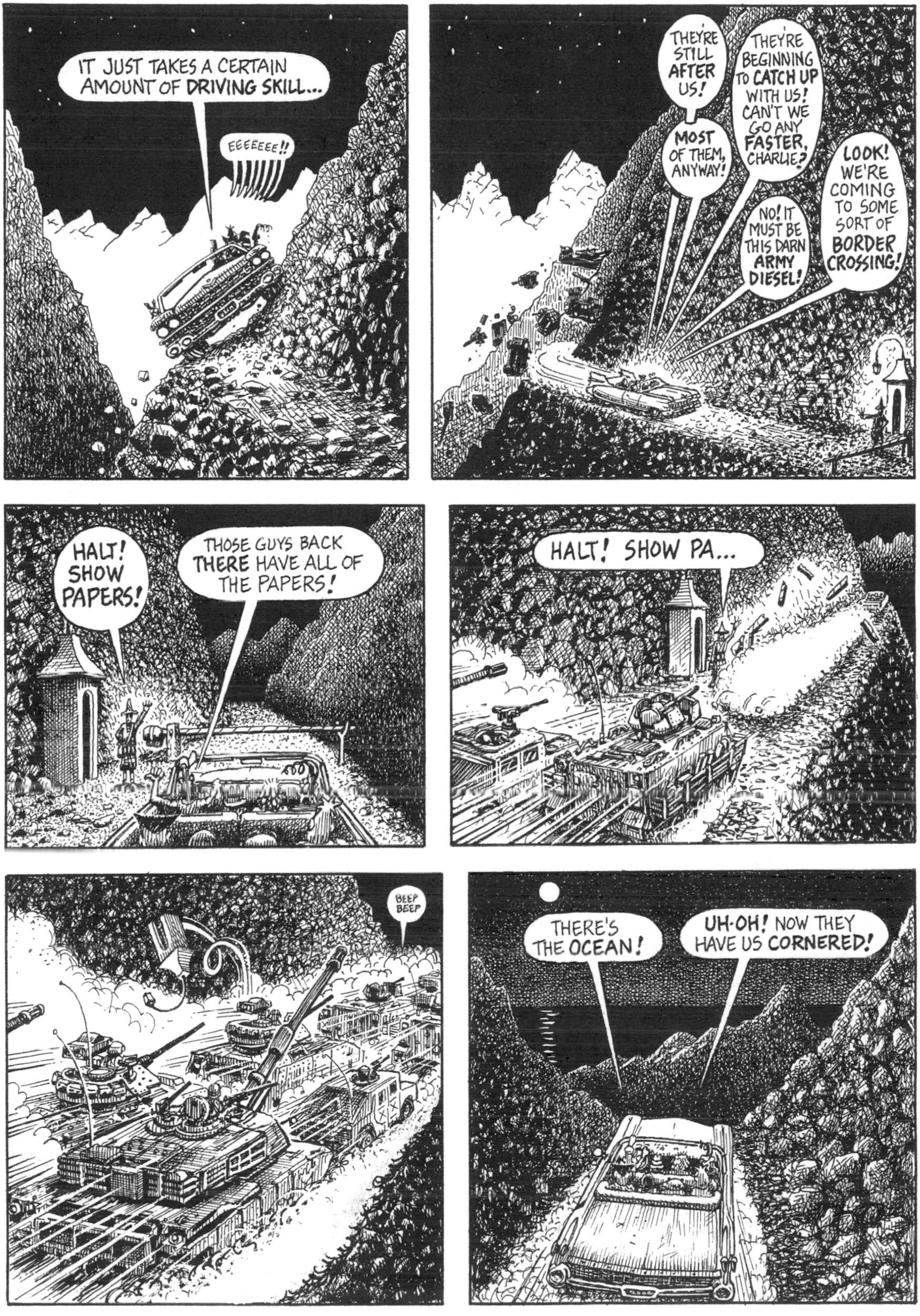
IT JUST TAKES A CERTAIN AMOUNT OF DRIVING SKILL...
EEEEEEE!!
THEY'RE STILL AFTER US!
MOST OF THEM, ANYWAY!
THEY'RE BEGINNING TO CATCH UP WITH US! CAN'T WE GO ANY FASTER, CHARLIE?
NO! IT MUST BE THIS DARN ARMY DIESEL!
LOOK! WE'RE COMING TO SOME SORT OF BORDER CROSSING!
HALT! SHOW PAPERS!
THOSE GUYS BACK THERE HAVE ALL OF THE PAPERS!
HALT! SHOW PA...
BEEP BEEP
THERE'S THE OCEAN!
UH-OH! NOW THEY HAVE US CORNERED!

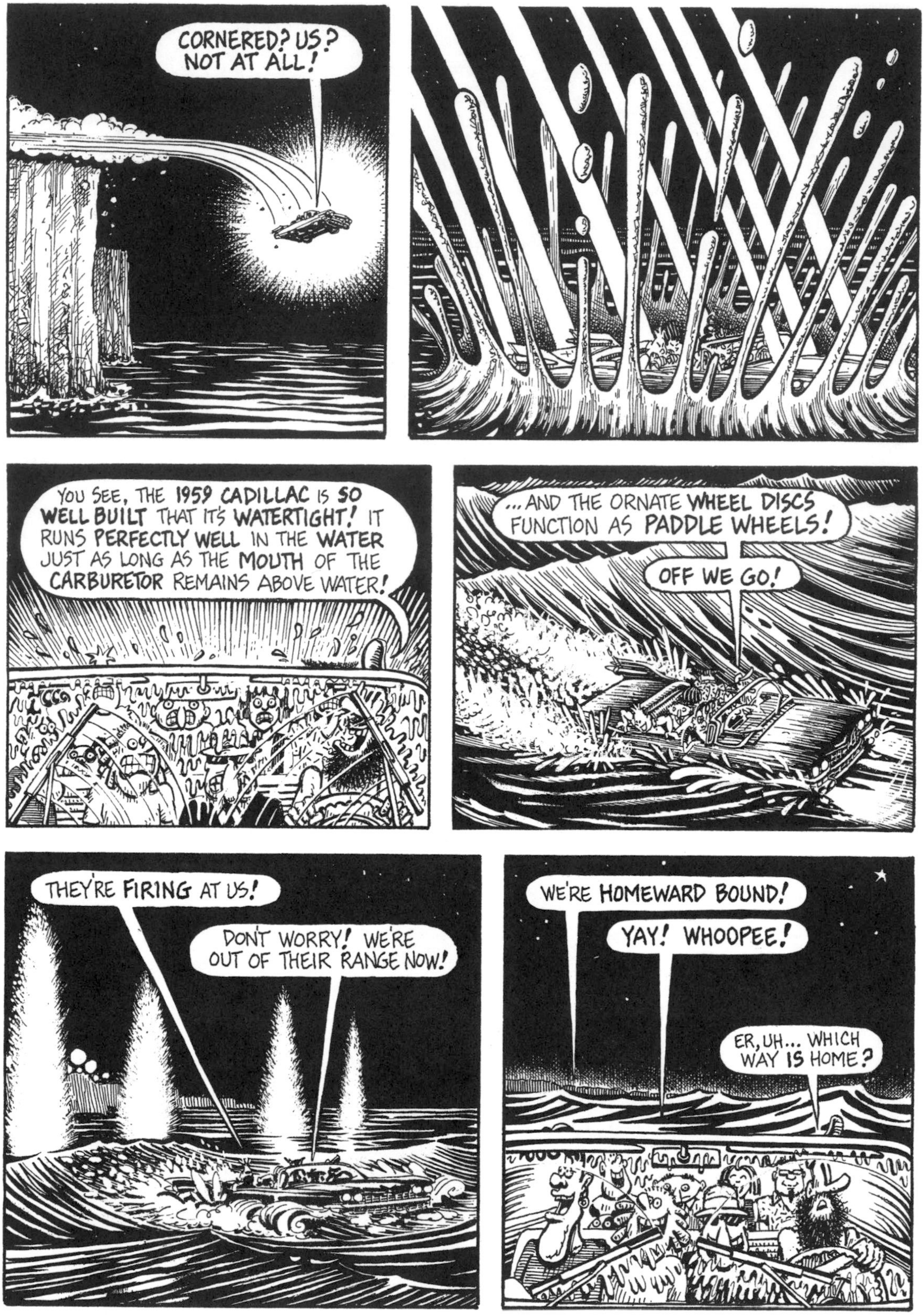
CORNERED? US? NOT AT ALL!
YOU SEE, THE 1959 CADILLAC IS SO WELL BUILT THAT IT'S WATERTIGHT! IT RUNS PERFECTLY WELL IN THE WATER JUST AS LONG AS THE MOUTH OF THE CARBURETOR REMAINS ABOVE WATER!
...AND THE ORNATE WHEEL DISCS FUNCTION AS PADDLE WHEELS!
OFF WE GO!
THEY'RE FIRING AT US!
DON'T WORRY! WE'RE OUT OF THEIR RANGE NOW!
WE'RE HOMEWARD BOUND!
YAY! WHOOPEE!
ER, UH... WHICH WAY IS HOME?

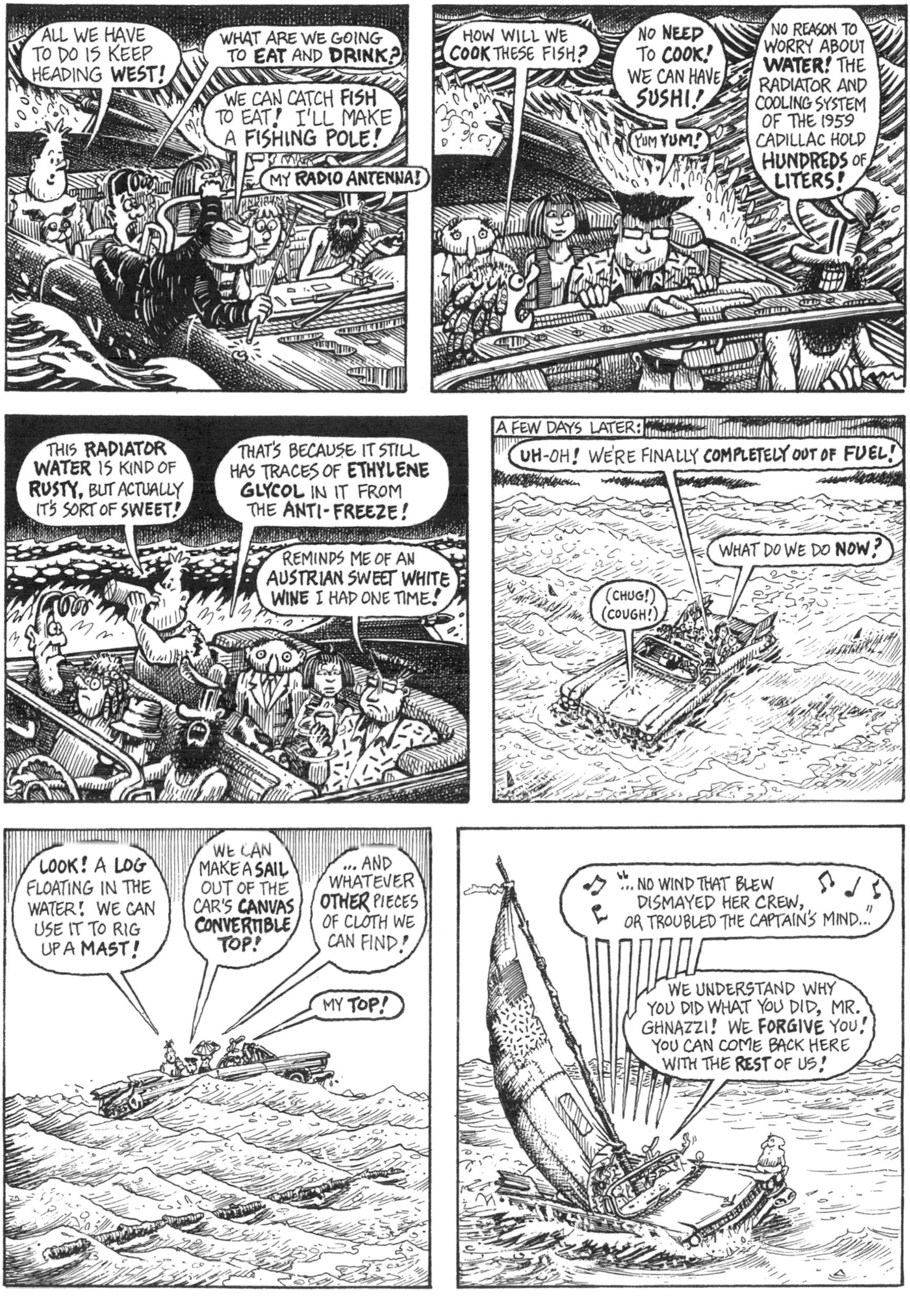
ALL WE HAVE TO DO IS KEEP HEADING WEST!
WHAT ARE WE GOING TO EAT AND DRINK?
WE CAN CATCH FISH TO EAT! I'LL MAKE A FISHING POLE!
MY RADIO ANTENNA!
HOW WILL WE COOK THESE FISH?
NO NEED TO COOK! WE CAN HAVE SUSHI!
YUM YUM!
NO REASON TO WORRY ABOUT WATER! THE RADIATOR AND COOLING SYSTEM OF THE 1959 CADILLAC HOLD HUNDREDS OF LITERS!
THIS RADIATOR WATER IS KIND OF RUSTY, BUT ACTUALLY IT'S SORT OF SWEET!
THAT'S BECAUSE IT STILL HAS TRACES OF ETHYLENE GLYCOL IN IT FROM THE ANTI-FREEZE!
REMINDS ME OF AN AUSTRIAN SWEET WHITE WINE I HAD ONE TIME!
A FEW DAYS LATER:
UH-OH! WE'RE FINALLY COMPLETELY OUT OF FUEL!
WHAT DO WE DO NOW?
(CHUG!) (COUGH!)
LOOK! A LOG FLOATING IN THE WATER! WE CAN USE IT TO RIG UP A MAST!
WE CAN MAKE A SAIL OUT OF THE CAR'S CANVAS CONVERTIBLE TOP!
...AND WHATEVER OTHER PIECES OF CLOTH WE CAN FIND!
MY TOP!
"...NO WIND THAT BLEW DISMAYED HER CREW, OR TROUBLED THE CAPTAIN'S MIND..."
WE UNDERSTAND WHY YOU DID WHAT YOU DID, MR. GHNAZZI! WE FORGIVE YOU! YOU CAN COME BACK HERE WITH THE REST OF US!

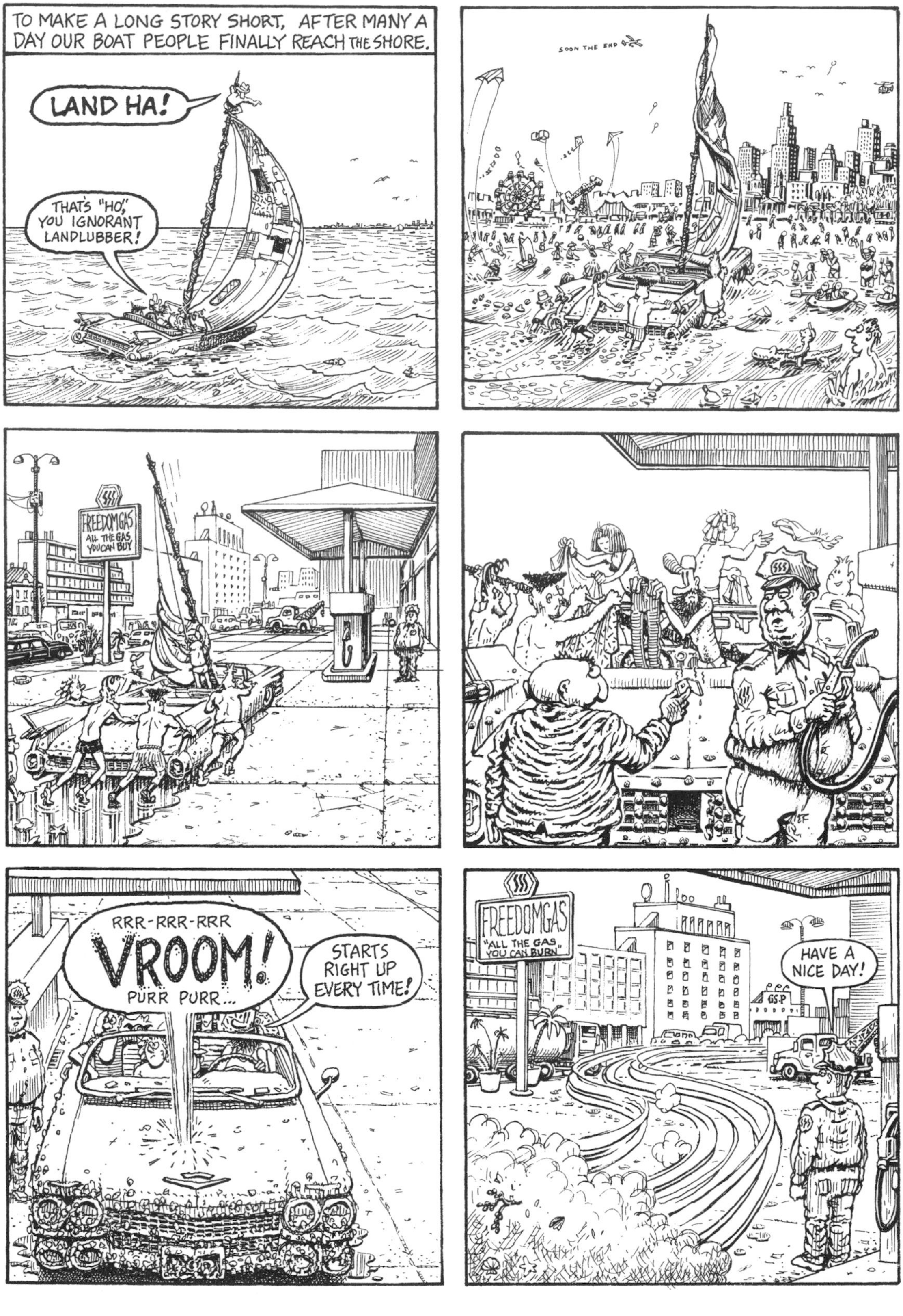
TO MAKE A LONG STORY SHORT, AFTER MANY A DAY OUR BOAT PEOPLE FINALLY REACH THE SHORE.
LAND HA!
THAT'S "HO," YOU IGNORANT LANDLUBBER!
SOON THE END
FREEDOMGAS ALL THE GAS YOU CAN BUY
RRR-RRR-RRR
VROOM!
PURR PURR...
STARTS RIGHT UP EVERY TIME!
FREEDOMGAS "ALL THE GAS YOU CAN BURN"
GS.P
HAVE A NICE DAY!

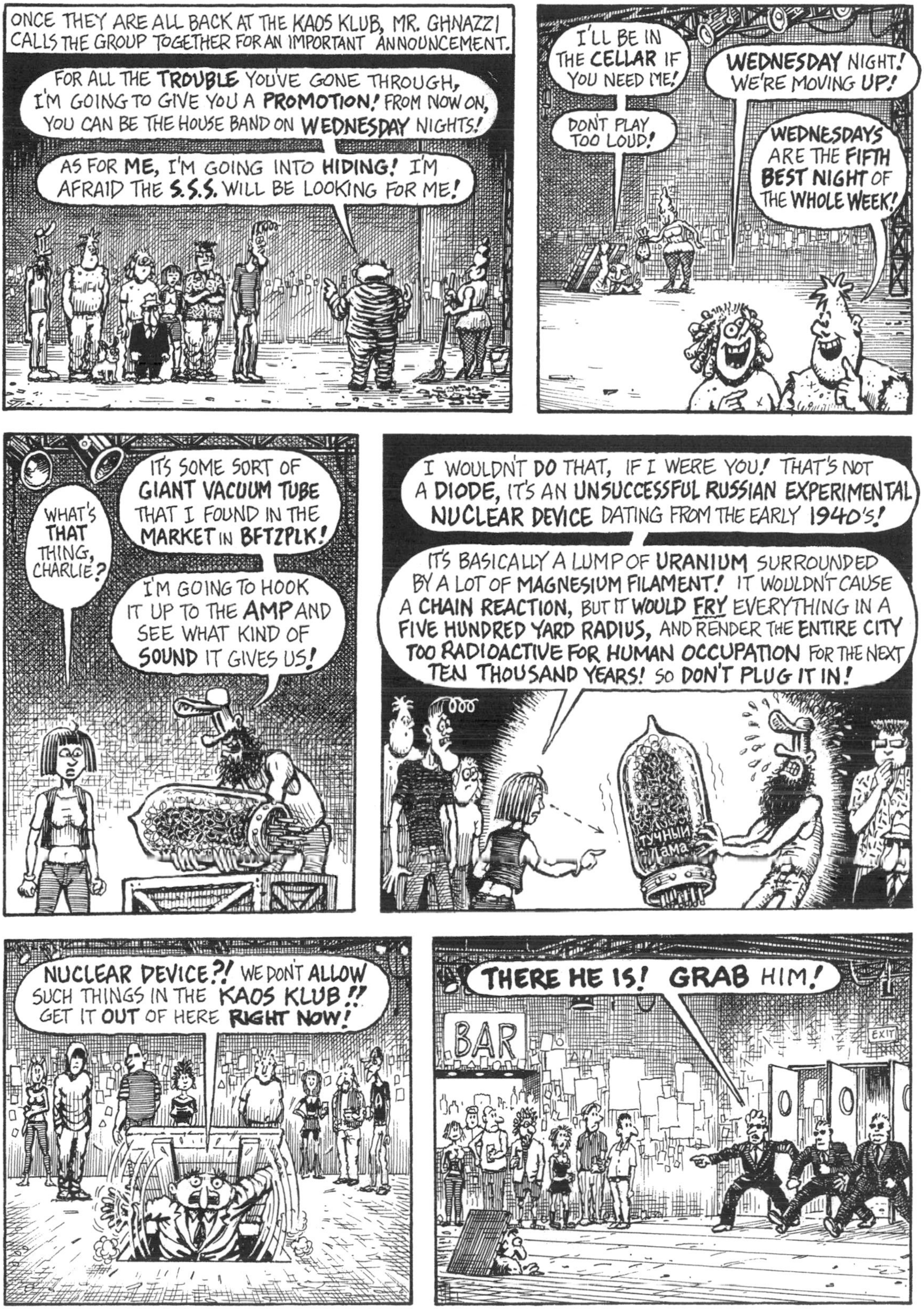
ONCE THEY ARE ALL BACK AT THE KAOS KLUB, MR. GHNAZZI CALLS THE GROUP TOGETHER FOR AN IMPORTANT ANNOUNCEMENT.
FOR ALL THE TROUBLE YOU'VE GONE THROUGH, I'M GOING TO GIVE YOU A PROMOTION! FROM NOW ON, YOU CAN BE THE HOUSE BAND ON WEDNESDAY NIGHTS!
AS FOR ME, I'M GOING INTO HIDING! I'M AFRAID THE S.S.S. WILL BE LOOKING FOR ME!
I'LL BE IN THE CELLAR IF YOU NEED ME!
DON'T PLAY TOO LOUD!
WEDNESDAY NIGHT! WE'RE MOVING UP!
WEDNESDAYS ARE THE FIFTH BEST NIGHT OF THE WHOLE WEEK!
WHAT'S THAT THING, CHARLIE?
IT'S SOME SORT OF GIANT VACUUM TUBE THAT I FOUND IN THE MARKET IN BFTZPLK!
I'M GOING TO HOOK IT UP TO THE AMP AND SEE WHAT KIND OF SOUND IT GIVES US!
I WOULDN'T DO THAT, IF I WERE YOU! THAT'S NOT A DIODE, IT'S AN UNSUCCESSFUL RUSSIAN EXPERIMENTAL NUCLEAR DEVICE DATING FROM THE EARLY 1940'S!
IT'S BASICALLY A LUMP OF URANIUM SURROUNDED BY A LOT OF MAGNESIUM FILAMENT! IT WOULDN'T CAUSE A CHAIN REACTION, BUT IT WOULD FRY EVERYTHING IN A FIVE HUNDRED YARD RADIUS, AND RENDER THE ENTIRE CITY TOO RADIOACTIVE FOR HUMAN OCCUPATION FOR THE NEXT TEN THOUSAND YEARS! SO DON'T PLUG IT IN!
NUCLEAR DEVICE?! WE DON'T ALLOW SUCH THINGS IN THE KAOS KLUB!! GET IT OUT OF HERE RIGHT NOW!
THERE HE IS! GRAB HIM!
BAR
EXIT

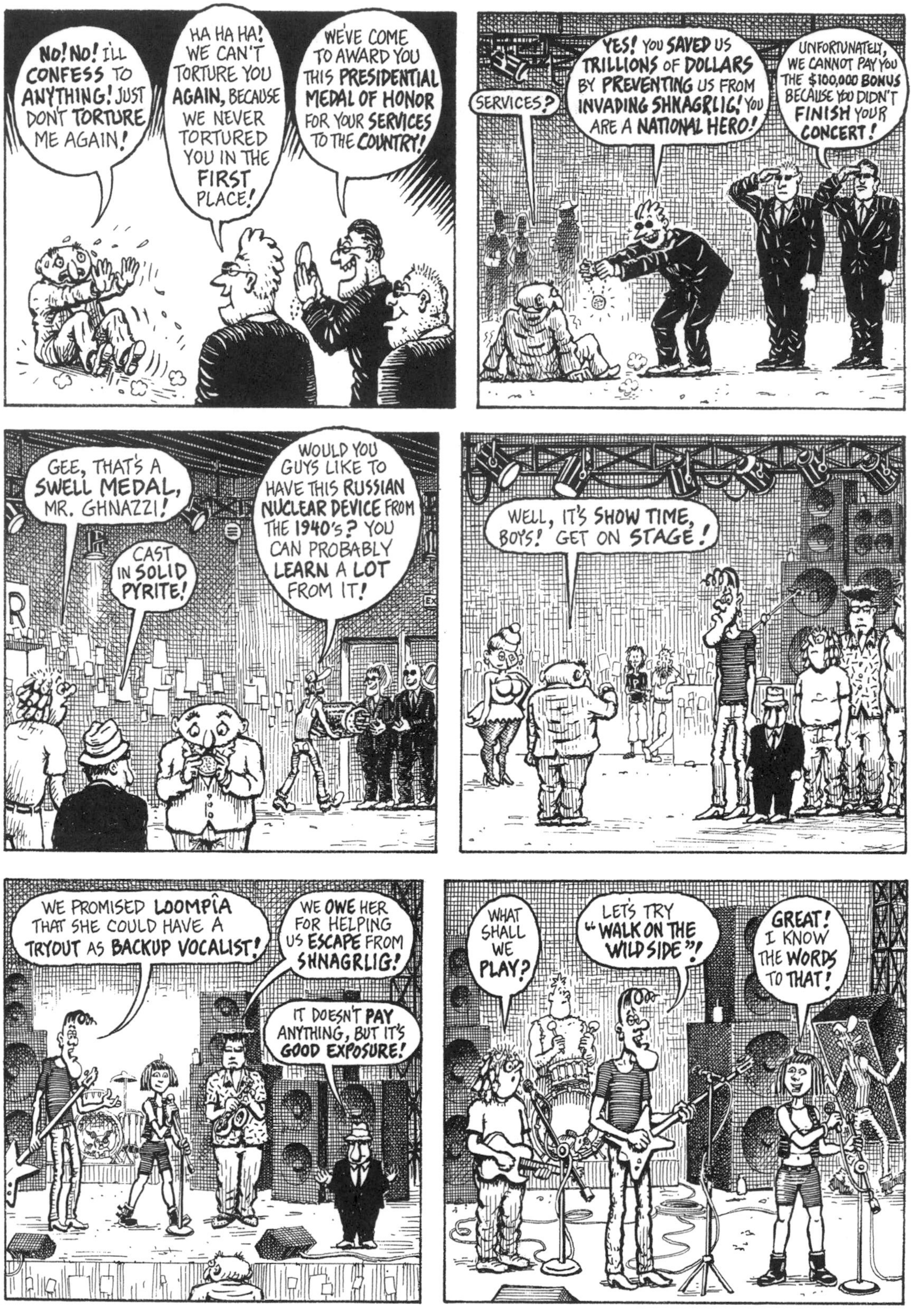
NO! NO! I'LL CONFESS TO ANYTHING! JUST DON'T TORTURE ME AGAIN!
HA HA HA! WE CAN'T TORTURE YOU AGAIN, BECAUSE WE NEVER TORTURED YOU IN THE FIRST PLACE!
WE'VE COME TO AWARD YOU THIS PRESIDENTIAL MEDAL OF HONOR FOR YOUR SERVICES TO THE COUNTRY!
SERVICES?
YES! YOU SAVED US TRILLIONS OF DOLLARS BY PREVENTING US FROM INVADING SHNAGRLIG! YOU ARE A NATIONAL HERO!
UNFORTUNATELY, WE CANNOT PAY YOU THE $100,000 BONUS BECAUSE YOU DIDN'T FINISH YOUR CONCERT!
GEE, THAT'S A SWELL MEDAL, MR. GHNAZZI!
CAST IN SOLID PYRITE!
WOULD YOU GUYS LIKE TO HAVE THIS RUSSIAN NUCLEAR DEVICE FROM THE 1940's? YOU CAN PROBABLY LEARN A LOT FROM IT!
WELL, IT'S SHOW TIME, BOYS! GET ON STAGE!
WE PROMISED LOOMPÎA THAT SHE COULD HAVE A TRYOUT AS BACKUP VOCALIST!
WE OWE HER FOR HELPING US ESCAPE FROM SHNAGRLIG!
IT DOESN'T PAY ANYTHING, BUT IT'S GOOD EXPOSURE!
WHAT SHALL WE PLAY?
LET'S TRY "WALK ON THE WILD SIDE"!
GREAT! I KNOW THE WORDS TO THAT!

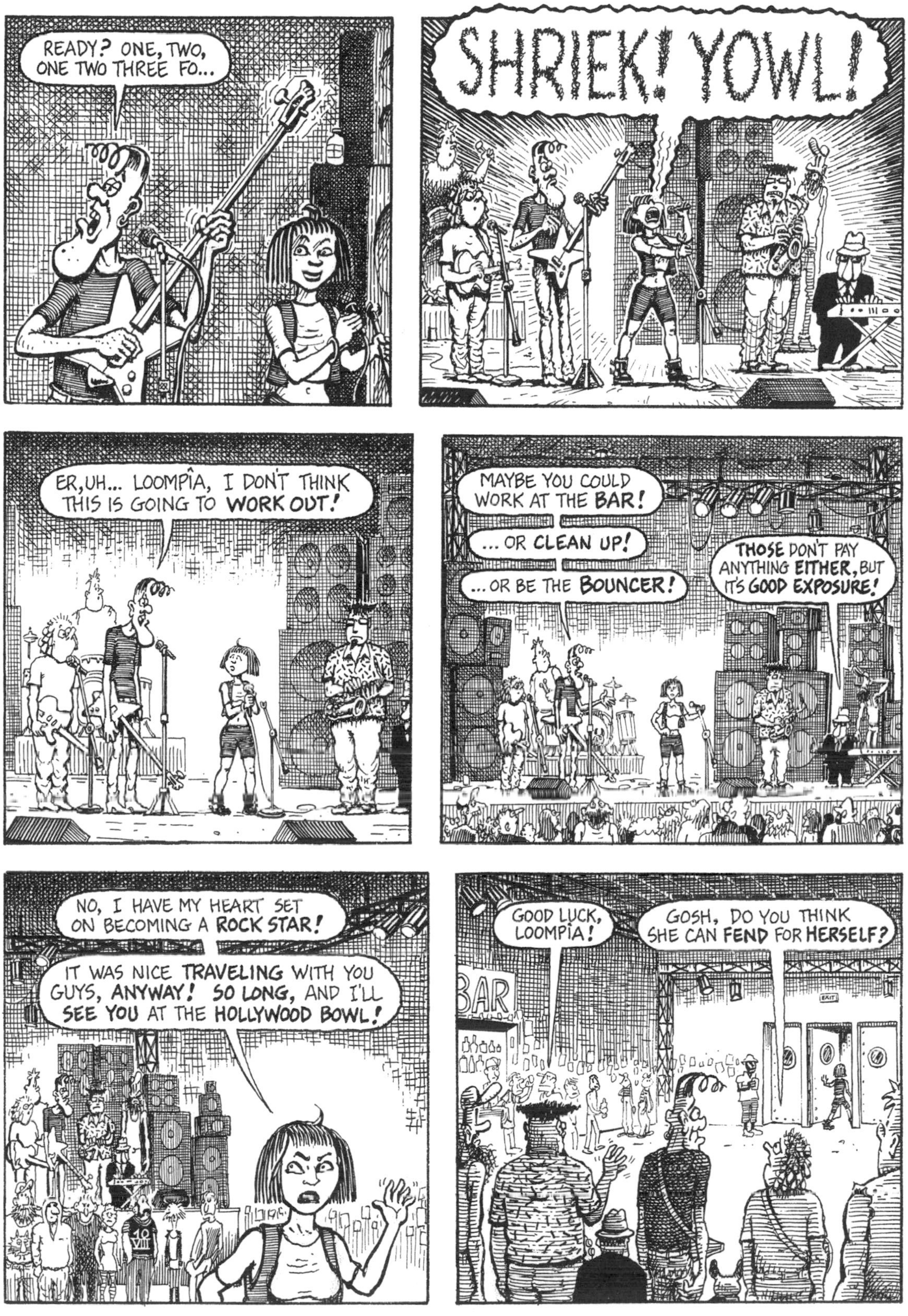
READY? ONE, TWO, ONE TWO THREE FO...
SHRIEK! YOWL!
ER, UH... LOOMPÎA, I DON'T THINK THIS IS GOING TO WORK OUT!
MAYBE YOU COULD WORK AT THE BAR!
... OR CLEAN UP!
... OR BE THE BOUNCER!
THOSE DON'T PAY ANYTHING EITHER, BUT IT'S GOOD EXPOSURE!
NO, I HAVE MY HEART SET ON BECOMING A ROCK STAR!
IT WAS NICE TRAVELING WITH YOU GUYS, ANYWAY! SO LONG, AND I'LL SEE YOU AT THE HOLLYWOOD BOWL!
BAR
EXIT
GOOD LUCK, LOOMPÎA!
GOSH, DO YOU THINK SHE CAN FEND FOR HERSELF?

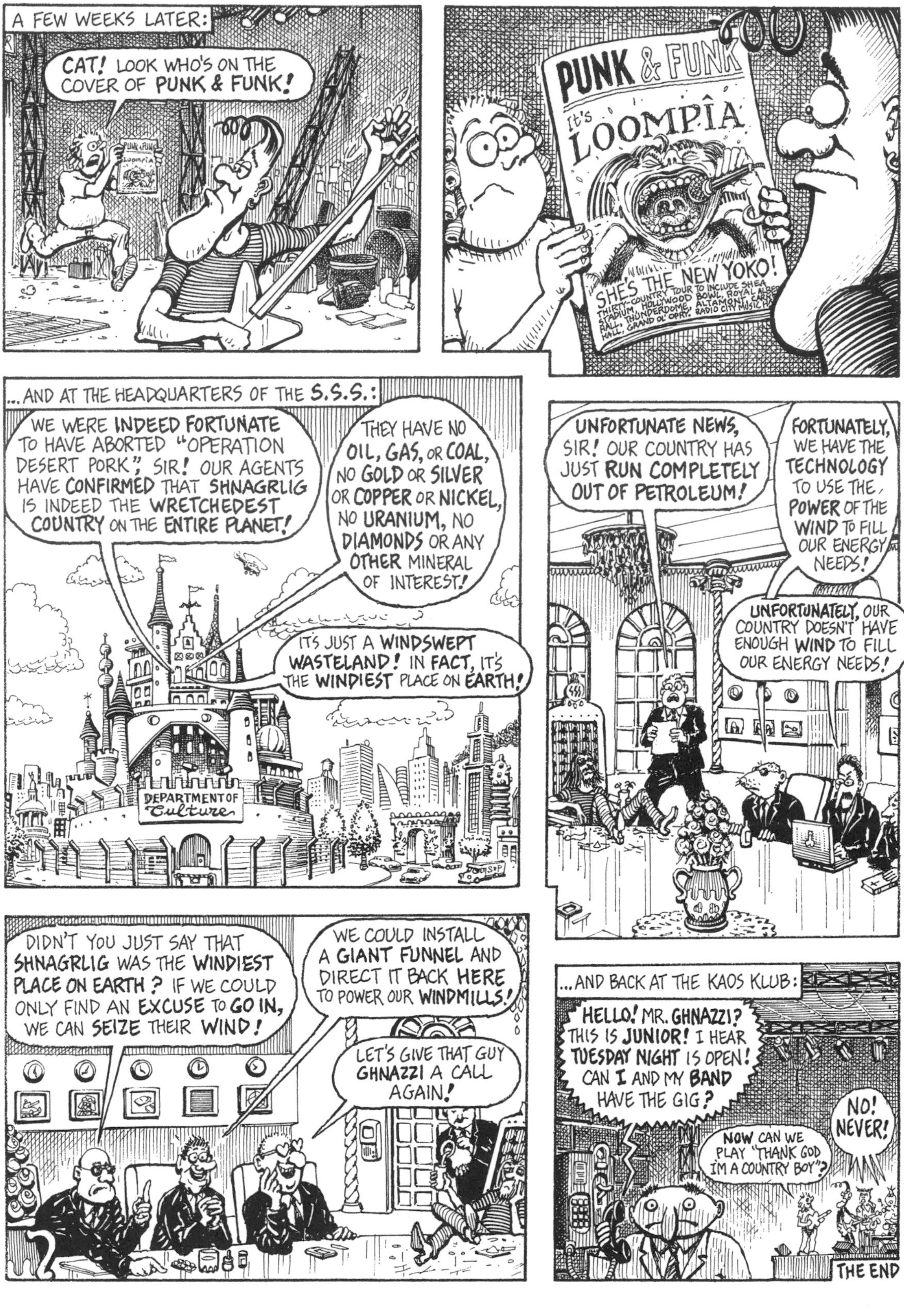
A FEW WEEKS LATER:
CAT! LOOK WHO'S ON THE COVER OF PUNK & FUNK!
PUNK & FUNK
It's LOOMPÎA
SHE'S THE NEW YOKO!
...AND AT THE HEADQUARTERS OF THE S.S.S.:
WE WERE INDEED FORTUNATE TO HAVE ABORTED "OPERATION DESERT PORK," SIR! OUR AGENTS HAVE CONFIRMED THAT SHNAGRLIG IS INDEED THE WRETCHEDEST COUNTRY ON THE ENTIRE PLANET!
THEY HAVE NO OIL, GAS, OR COAL, NO GOLD OR SILVER OR COPPER OR NICKEL, NO URANIUM, NO DIAMONDS OR ANY OTHER MINERAL OF INTEREST!
IT'S JUST A WINDSWEPT WASTELAND! IN FACT, IT'S THE WINDIEST PLACE ON EARTH!
DEPARTMENT OF Culture
UNFORTUNATE NEWS, SIR! OUR COUNTRY HAS JUST RUN COMPLETELY OUT OF PETROLEUM!
FORTUNATELY, WE HAVE THE TECHNOLOGY TO USE THE POWER OF THE WIND TO FILL OUR ENERGY NEEDS!
UNFORTUNATELY, OUR COUNTRY DOESN'T HAVE ENOUGH WIND TO FILL OUR ENERGY NEEDS!
DIDN'T YOU JUST SAY THAT SHNAGRLIG WAS THE WINDIEST PLACE ON EARTH? IF WE COULD ONLY FIND AN EXCUSE TO GO IN, WE CAN SEIZE THEIR WIND!
WE COULD INSTALL A GIANT FUNNEL AND DIRECT IT BACK HERE TO POWER OUR WINDMILLS!
LET'S GIVE THAT GUY GHNAZZI A CALL AGAIN!
...AND BACK AT THE KAOS KLUB:
HELLO! MR. GHNAZZI? THIS IS JUNIOR! I HEAR TUESDAY NIGHT IS OPEN! CAN I AND MY BAND HAVE THE GIG?
NO! NEVER!
NOW CAN WE PLAY "THANK GOD I'M A COUNTRY BOY"?
THE END

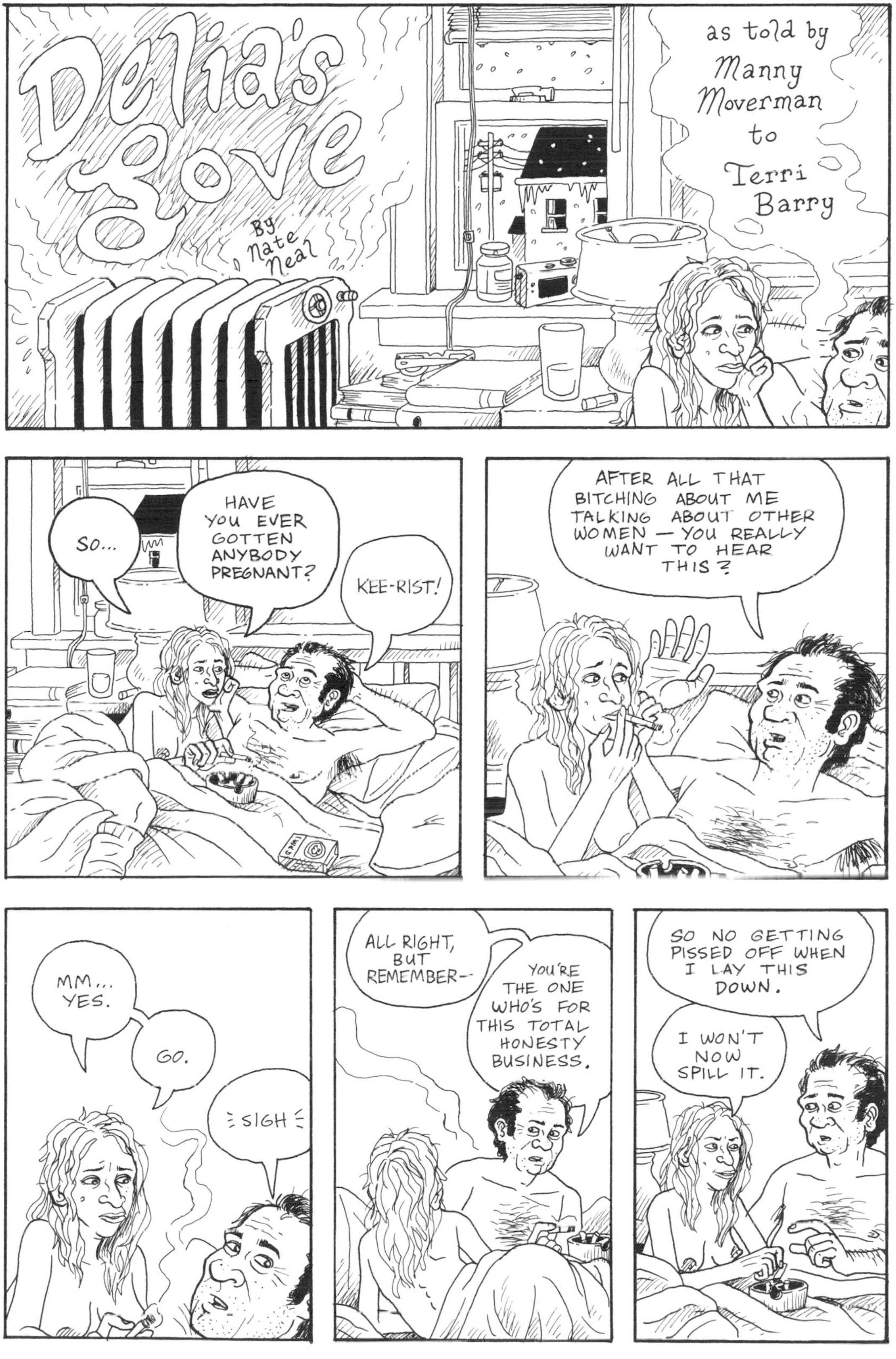

Delia's Love
By Nate Neal
as told by Manny Moverman to Terri Barry
SO...
HAVE YOU EVER GOTTEN ANYBODY PREGNANT?
KEE-RIST!
AFTER ALL THAT BITCHING ABOUT ME TALKING ABOUT OTHER WOMEN — YOU REALLY WANT TO HEAR THIS?
MM... YES.
GO.
SIGH
ALL RIGHT, BUT REMEMBER--
YOU'RE THE ONE WHO'S FOR THIS TOTAL HONESTY BUSINESS.
SO NO GETTING PISSED OFF WHEN I LAY THIS DOWN.
I WON'T NOW SPILL IT.

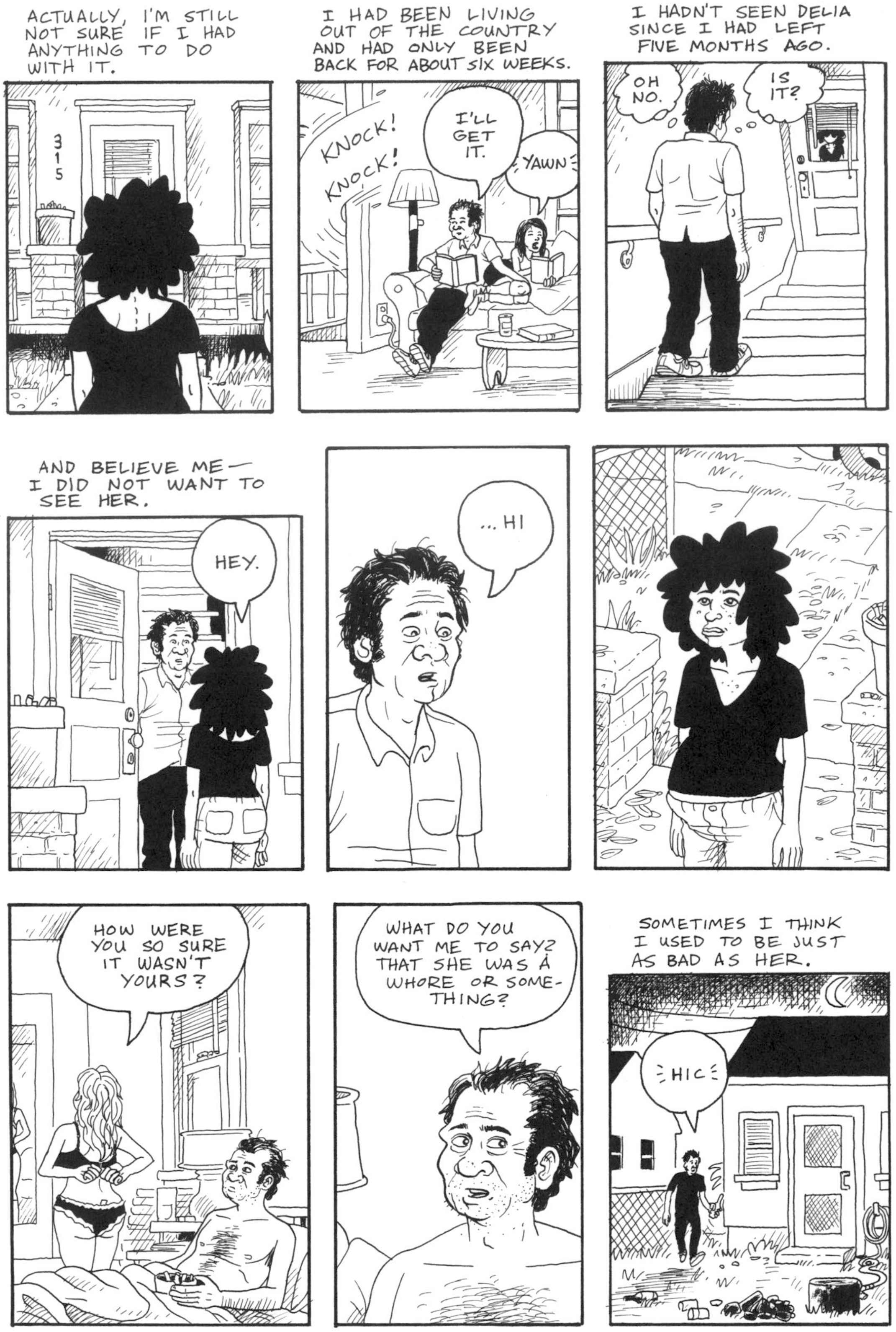
ACTUALLY, I'M STILL NOT SURE IF I HAD ANYTHING TO DO WITH IT.
315
I HAD BEEN LIVING OUT OF THE COUNTRY AND HAD ONLY BEEN BACK FOR ABOUT SIX WEEKS.
KNOCK! KNOCK!
I'LL GET IT.
YAWN
I HADN'T SEEN DELIA SINCE I HAD LEFT FIVE MONTHS AGO.
OH NO.
IS IT?
AND BELIEVE ME— I DID NOT WANT TO SEE HER.
HEY.
...HI
HOW WERE YOU SO SURE IT WASN'T YOURS?
WHAT DO YOU WANT ME TO SAY? THAT SHE WAS A WHORE OR SOME-THING?
SOMETIMES I THINK I USED TO BE JUST AS BAD AS HER.
HIC

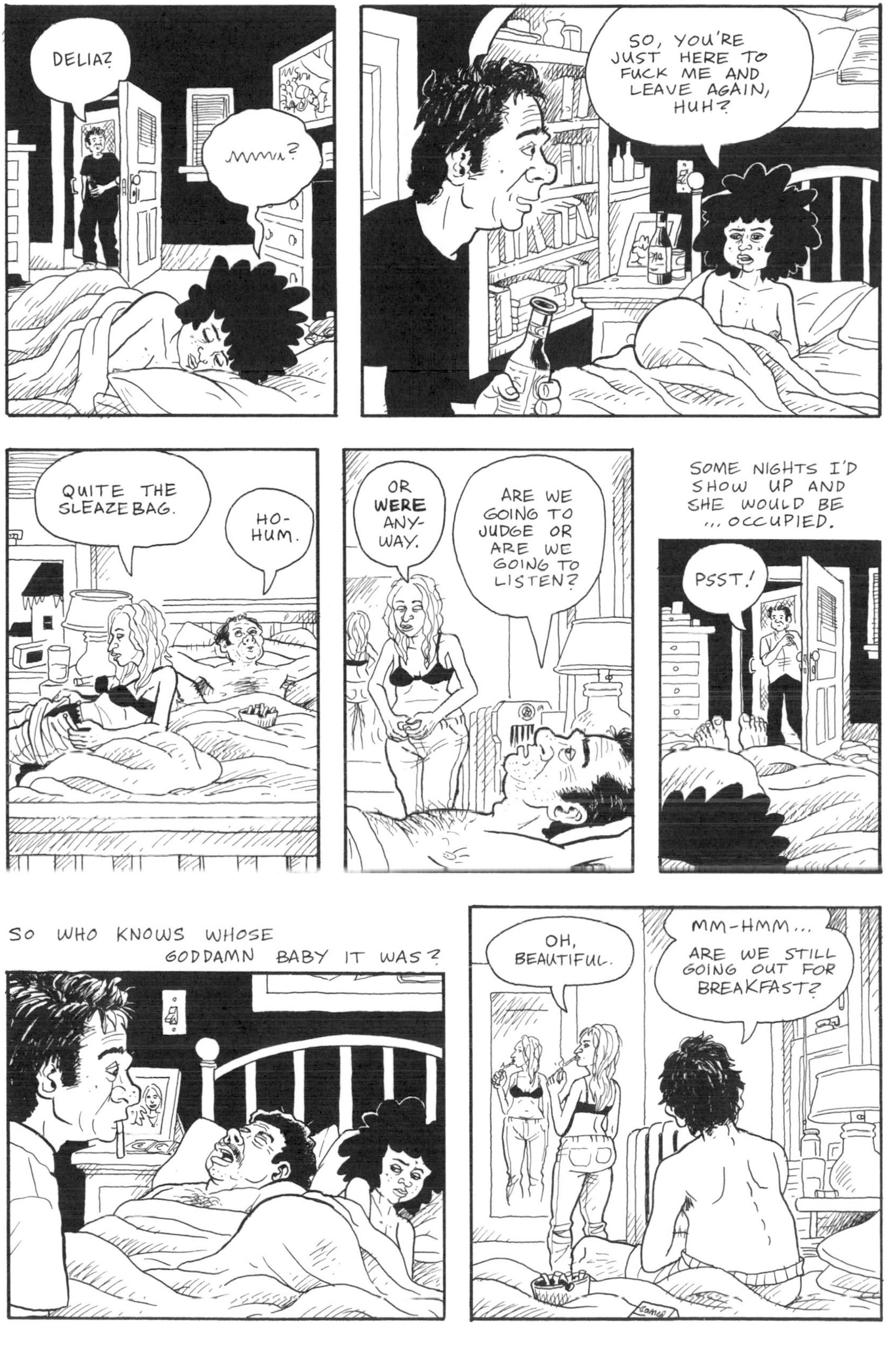

DELIA?
mmm?
SO, YOU'RE JUST HERE TO FUCK ME AND LEAVE AGAIN, HUH?
QUITE THE SLEAZEBAG.
HO-HUM.
OR **WERE** ANY-WAY.
ARE WE GOING TO JUDGE OR ARE WE GOING TO LISTEN?
SOME NIGHTS I'D SHOW UP AND SHE WOULD BE ...OCCUPIED.
PSST!
SO WHO KNOWS WHOSE GODDAMN BABY IT WAS?
OH, BEAUTIFUL.
MM-HMM... ARE WE STILL GOING OUT FOR BREAKFAST?

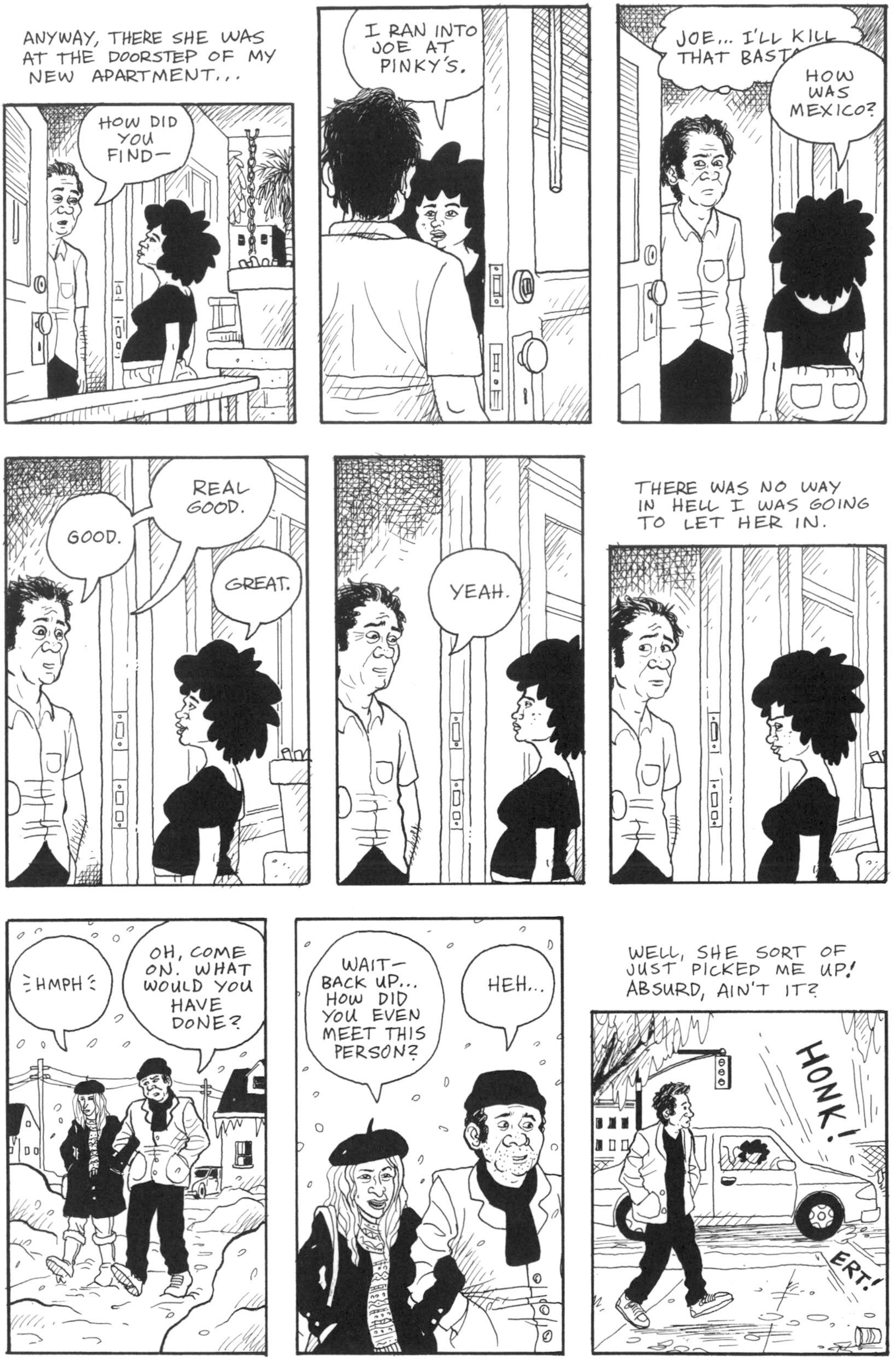

ANYWAY, THERE SHE WAS AT THE DOORSTEP OF MY NEW APARTMENT...
HOW DID YOU FIND—
I RAN INTO JOE AT PINKY'S.
JOE... I'LL KILL THAT BAST
HOW WAS MEXICO?
GOOD.
REAL GOOD.
GREAT.
YEAH.
THERE WAS NO WAY IN HELL I WAS GOING TO LET HER IN.
HMPH
OH, COME ON. WHAT WOULD YOU HAVE DONE?
WAIT— BACK UP... HOW DID YOU EVEN MEET THIS PERSON?
HEH...
WELL, SHE SORT OF JUST PICKED ME UP! ABSURD, AIN'T IT?
HONK!
ERT!

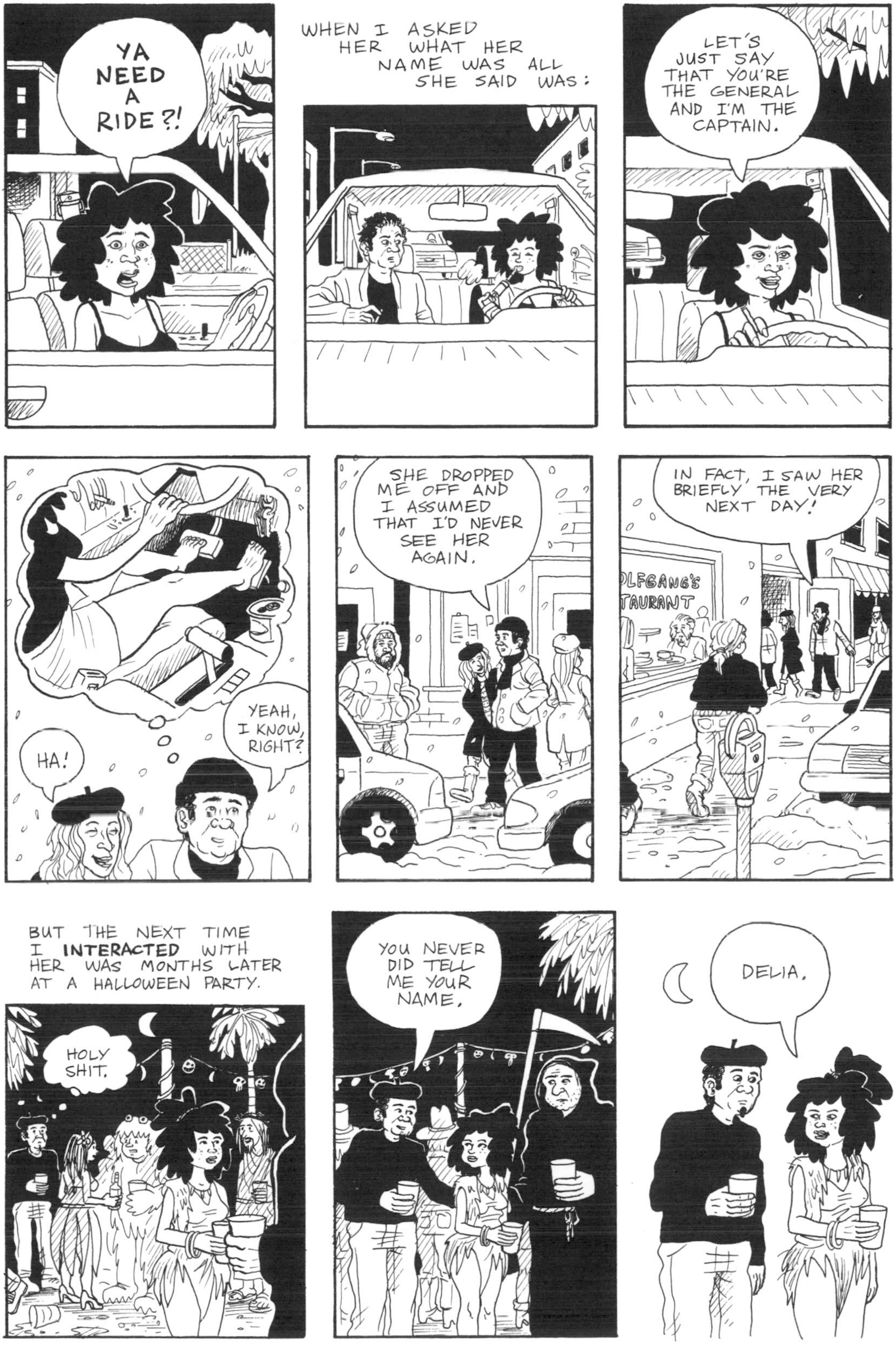
YA NEED A RIDE?!
WHEN I ASKED HER WHAT HER NAME WAS ALL SHE SAID WAS:
LET'S JUST SAY THAT YOU'RE THE GENERAL AND I'M THE CAPTAIN.
HA!
YEAH, I KNOW, RIGHT?
SHE DROPPED ME OFF AND I ASSUMED THAT I'D NEVER SEE HER AGAIN.
IN FACT, I SAW HER BRIEFLY THE VERY NEXT DAY!
OLFGANG'S
TAURANT
BUT THE NEXT TIME I INTERACTED WITH HER WAS MONTHS LATER AT A HALLOWEEN PARTY.
HOLY SHIT.
YOU NEVER DID TELL ME YOUR NAME.
DELIA.

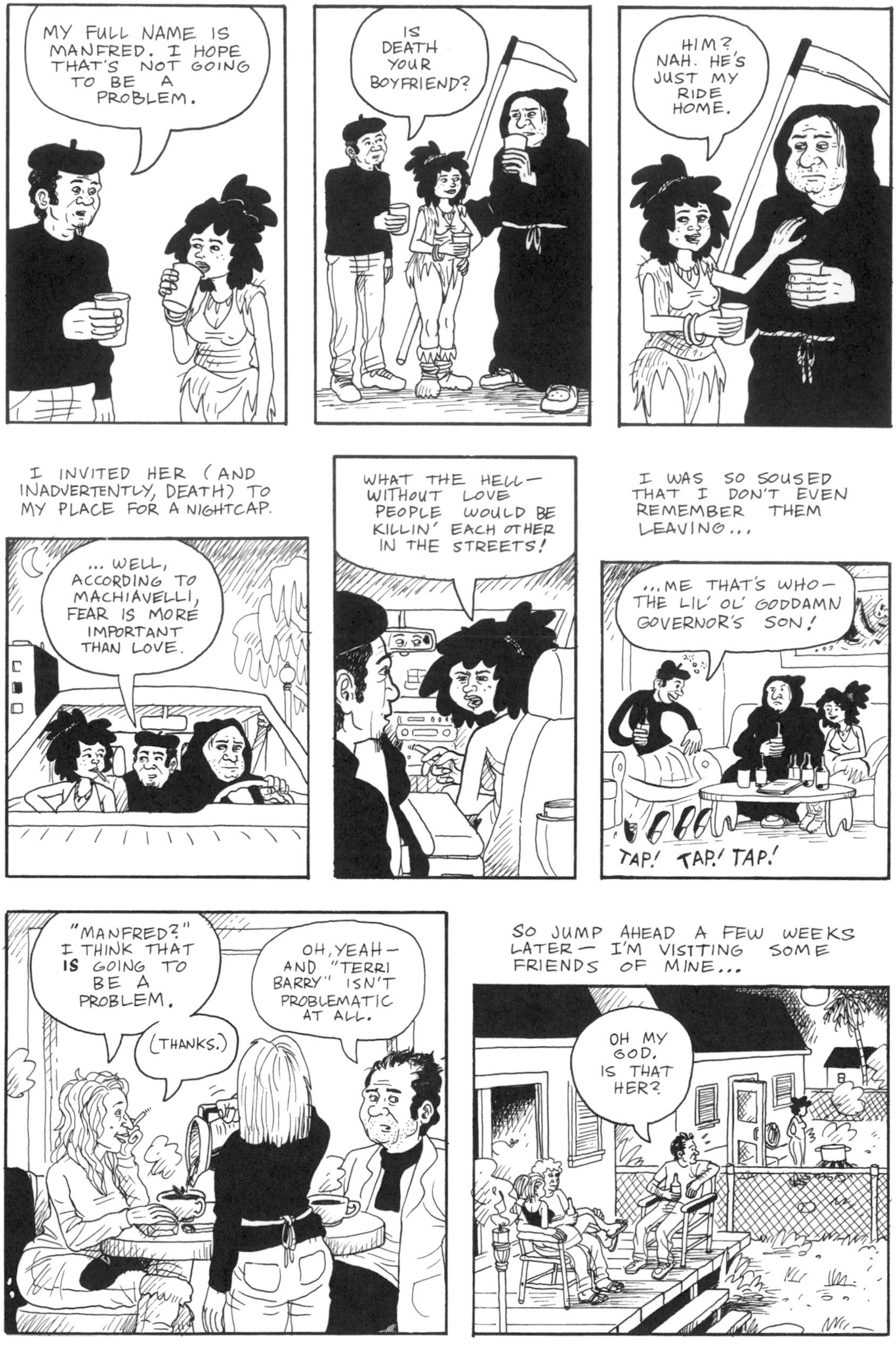
MY FULL NAME IS MANFRED. I HOPE THAT'S NOT GOING TO BE A PROBLEM.
IS DEATH YOUR BOYFRIEND?
HIM? NAH. HE'S JUST MY RIDE HOME.
I INVITED HER (AND INADVERTENTLY, DEATH) TO MY PLACE FOR A NIGHTCAP.
... WELL, ACCORDING TO MACHIAVELLI, FEAR IS MORE IMPORTANT THAN LOVE.
WHAT THE HELL— WITHOUT LOVE PEOPLE WOULD BE KILLIN' EACH OTHER IN THE STREETS!
I WAS SO SOUSED THAT I DON'T EVEN REMEMBER THEM LEAVING...
...ME THAT'S WHO— THE LIL' OL' GODDAMN GOVERNOR'S SON!
TAP! TAP! TAP!
"MANFRED?" I THINK THAT **IS** GOING TO BE A PROBLEM.
(THANKS.)
OH, YEAH— AND "TERRI BARRY" ISN'T PROBLEMATIC AT ALL.
SO JUMP AHEAD A FEW WEEKS LATER— I'M VISITING SOME FRIENDS OF MINE...
OH MY GOD. IS THAT HER?

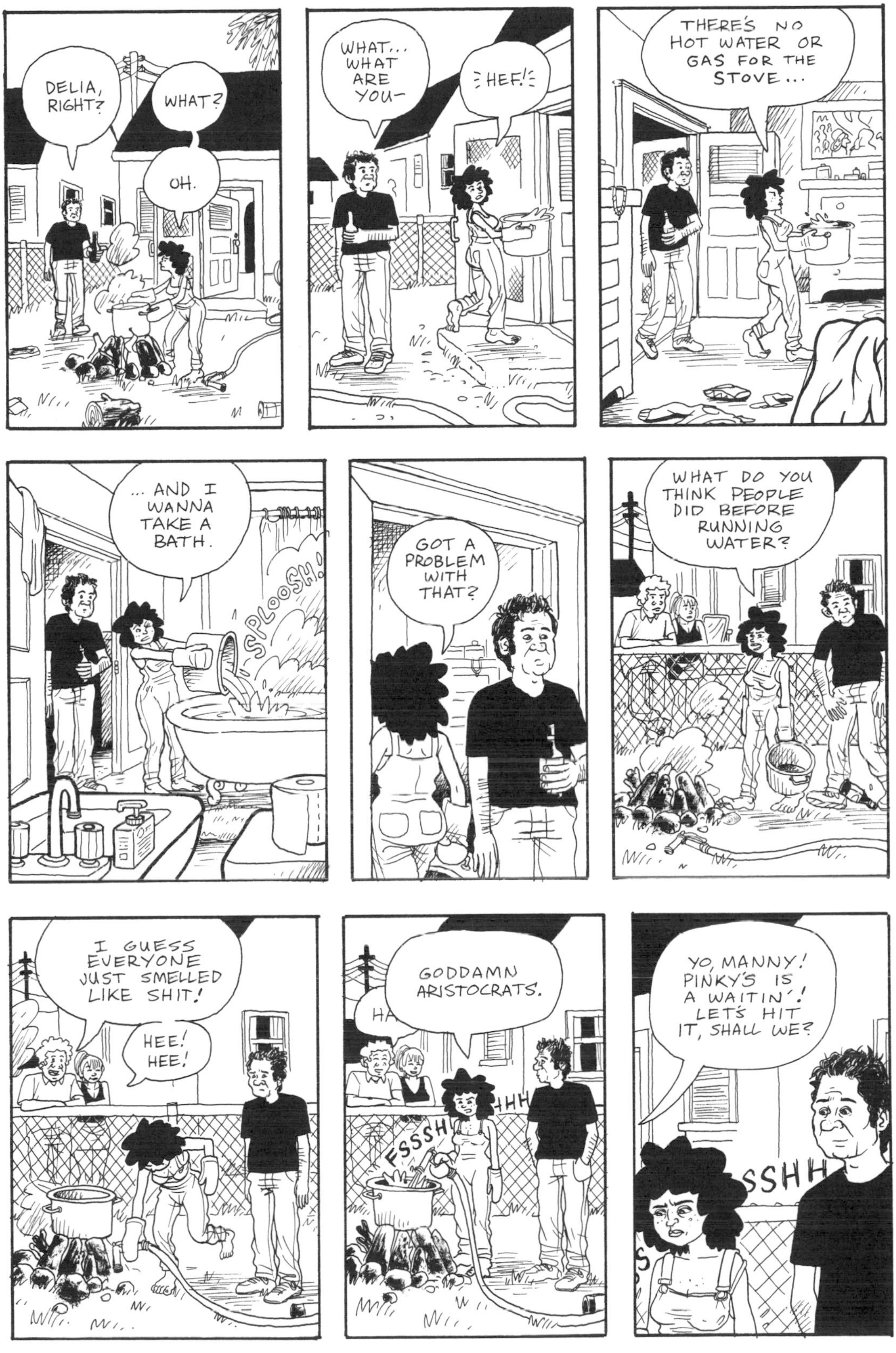
DELIA, RIGHT?
WHAT?
OH.
WHAT... WHAT ARE YOU-
HEF!
THERE'S NO HOT WATER OR GAS FOR THE STOVE...
...AND I WANNA TAKE A BATH.
SPLOOSH!
GOT A PROBLEM WITH THAT?
WHAT DO YOU THINK PEOPLE DID BEFORE RUNNING WATER?
I GUESS EVERYONE JUST SMELLED LIKE SHIT!
HEE! HEE!
GODDAMN ARISTOCRATS!
FSSSH
YO, MANNY! PINKY'S IS A WAITIN'! LET'S HIT IT, SHALL WE?
SSHH

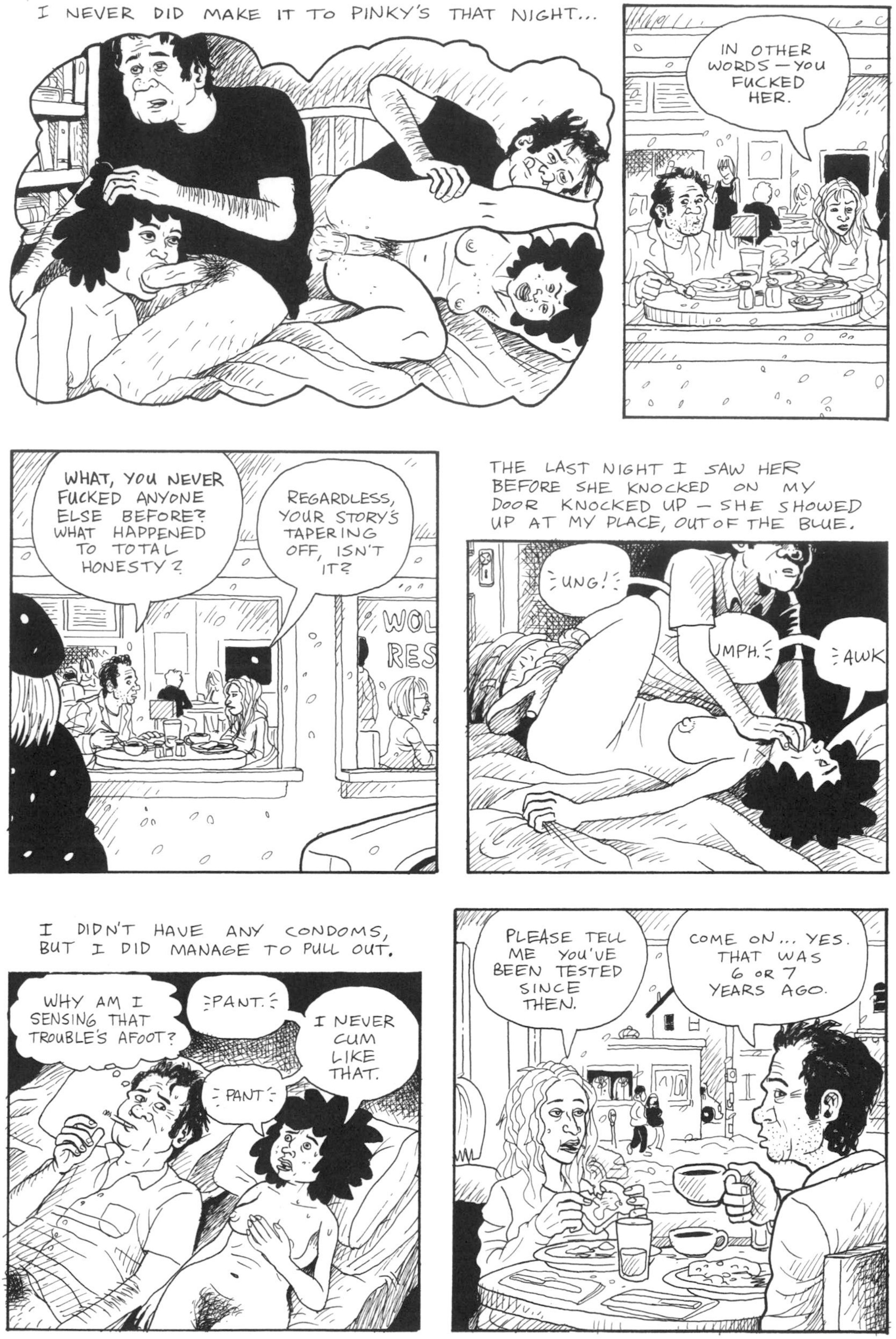
I NEVER DID MAKE IT TO PINKY'S THAT NIGHT...
IN OTHER WORDS — YOU FUCKED HER.
WHAT, YOU NEVER FUCKED ANYONE ELSE BEFORE? WHAT HAPPENED TO TOTAL HONESTY?
REGARDLESS, YOUR STORY'S TAPERING OFF, ISN'T IT?
WOL
RES
THE LAST NIGHT I SAW HER BEFORE SHE KNOCKED ON MY DOOR KNOCKED UP — SHE SHOWED UP AT MY PLACE, OUT OF THE BLUE.
UNG!
UMPH.
AWK
I DIDN'T HAVE ANY CONDOMS, BUT I DID MANAGE TO PULL OUT.
WHY AM I SENSING THAT TROUBLE'S AFOOT?
PANT.
I NEVER CUM LIKE THAT.
PANT
PLEASE TELL ME YOU'VE BEEN TESTED SINCE THEN.
COME ON... YES. THAT WAS 6 OR 7 YEARS AGO.

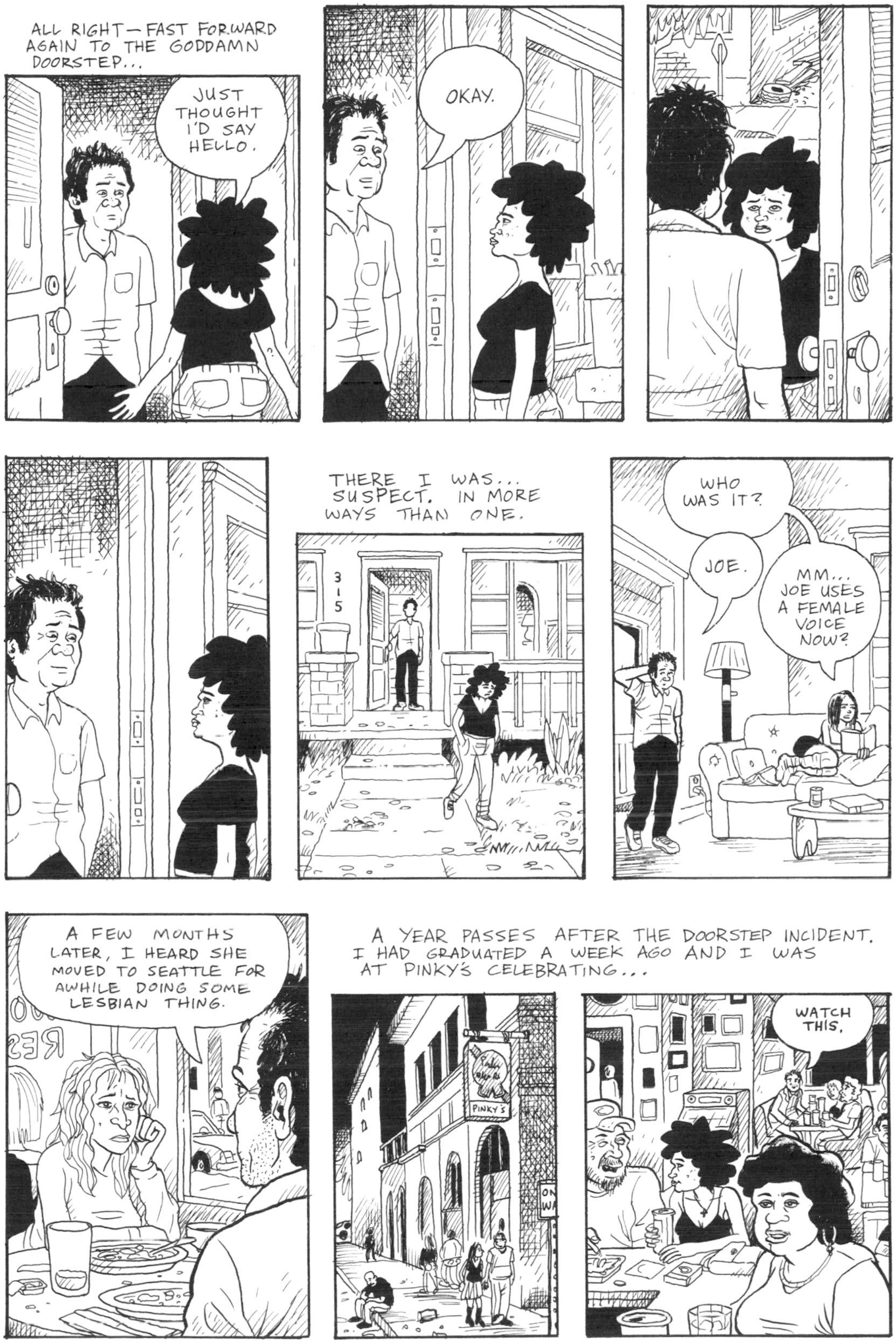
ALL RIGHT—FAST FORWARD AGAIN TO THE GODDAMN DOORSTEP...
JUST THOUGHT I'D SAY HELLO.
OKAY.
THERE I WAS... SUSPECT. IN MORE WAYS THAN ONE.
3 1 5
WHO WAS IT?
JOE.
MM... JOE USES A FEMALE VOICE NOW?
A FEW MONTHS LATER, I HEARD SHE MOVED TO SEATTLE FOR AWHILE DOING SOME LESBIAN THING.
A YEAR PASSES AFTER THE DOORSTEP INCIDENT. I HAD GRADUATED A WEEK AGO AND I WAS AT PINKY'S CELEBRATING...
PINKY'S
WATCH THIS.

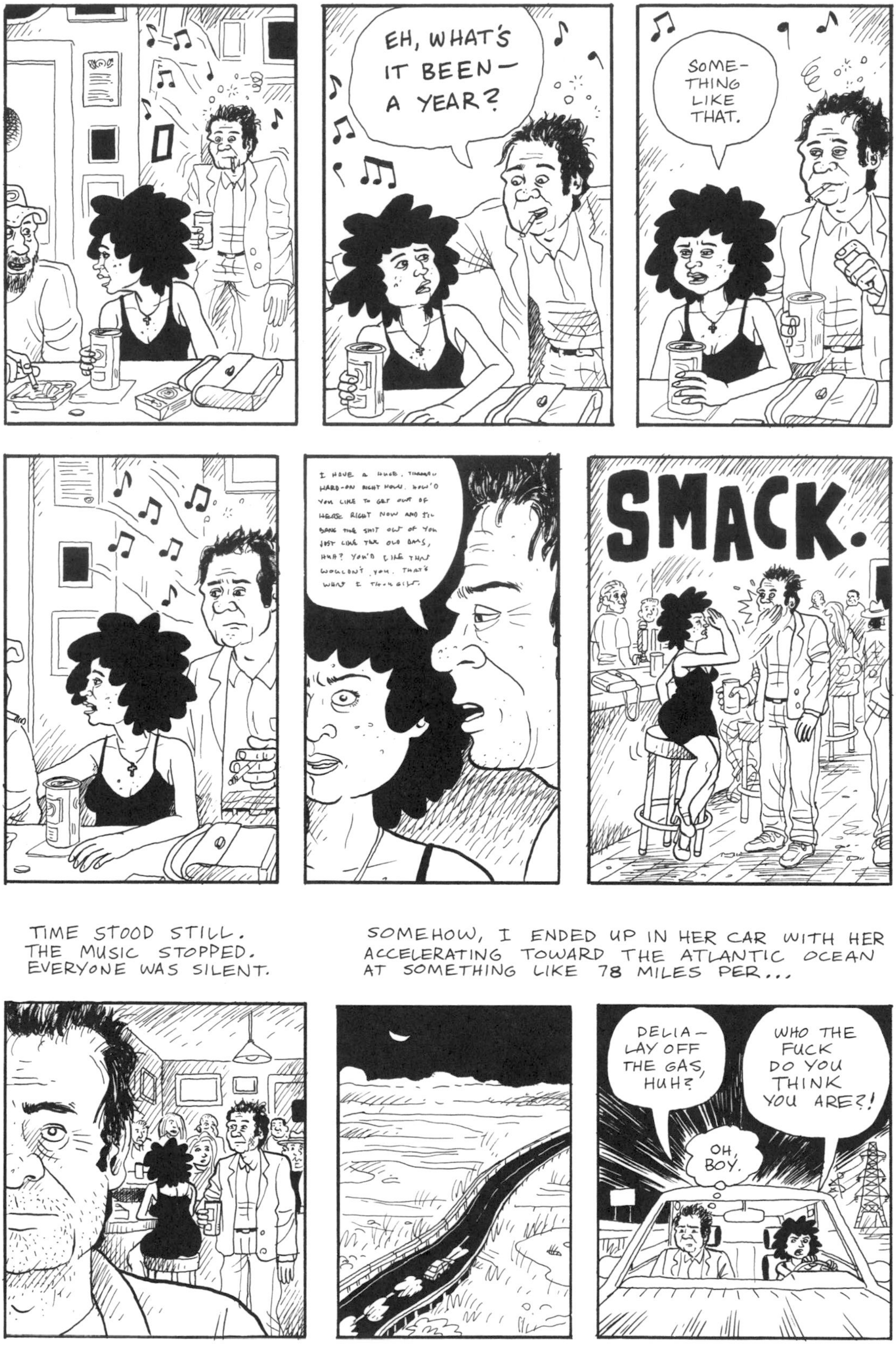
EH, WHAT'S IT BEEN— A YEAR?
SOME-THING LIKE THAT.
I HAVE A HUGE, THROBBING HARD-ON RIGHT NOW. HOW'D YOU LIKE TO GET OUT OF HERE RIGHT NOW AND I'LL BANG THE SHIT OUT OF YOU JUST LIKE THE OLD DAYS, HUH? YOU'D LIKE THAT WOULDN'T YOU. THAT'S WHAT I THOUGHT.
SMACK.
TIME STOOD STILL. THE MUSIC STOPPED. EVERYONE WAS SILENT.
SOMEHOW, I ENDED UP IN HER CAR WITH HER ACCELERATING TOWARD THE ATLANTIC OCEAN AT SOMETHING LIKE 78 MILES PER...
DELIA— LAY OFF THE GAS, HUH?
OH, BOY.
WHO THE FUCK DO YOU THINK YOU ARE?!

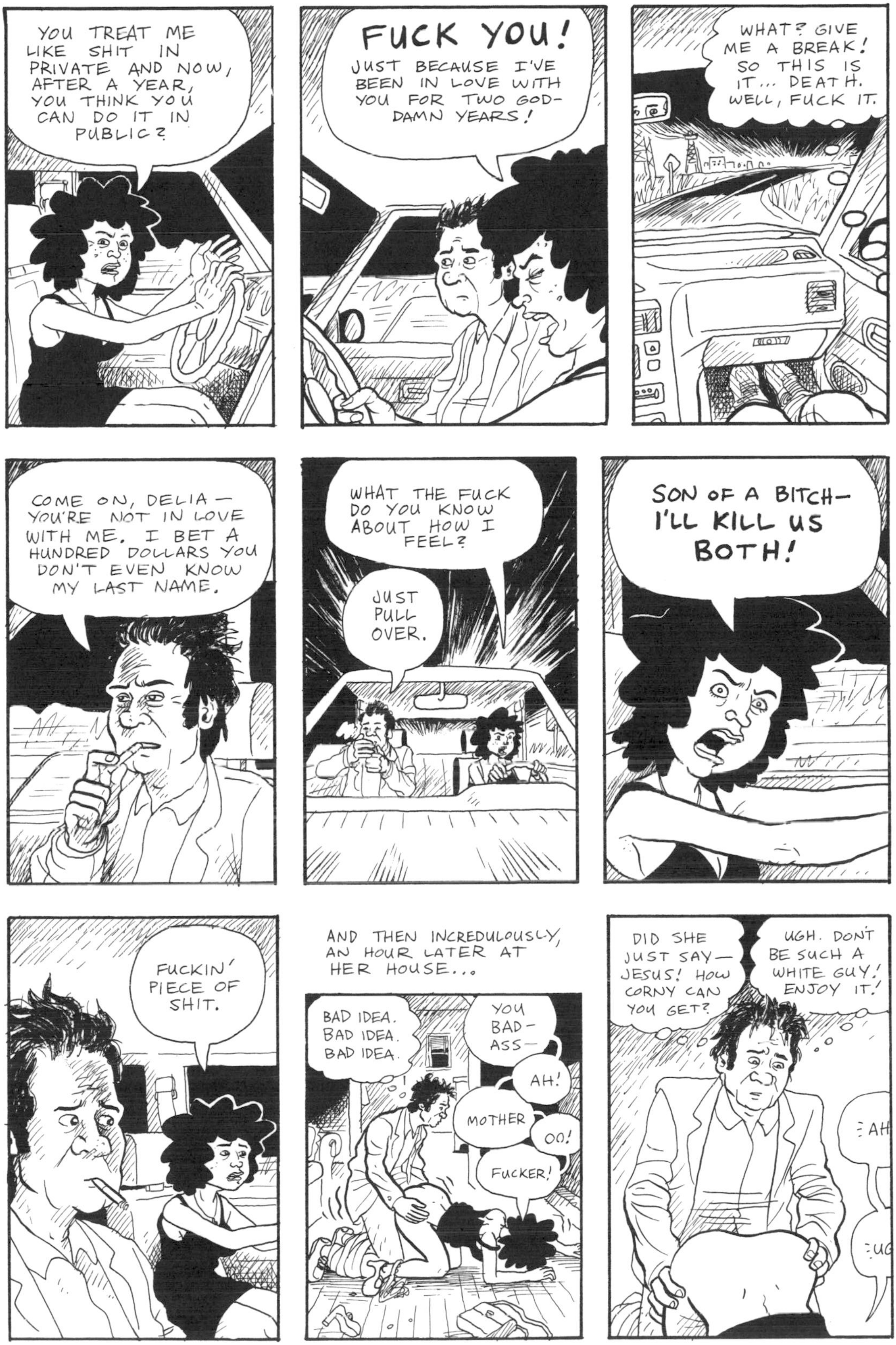
YOU TREAT ME LIKE SHIT IN PRIVATE AND NOW, AFTER A YEAR, YOU THINK YOU CAN DO IT IN PUBLIC?
FUCK YOU! JUST BECAUSE I'VE BEEN IN LOVE WITH YOU FOR TWO GOD-DAMN YEARS!
WHAT? GIVE ME A BREAK! SO THIS IS IT... DEATH. WELL, FUCK IT.
COME ON, DELIA— YOU'RE NOT IN LOVE WITH ME. I BET A HUNDRED DOLLARS YOU DON'T EVEN KNOW MY LAST NAME.
WHAT THE FUCK DO YOU KNOW ABOUT HOW I FEEL?
JUST PULL OVER.
SON OF A BITCH— I'LL KILL US BOTH!
FUCKIN' PIECE OF SHIT.
AND THEN INCREDULOUSLY, AN HOUR LATER AT HER HOUSE...
BAD IDEA. BAD IDEA. BAD IDEA.
YOU BAD-ASS—
AH!
MOTHER
OO!
FUCKER!
DID SHE JUST SAY— JESUS! HOW CORNY CAN YOU GET?
UGH. DON'T BE SUCH A WHITE GUY! ENJOY IT!

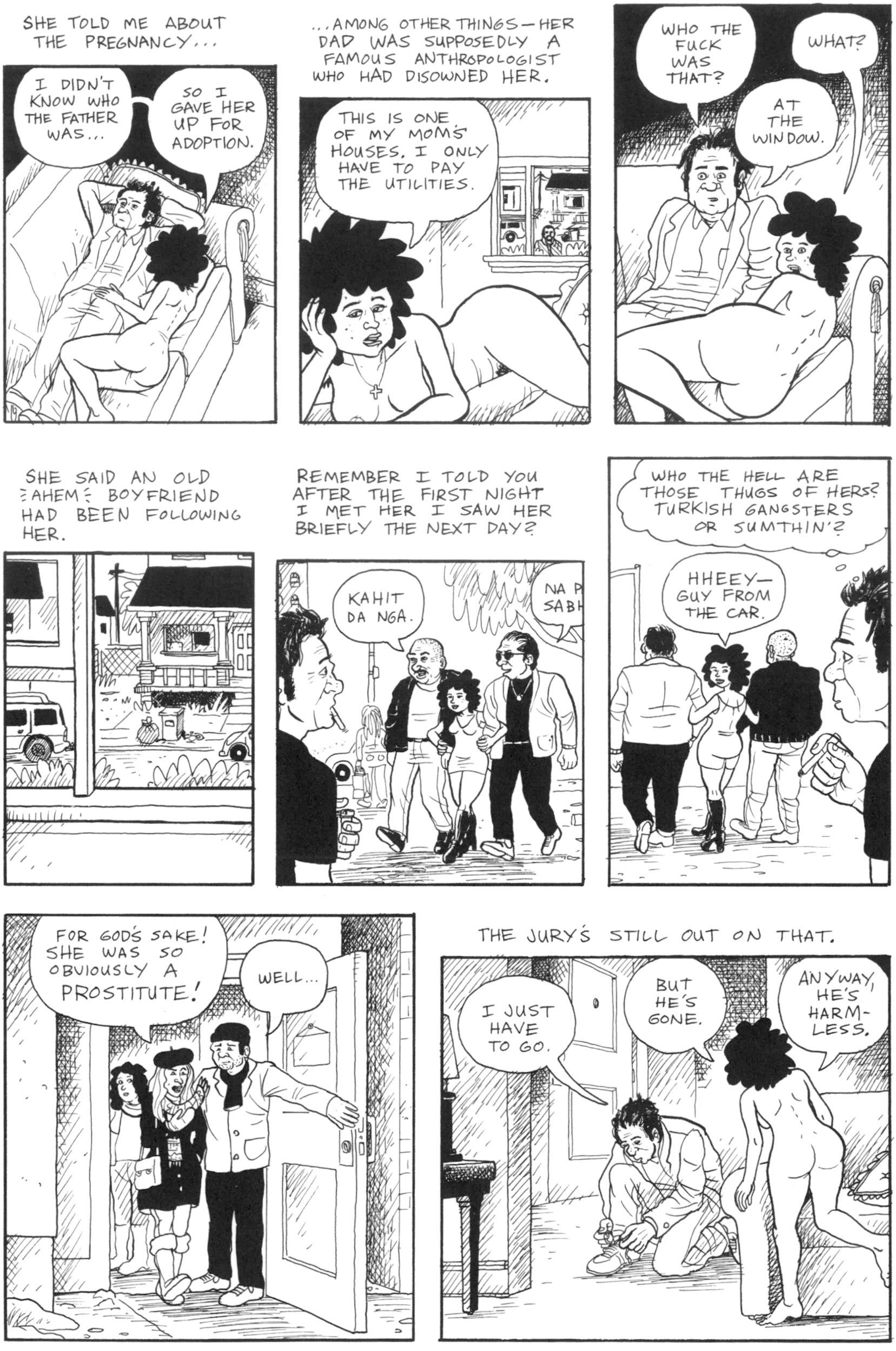
SHE TOLD ME ABOUT THE PREGNANCY...
I DIDN'T KNOW WHO THE FATHER WAS...
SO I GAVE HER UP FOR ADOPTION.
...AMONG OTHER THINGS—HER DAD WAS SUPPOSEDLY A FAMOUS ANTHROPOLOGIST WHO HAD DISOWNED HER.
THIS IS ONE OF MY MOM'S HOUSES. I ONLY HAVE TO PAY THE UTILITIES.
WHO THE FUCK WAS THAT?
WHAT?
AT THE WINDOW.
SHE SAID AN OLD ≡AHEM≡ BOYFRIEND HAD BEEN FOLLOWING HER.
REMEMBER I TOLD YOU AFTER THE FIRST NIGHT I MET HER I SAW HER BRIEFLY THE NEXT DAY?
KAHIT DA NGA.
NA P SABH
WHO THE HELL ARE THOSE THUGS OF HERS? TURKISH GANGSTERS OR SUMTHIN'?
HHEEY— GUY FROM THE CAR.
FOR GOD'S SAKE! SHE WAS SO OBVIOUSLY A PROSTITUTE!
WELL...
THE JURY'S STILL OUT ON THAT.
I JUST HAVE TO GO.
BUT HE'S GONE.
ANYWAY, HE'S HARMLESS.

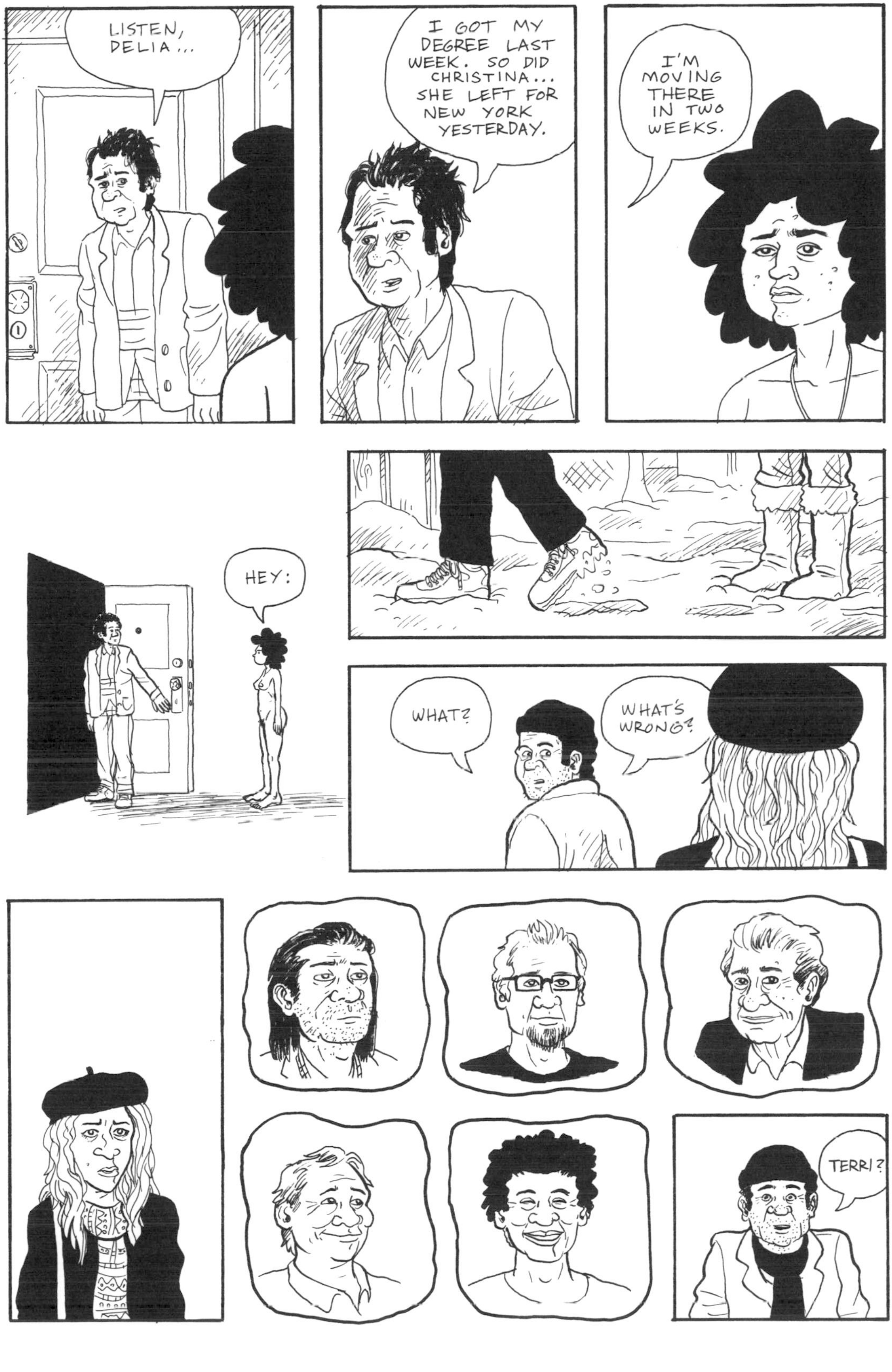
LISTEN, DELIA...
I GOT MY DEGREE LAST WEEK. SO DID CHRISTINA... SHE LEFT FOR NEW YORK YESTERDAY.
I'M MOVING THERE IN TWO WEEKS.
HEY:
WHAT?
WHAT'S WRONG?
TERRI?

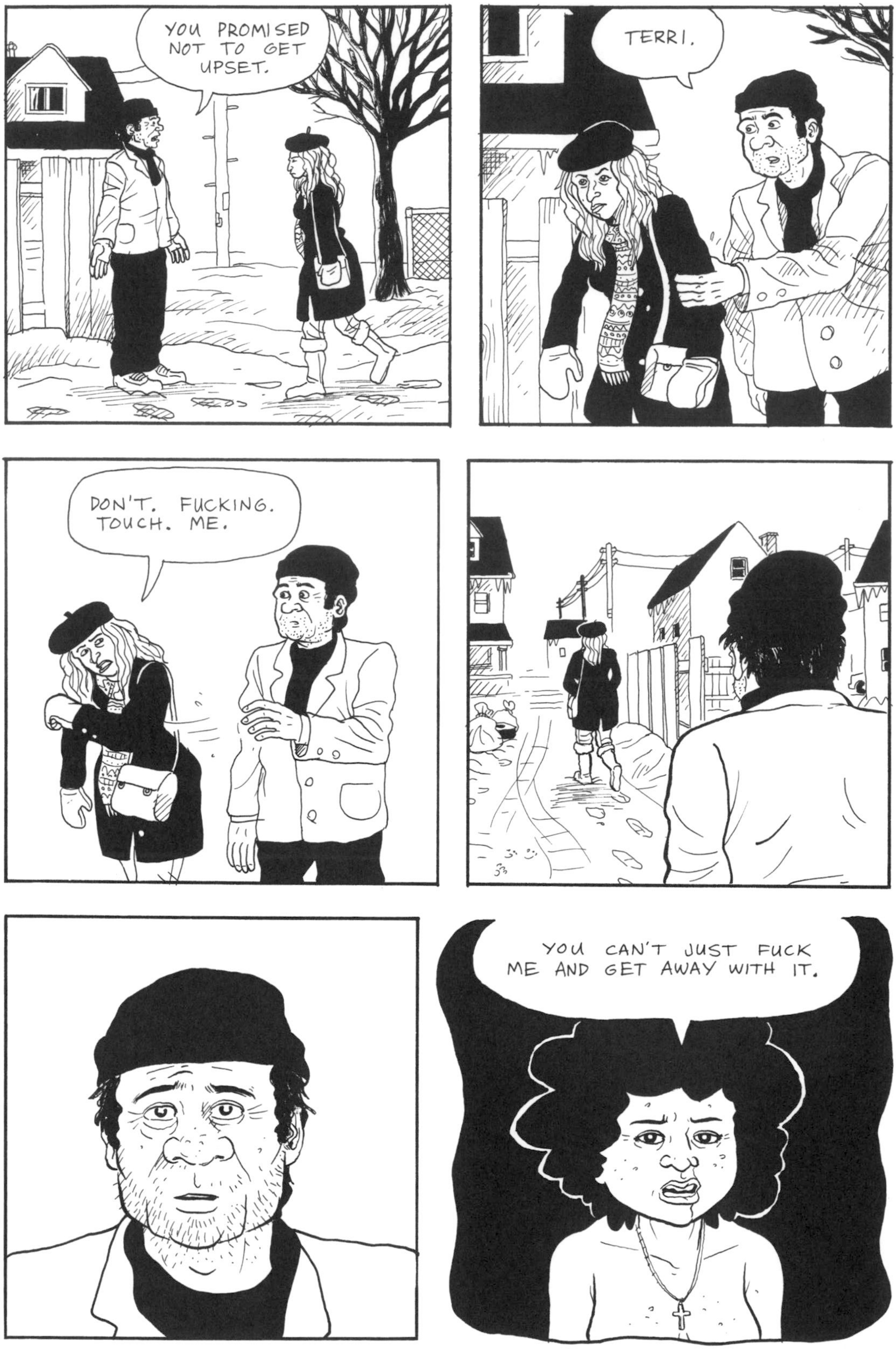

YOU PROMISED NOT TO GET UPSET.
TERRI.
DON'T. FUCKING. TOUCH. ME.
YOU CAN'T JUST FUCK ME AND GET AWAY WITH IT.

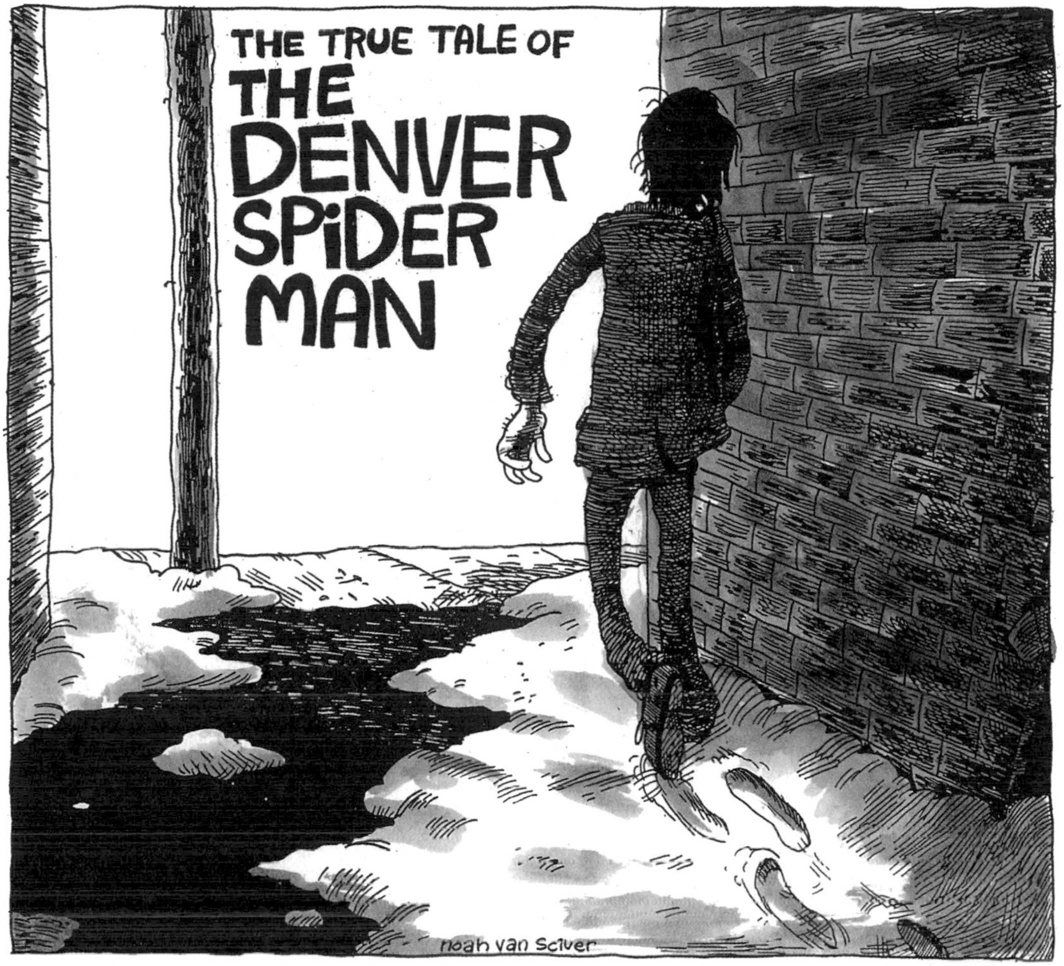
THE TRUE TALE OF
THE DENVER SPIDER MAN
noah van sciver

Theodore edward coneys was born in Petersburg illinois in 1882. His father was a Canadian immigrant who owned a hardware store.

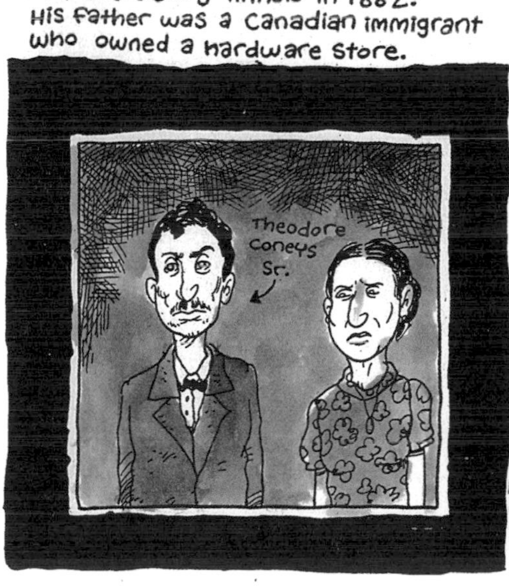
Theodore Coneys Sr.

From the time he was born he was a frail, sickly child. The doctors said he would not live to see his 18th birthday. consequently, he never finished school.

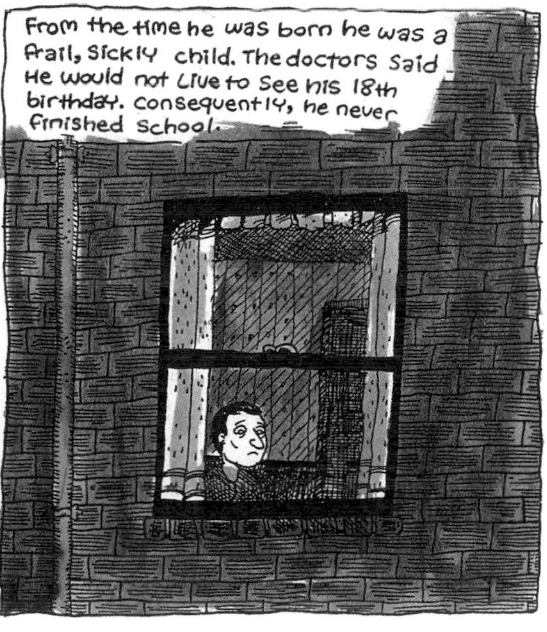

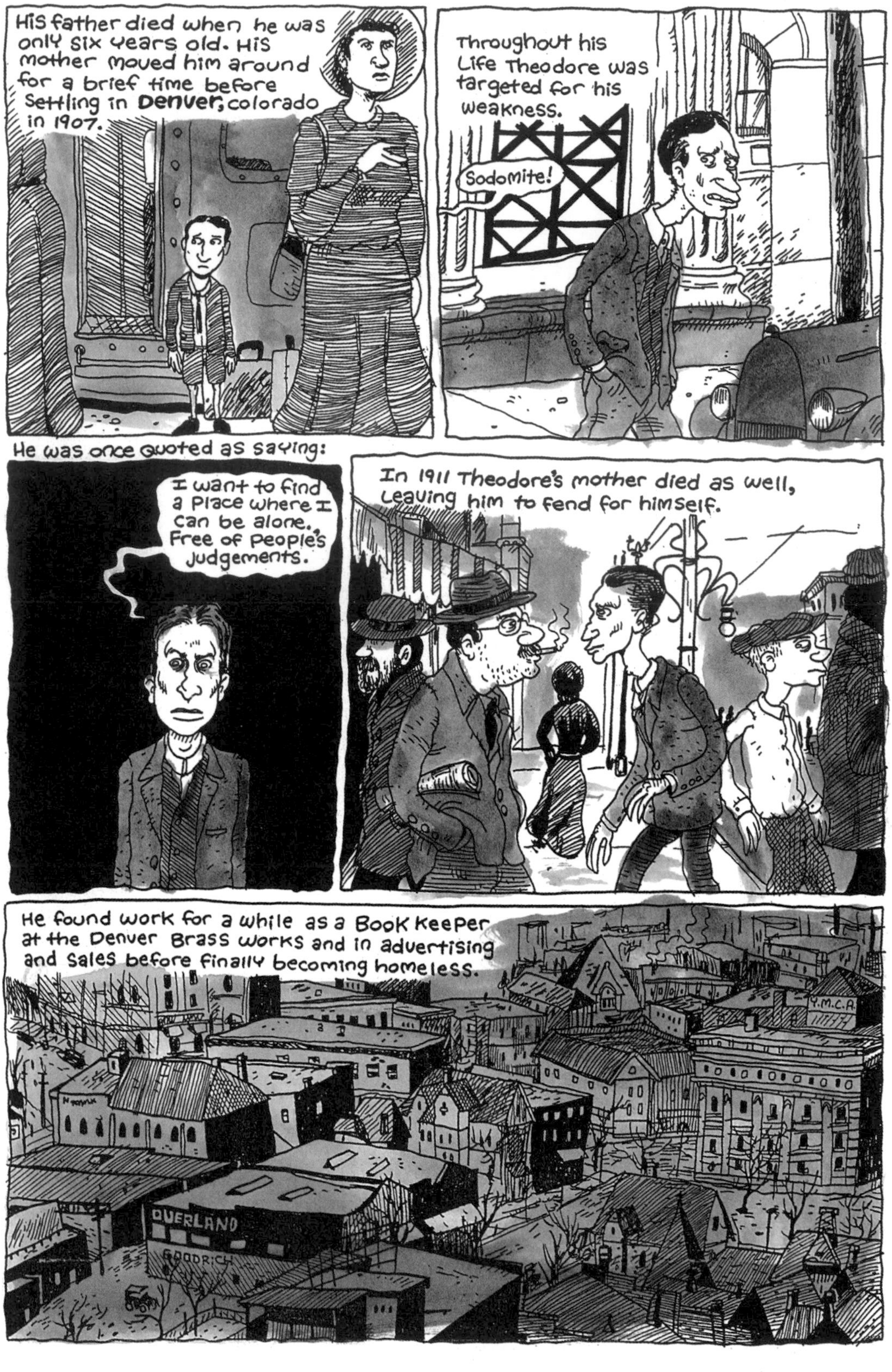
His father died when he was only six years old. His mother moved him around for a brief time before settling in Denver, colorado in 1907.
Throughout his Life Theodore was targeted for his weakness.
Sodomite!
He was once quoted as saying:
I want to find a place where I can be alone. Free of people's judgements.
In 1911 Theodore's mother died as well, leaving him to fend for himself.
He found work for a while as a Book Keeper at the Denver Brass works and in advertising and sales before finally becoming homeless.
Y.M.C.A
OVERLAND
GOODRICH

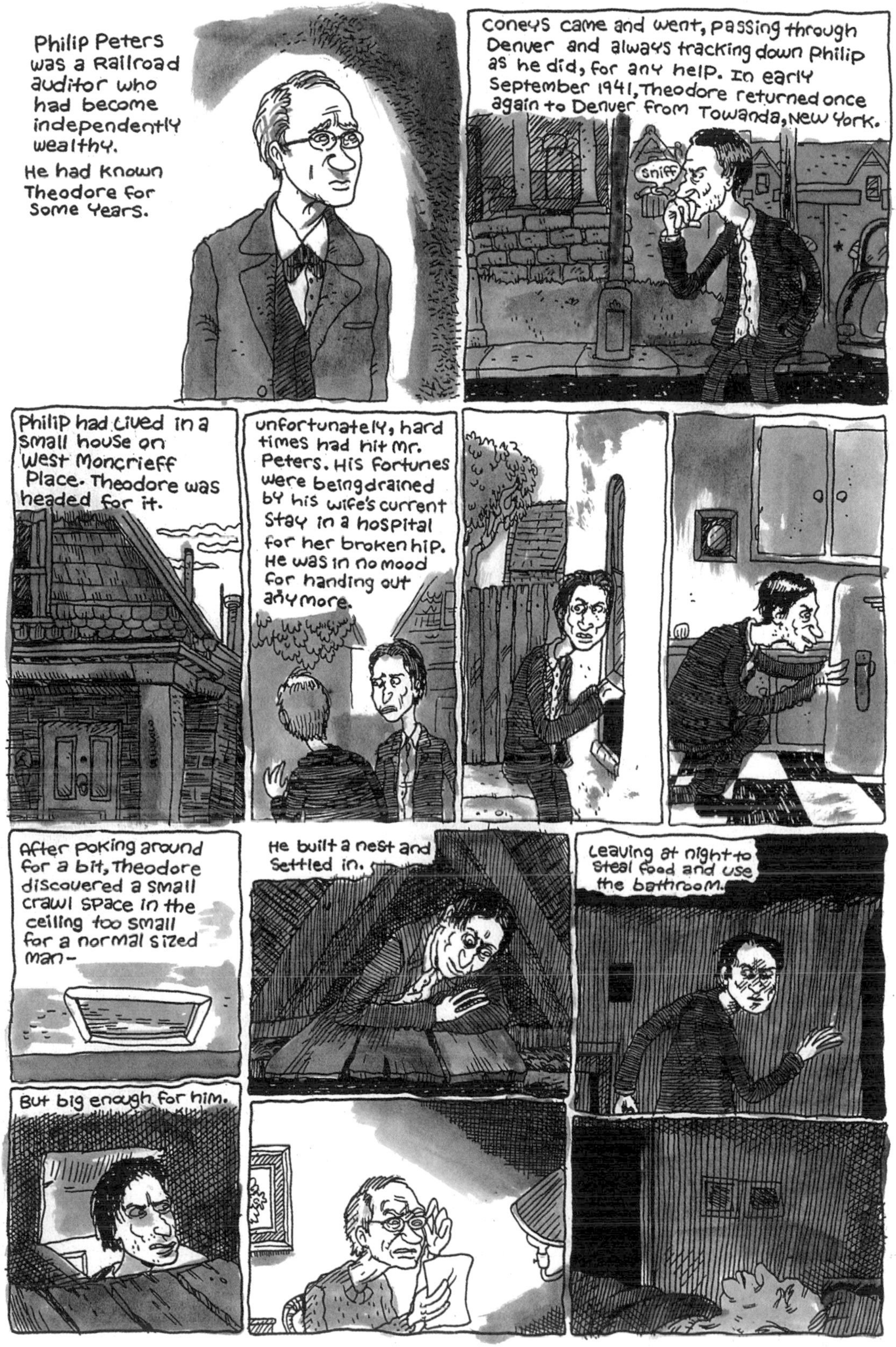
Philip Peters was a Railroad auditor who had become independently wealthy.
He had Known Theodore for some years.
Coneys came and went, passing through Denver and always tracking down Philip as he did, for any help. In early September 1941, Theodore returned once again to Denver from Towanda, New York.
sniff
Philip had lived in a small house on West Moncrieff Place. Theodore was headed for it.
Unfortunately, hard times had hit Mr. Peters. His fortunes were being drained by his wife's current stay in a hospital for her broken hip. He was in no mood for handing out any more.
After poking around for a bit, Theodore discovered a small crawl space in the ceiling too small for a normal sized man-
He built a nest and settled in.
Leaving at night to steal food and use the bathroom.
But big enough for him.

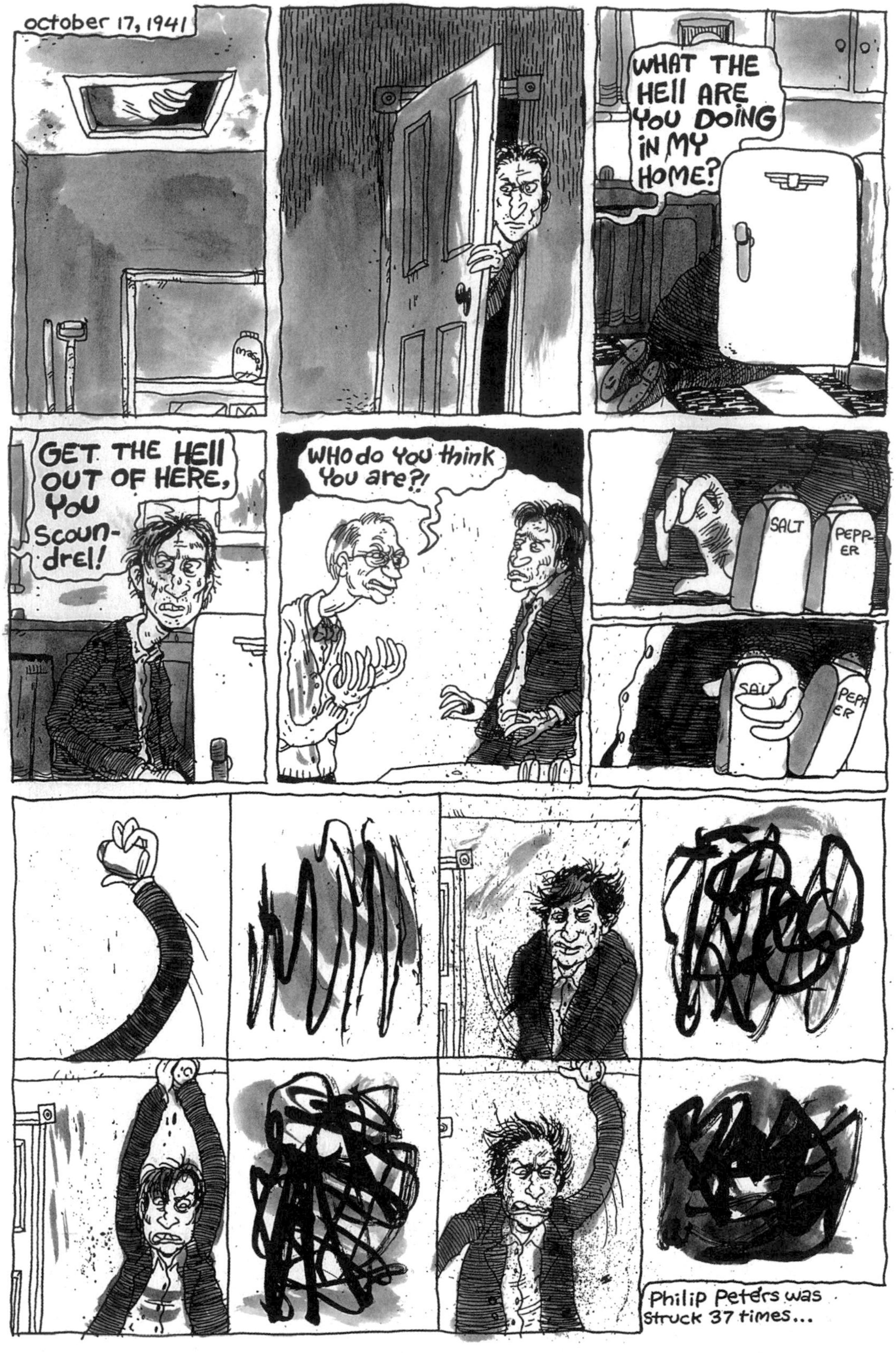
october 17, 1941
WHAT THE HEll ARE YOU DOING IN MY HOME?
GET THE HEll OUT OF HERE, YOU Scoundrel!
WHO do You think You are?!
SALT
PEPPER
Philip Peters was struck 37 times...

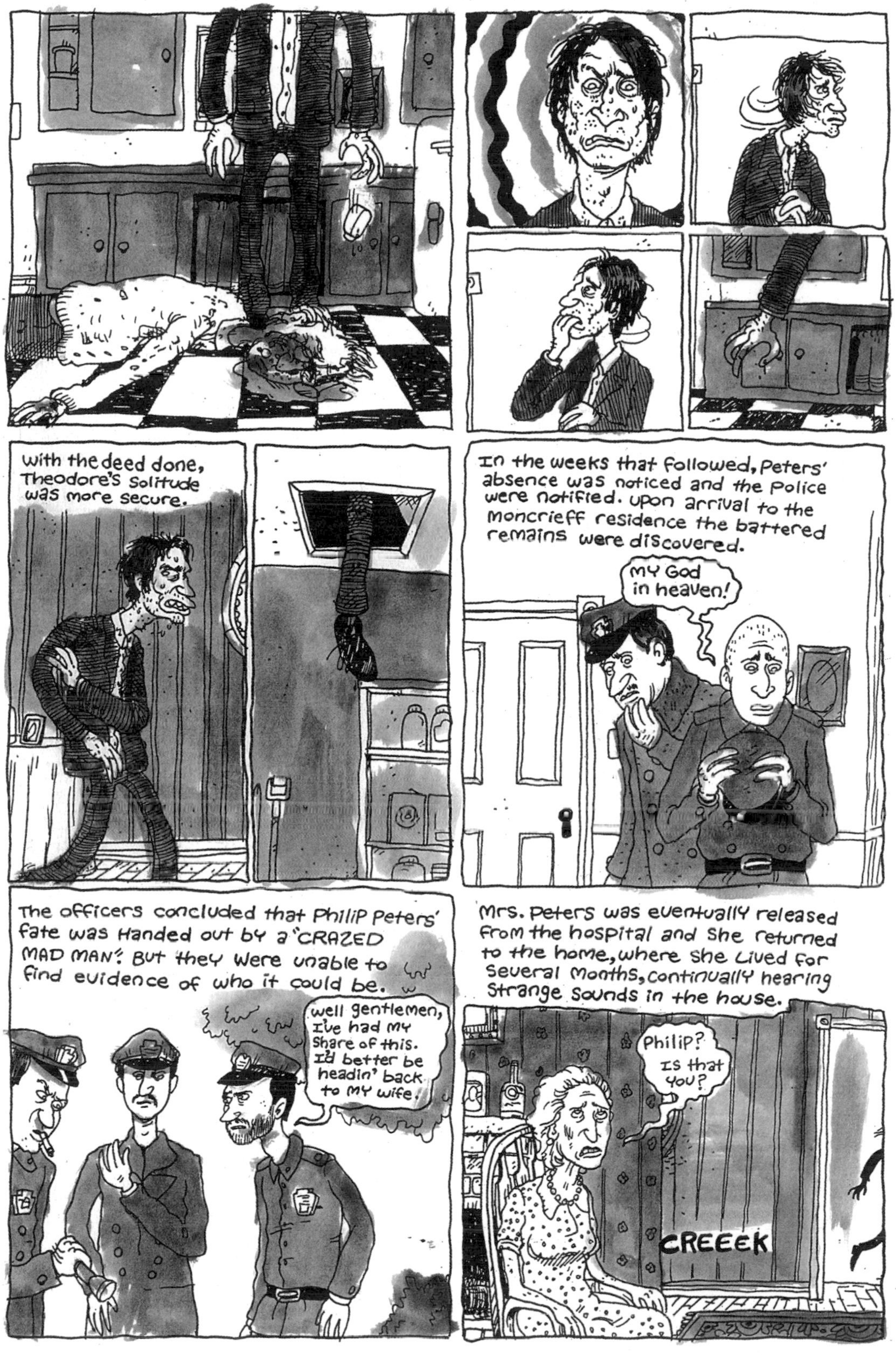
With the deed done, Theodore's Solitude was more secure.
In the weeks that followed, Peters' absence was noticed and the Police were notified. Upon arrival to the Moncrieff residence the battered remains were discovered.
MY God in heaven!
The officers concluded that Philip Peters' fate was Handed out by a "CRAZED MAD MAN". But they were unable to find evidence of who it could be.
Well gentlemen, I've had MY share of this. I'd better be headin' back to MY wife.
Mrs. Peters was eventually released from the hospital and she returned to the home, where she lived for several months, continually hearing strange sounds in the house.
Philip? Is that you?
CREEEK

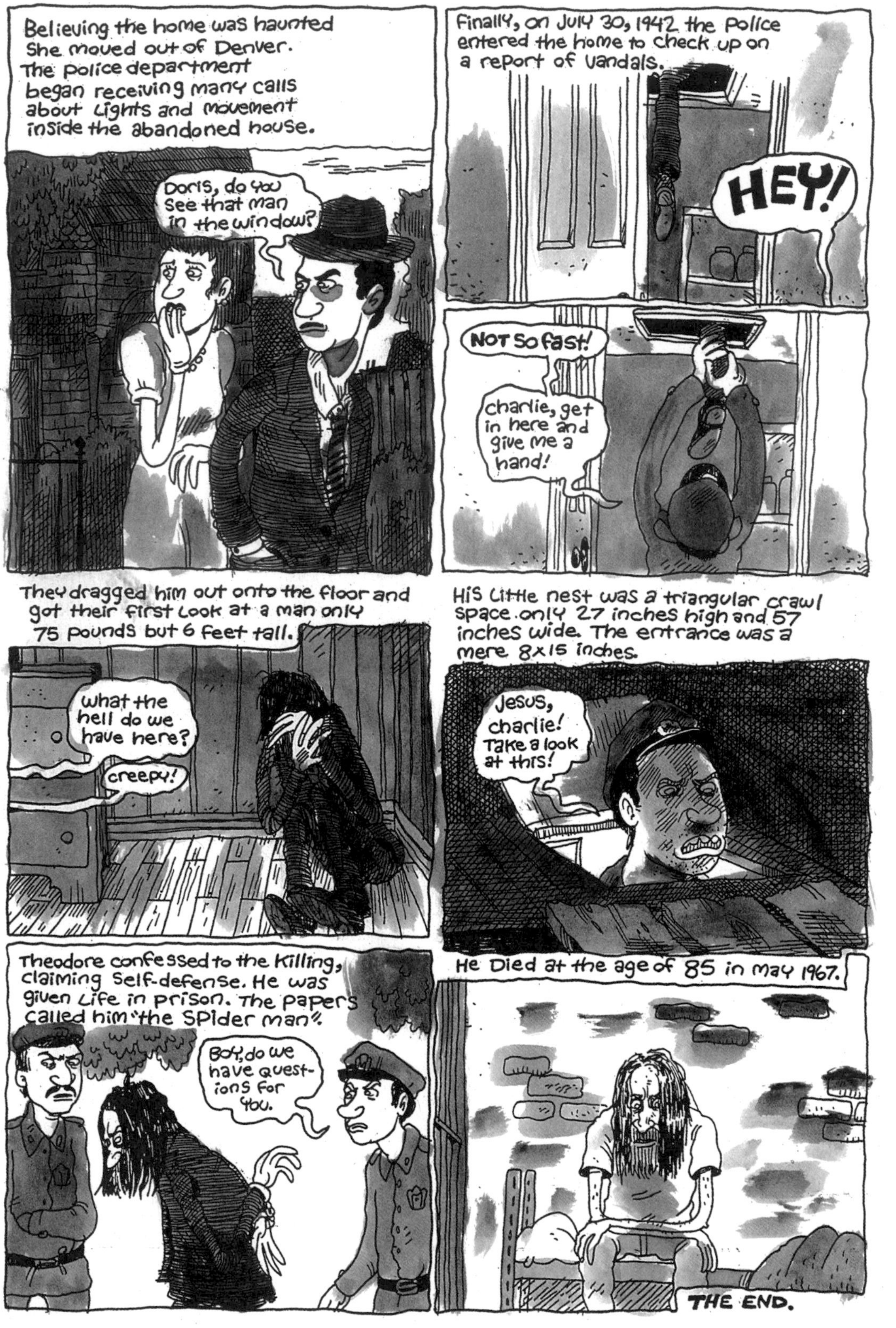

Believing the home was haunted She moved out of Denver. The police department began receiving many calls about lights and movement inside the abandoned house.
Doris, do you see that man in the window?
Finally, on July 30, 1942 the Police entered the home to check up on a report of vandals.
HEY!
NOT so fast!
charlie, get in here and give me a hand!
They dragged him out onto the floor and got their first look at a man only 75 pounds but 6 feet tall.
what the hell do we have here?
creepy!
His little nest was a triangular crawl space only 27 inches high and 57 inches wide. The entrance was a mere 8x15 inches.
Jesus, charlie! Take a look at this!
Theodore confessed to the killing, claiming self-defense. He was given life in prison. The papers called him "the Spider man".
Boy, do we have quest-ions for you.
He Died at the age of 85 in May 1967.
THE END.

LIVING LIKE A PIG

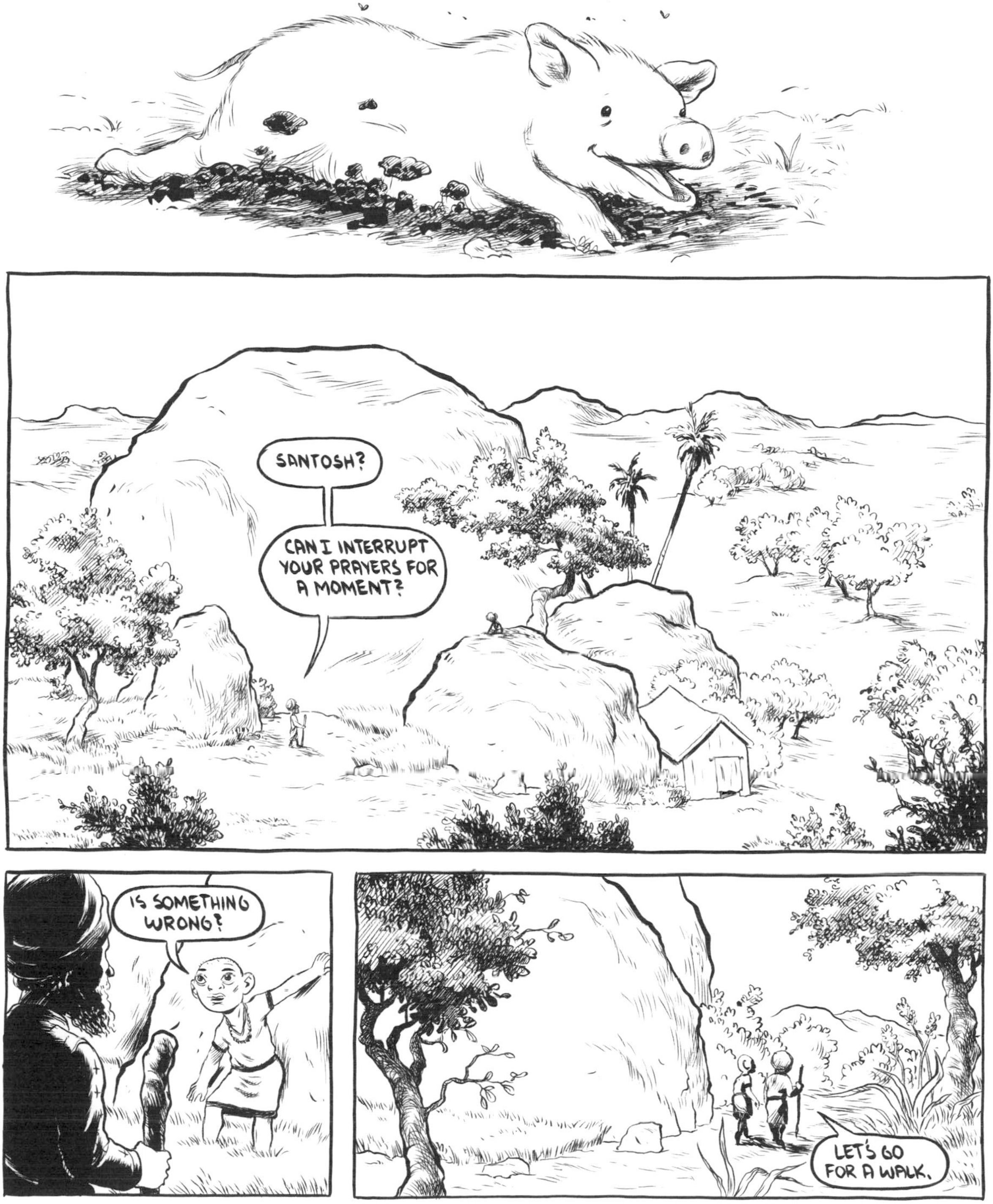
SANTOSH?
CAN I INTERRUPT YOUR PRAYERS FOR A MOMENT?
IS SOMETHING WRONG?
LET'S GO FOR A WALK.

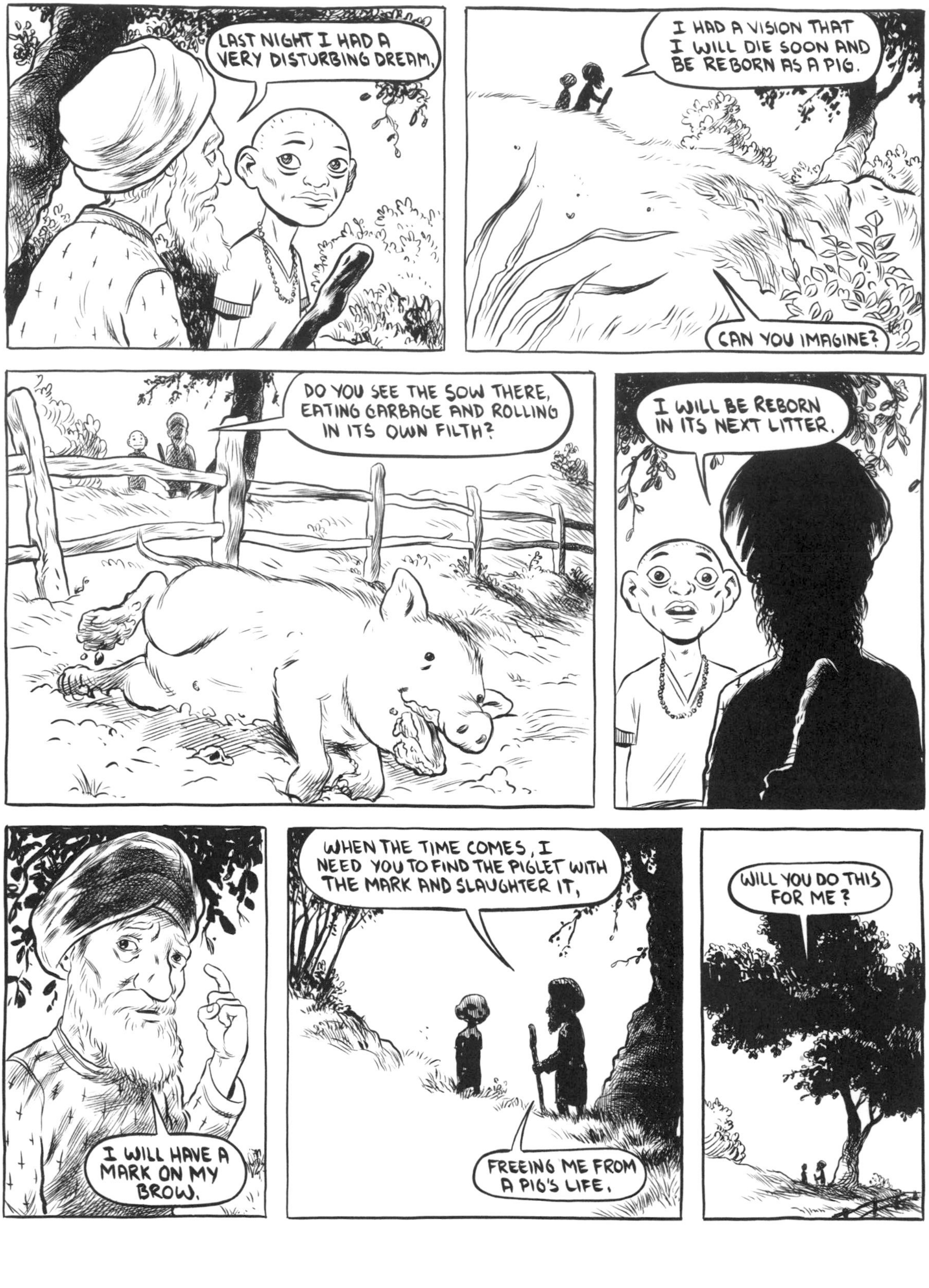
LAST NIGHT I HAD A VERY DISTURBING DREAM,
I HAD A VISION THAT I WILL DIE SOON AND BE REBORN AS A PIG.
CAN YOU IMAGINE?
DO YOU SEE THE SOW THERE, EATING GARBAGE AND ROLLING IN ITS OWN FILTH?
I WILL BE REBORN IN ITS NEXT LITTER.
I WILL HAVE A MARK ON MY BROW.
WHEN THE TIME COMES, I NEED YOU TO FIND THE PIGLET WITH THE MARK AND SLAUGHTER IT,
FREEING ME FROM A PIG'S LIFE.
WILL YOU DO THIS FOR ME?

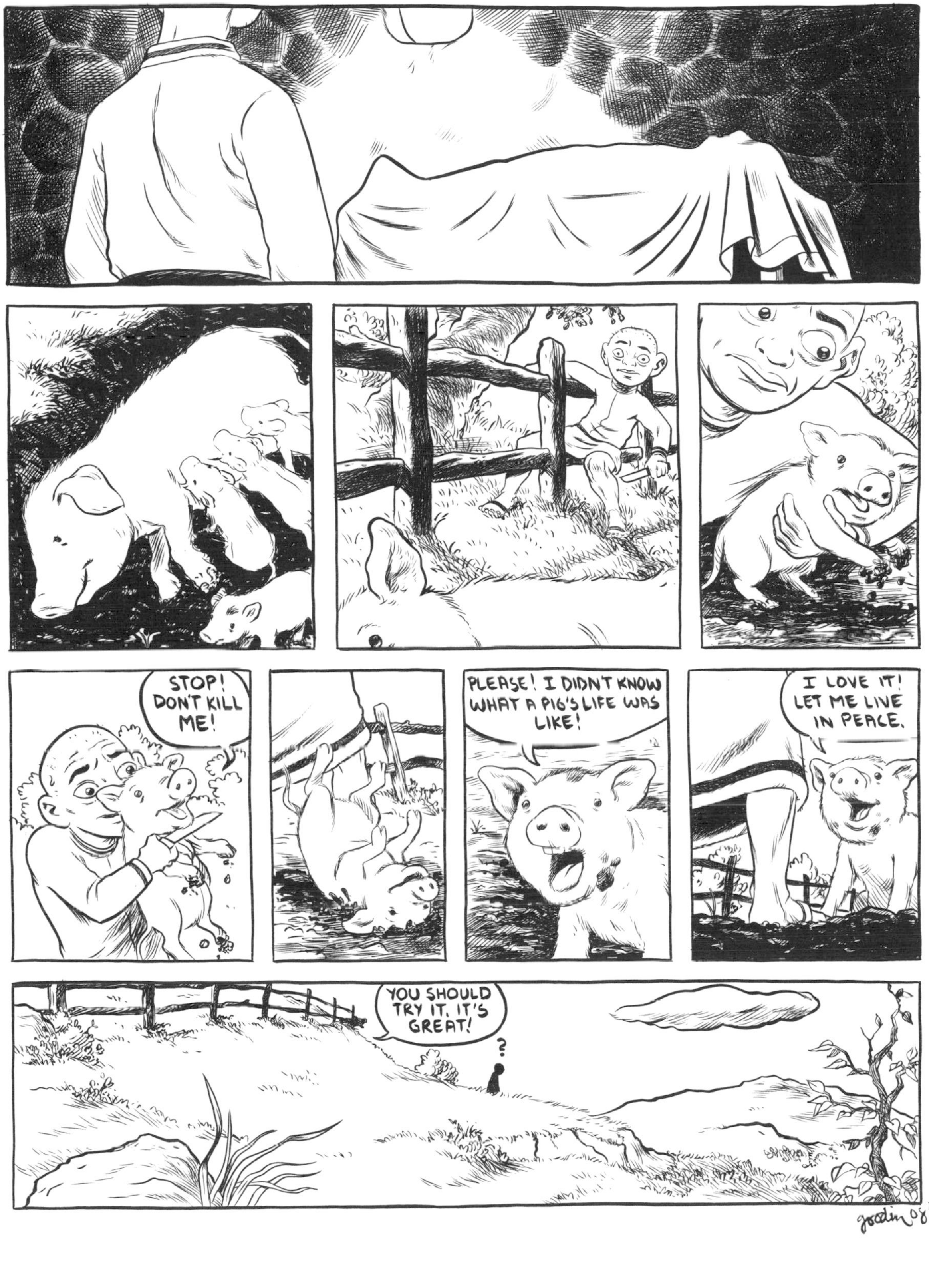
STOP! DON'T KILL ME!
PLEASE! I DIDN'T KNOW WHAT A PIG'S LIFE WAS LIKE!
I LOVE IT! LET ME LIVE IN PEACE.
YOU SHOULD TRY IT, IT'S GREAT!
?
godin 08'

MY ENTIRE HIGH SCHOOL... SINKING INTO THE SEA!

BY DASH SHAW FEB '09

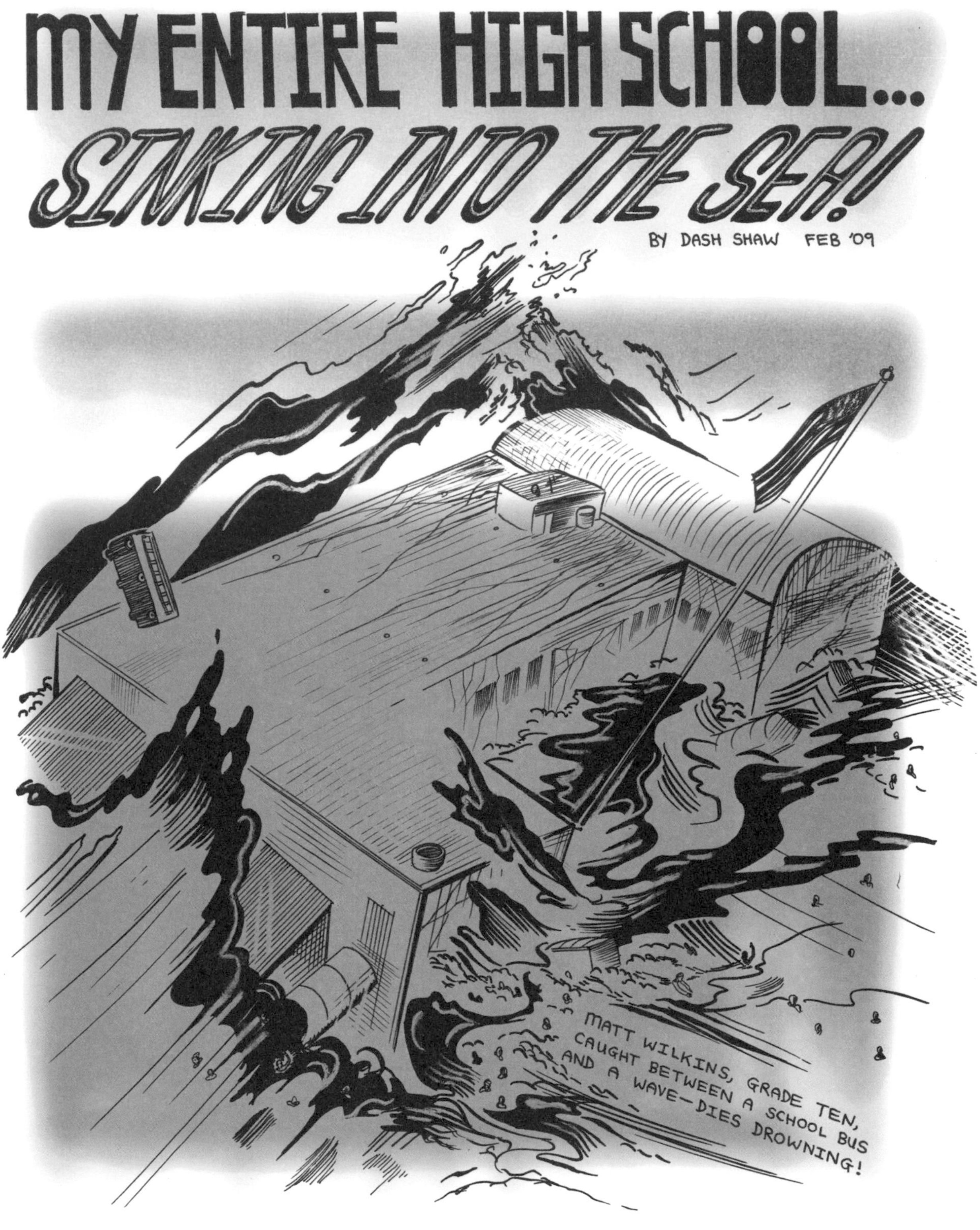
MATT WILKINS, GRADE TEN, CAUGHT BETWEEN A SCHOOL BUS AND A WAVE—DIES DROWNING!

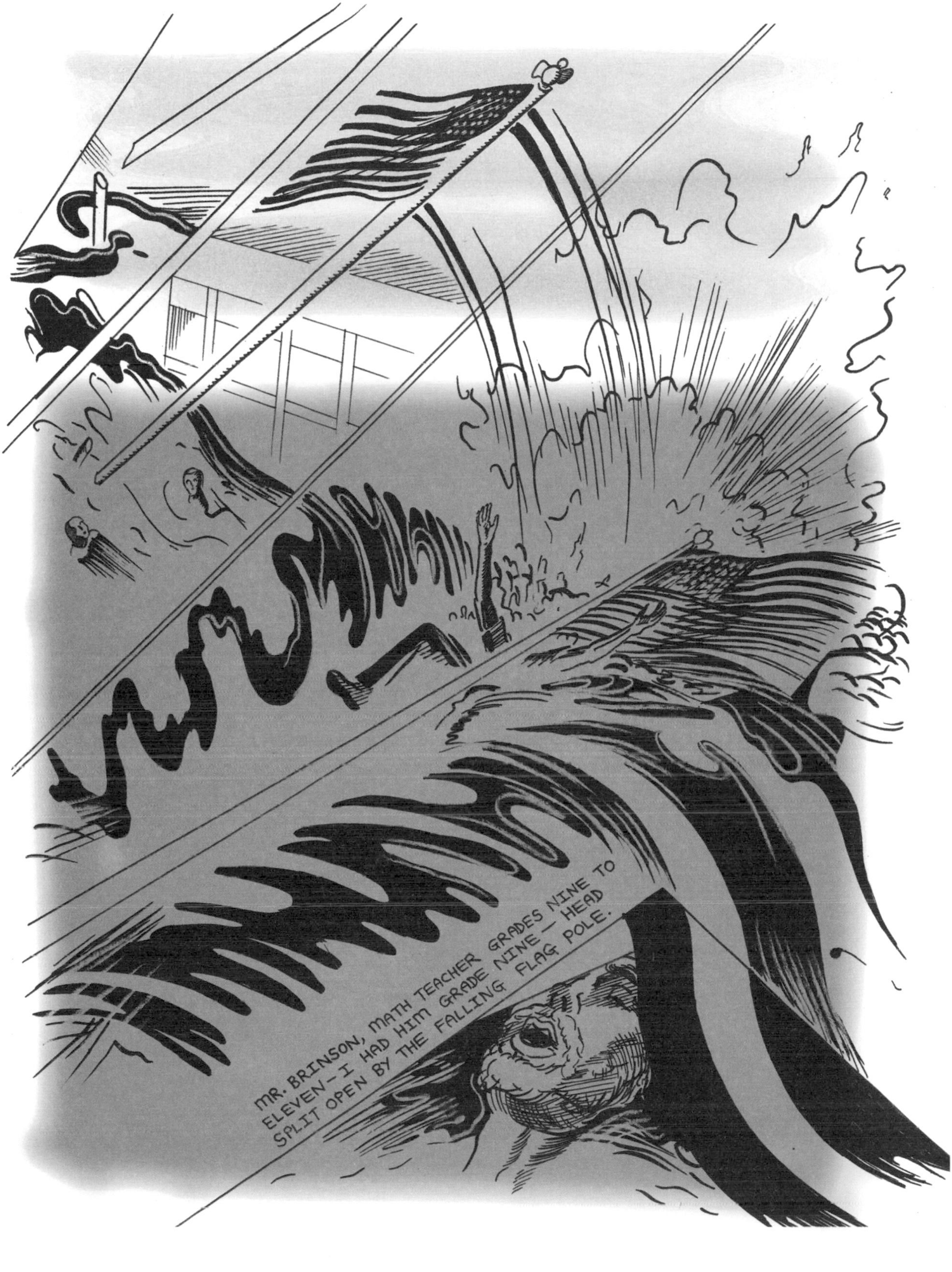
MR. BRINSON, MATH TEACHER GRADES NINE TO ELEVEN—I HAD HIM GRADE NINE—HEAD SPLIT OPEN BY THE FALLING FLAG POLE.

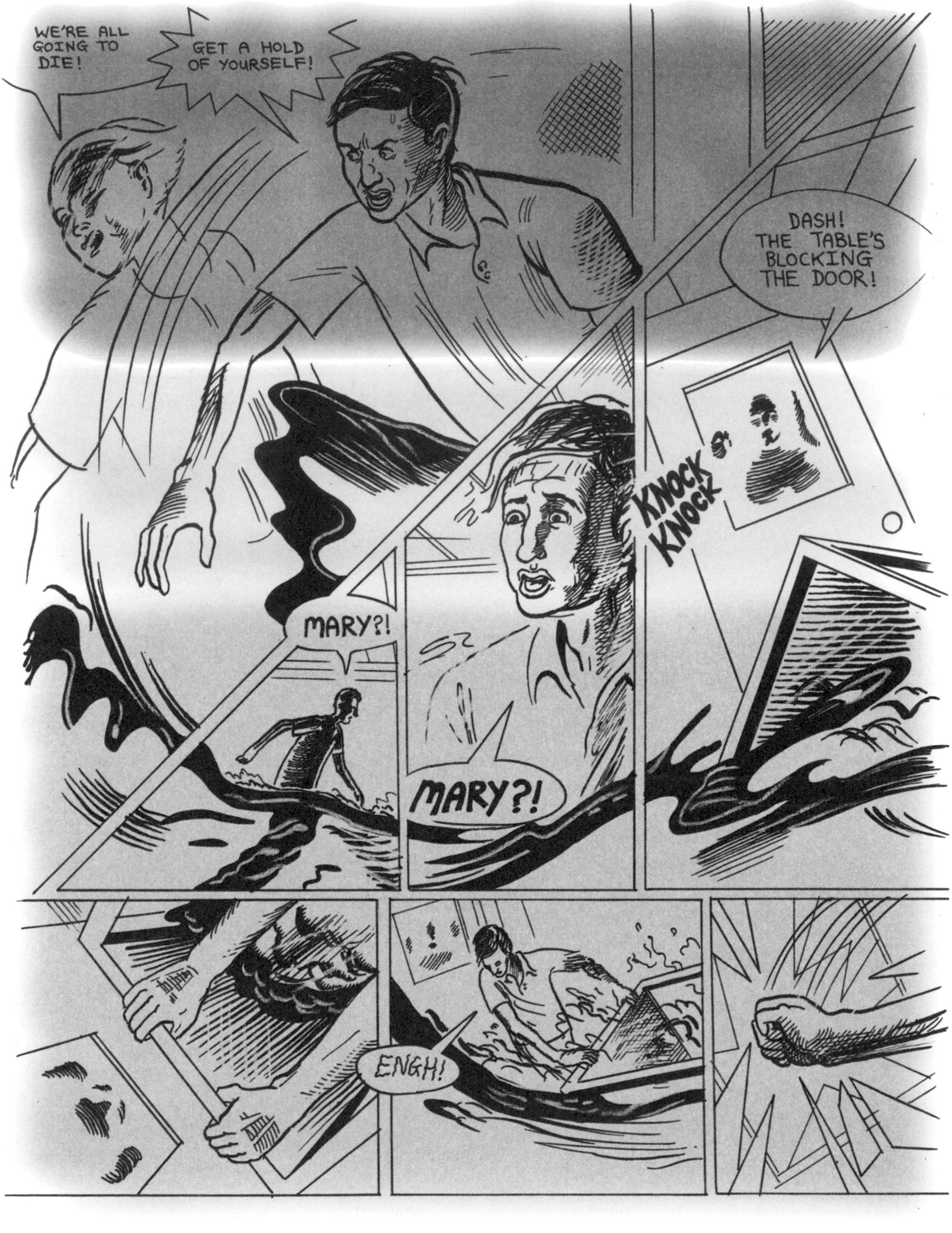
WE'RE ALL GOING TO DIE!
GET A HOLD OF YOURSELF!
DASH! THE TABLE'S BLOCKING THE DOOR!
KNOCK KNOCK
MARY?!
MARY?!
ENGH!

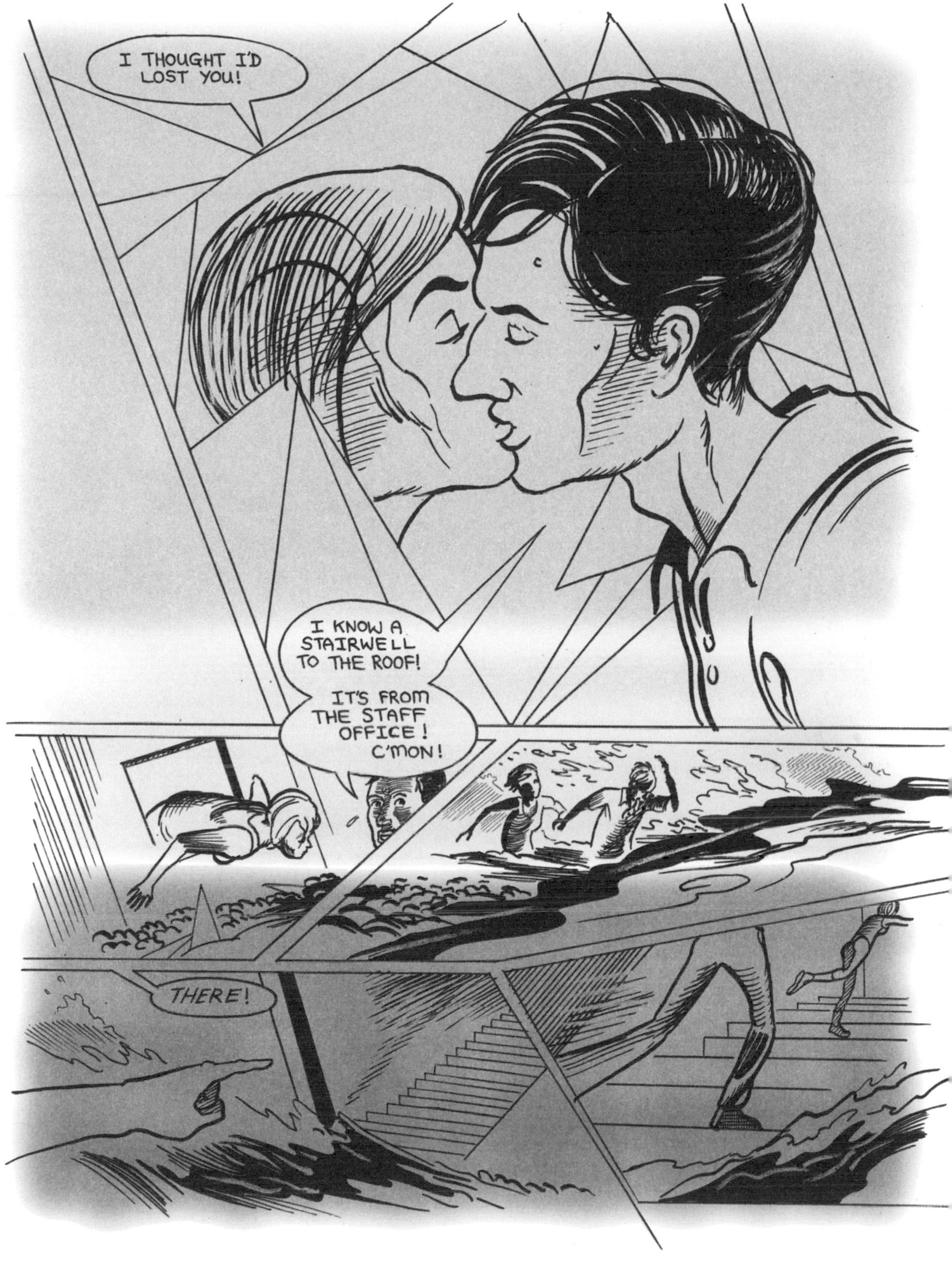
I THOUGHT I'D LOST YOU!
I KNOW A STAIRWELL TO THE ROOF!
IT'S FROM THE STAFF OFFICE! C'MON!
THERE!

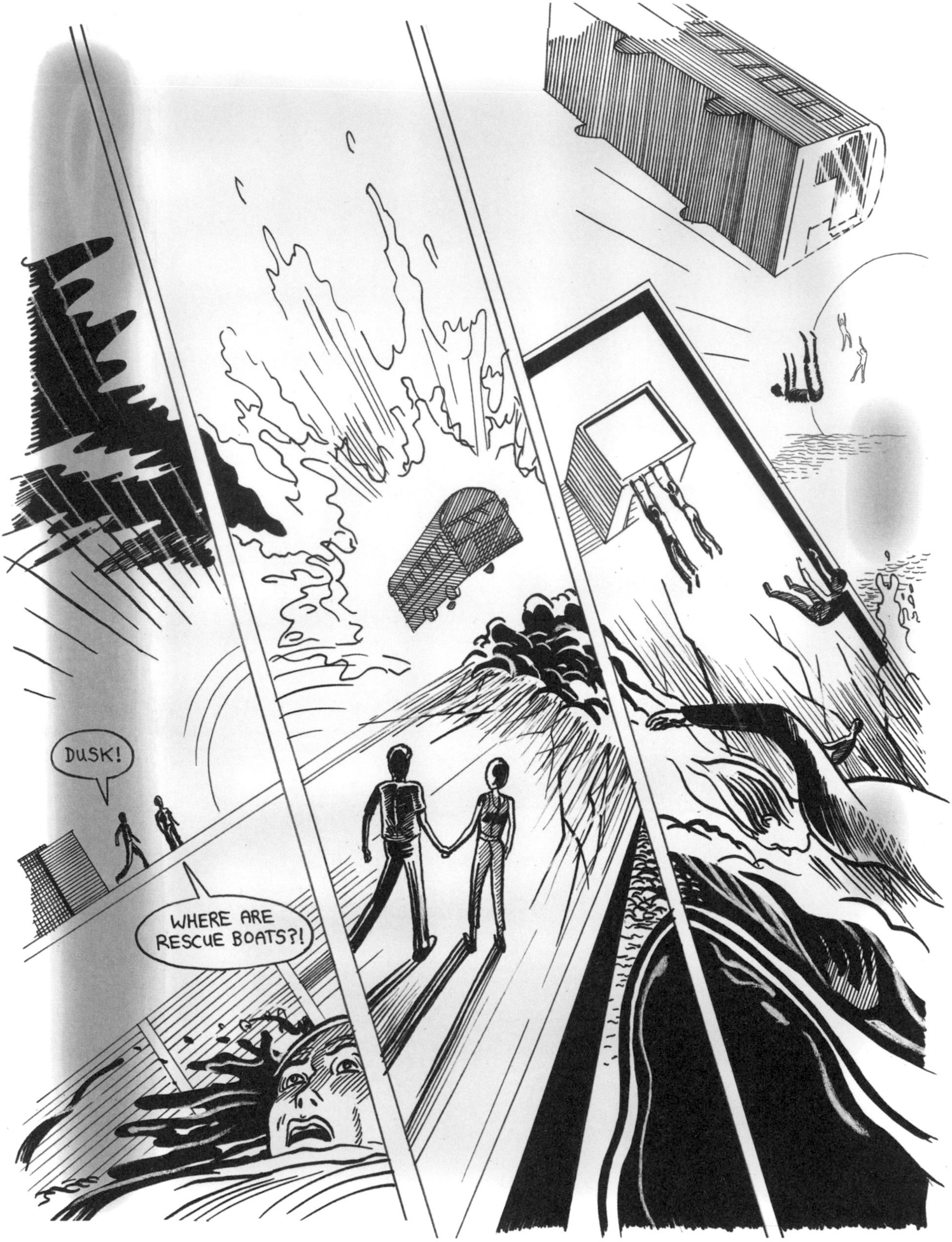
DUSK!
WHERE ARE RESCUE BOATS?!

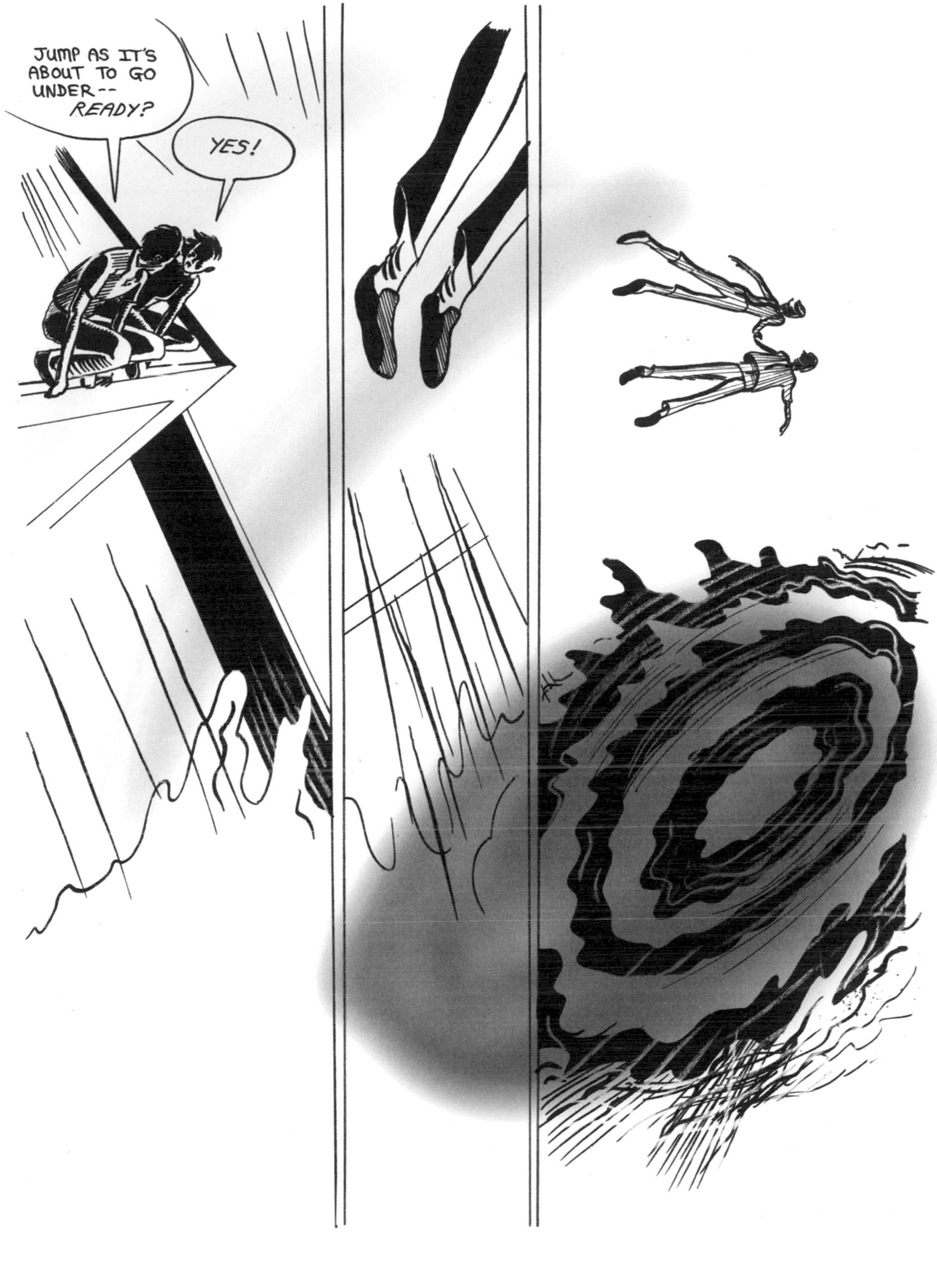

JUMP AS IT'S ABOUT TO GO UNDER-- READY?
YES!

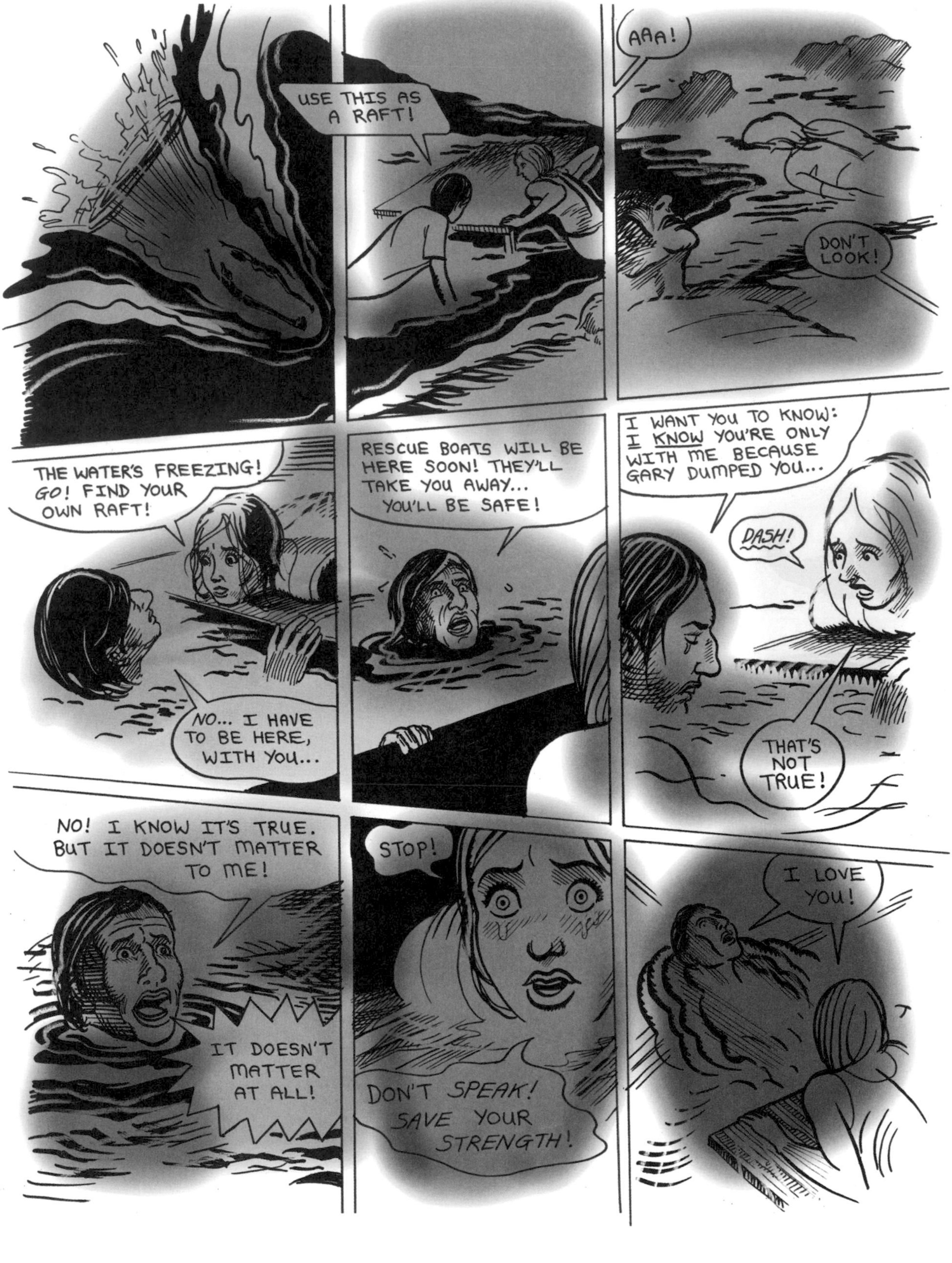
USE THIS AS A RAFT!
AAA!
DON'T LOOK!
THE WATER'S FREEZING! GO! FIND YOUR OWN RAFT!
NO... I HAVE TO BE HERE, WITH YOU...
RESCUE BOATS WILL BE HERE SOON! THEY'LL TAKE YOU AWAY... YOU'LL BE SAFE!
I WANT YOU TO KNOW: I KNOW YOU'RE ONLY WITH ME BECAUSE GARY DUMPED YOU...
DASH!
THAT'S NOT TRUE!
NO! I KNOW IT'S TRUE. BUT IT DOESN'T MATTER TO ME!
IT DOESN'T MATTER AT ALL!
STOP!
DON'T SPEAK! SAVE YOUR STRENGTH!
I LOVE YOU!

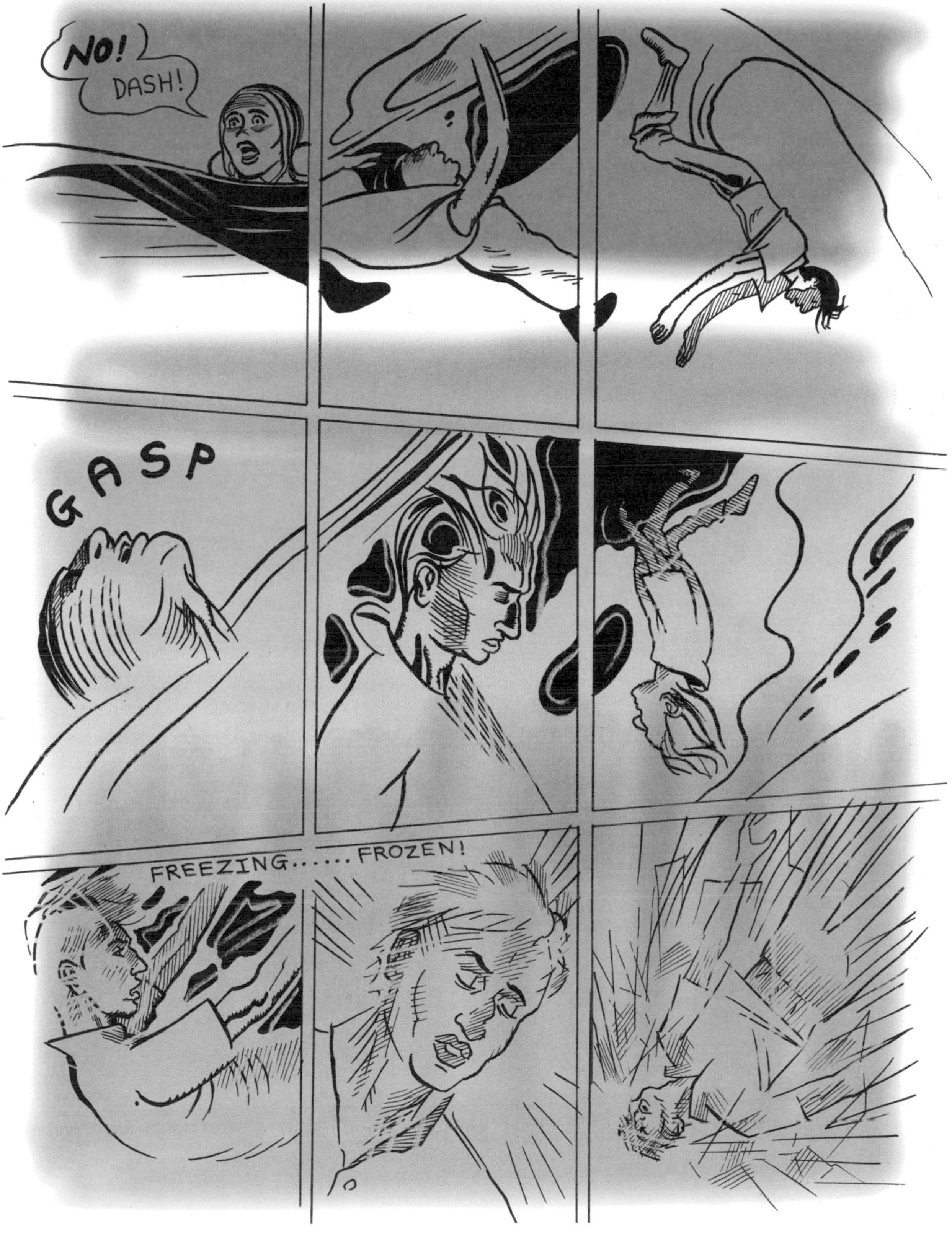
NO! DASH!
GASP
FREEZING...... FROZEN!

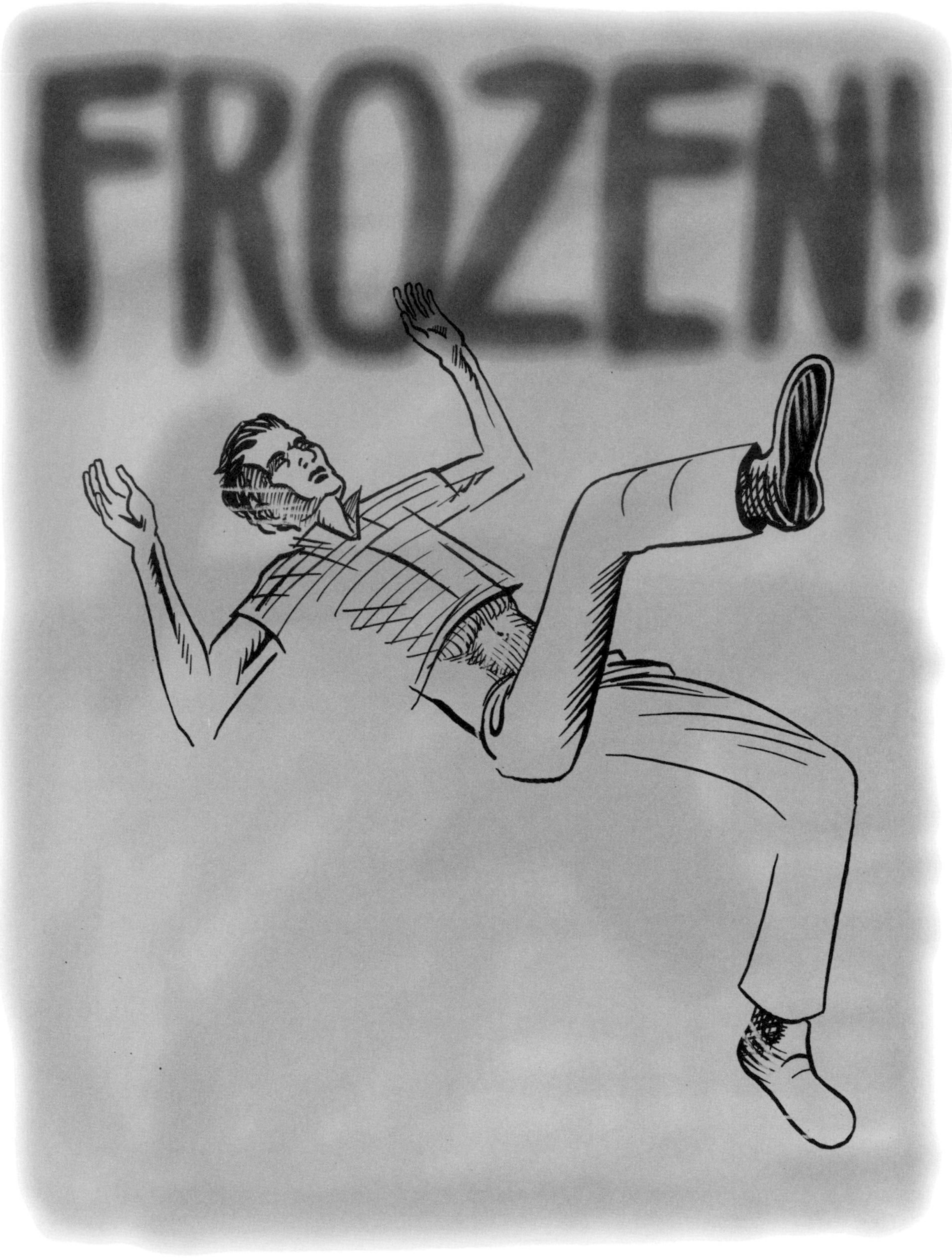
FROZEN!

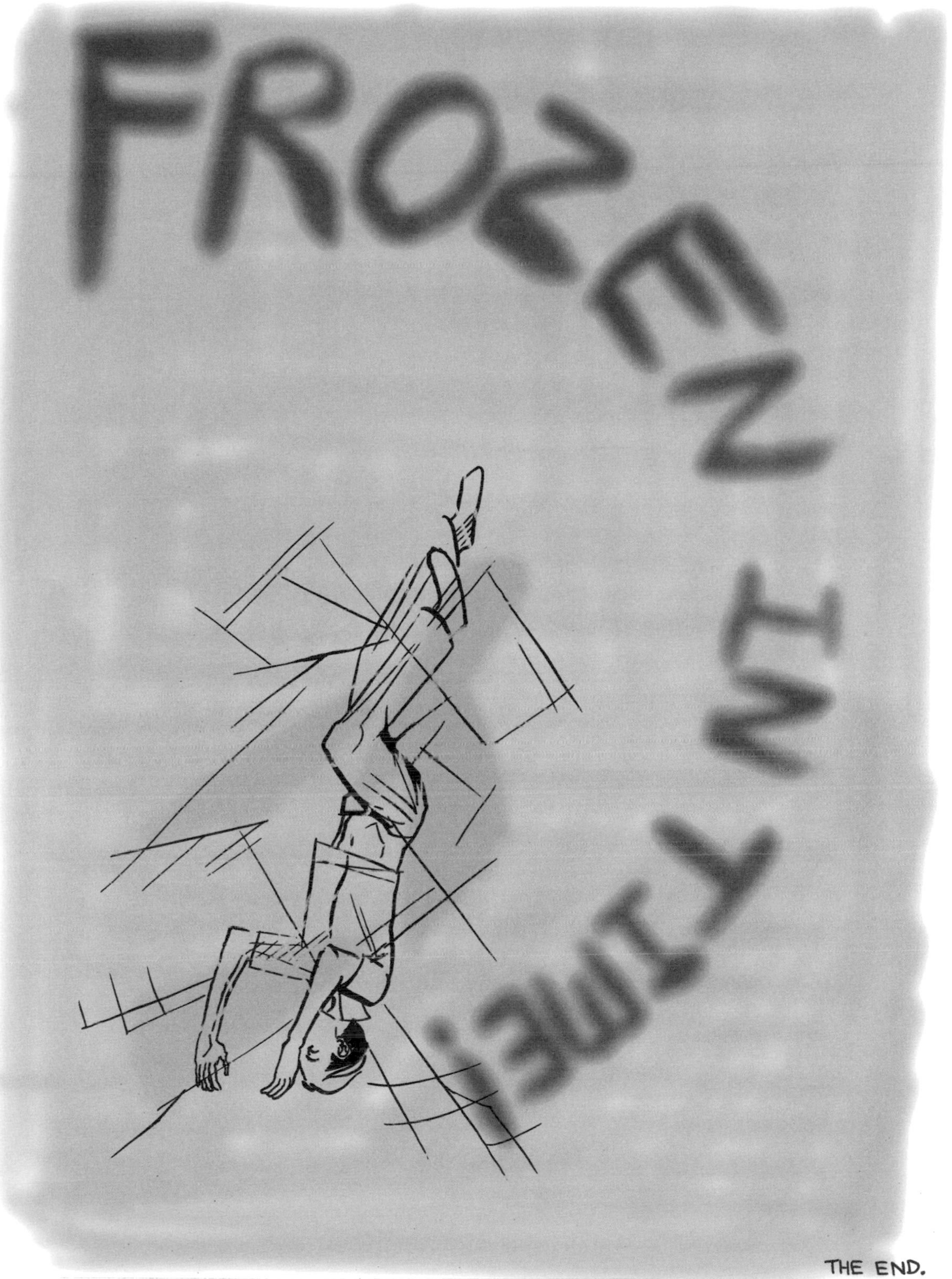
FROZEN IN TIME!

THE END.

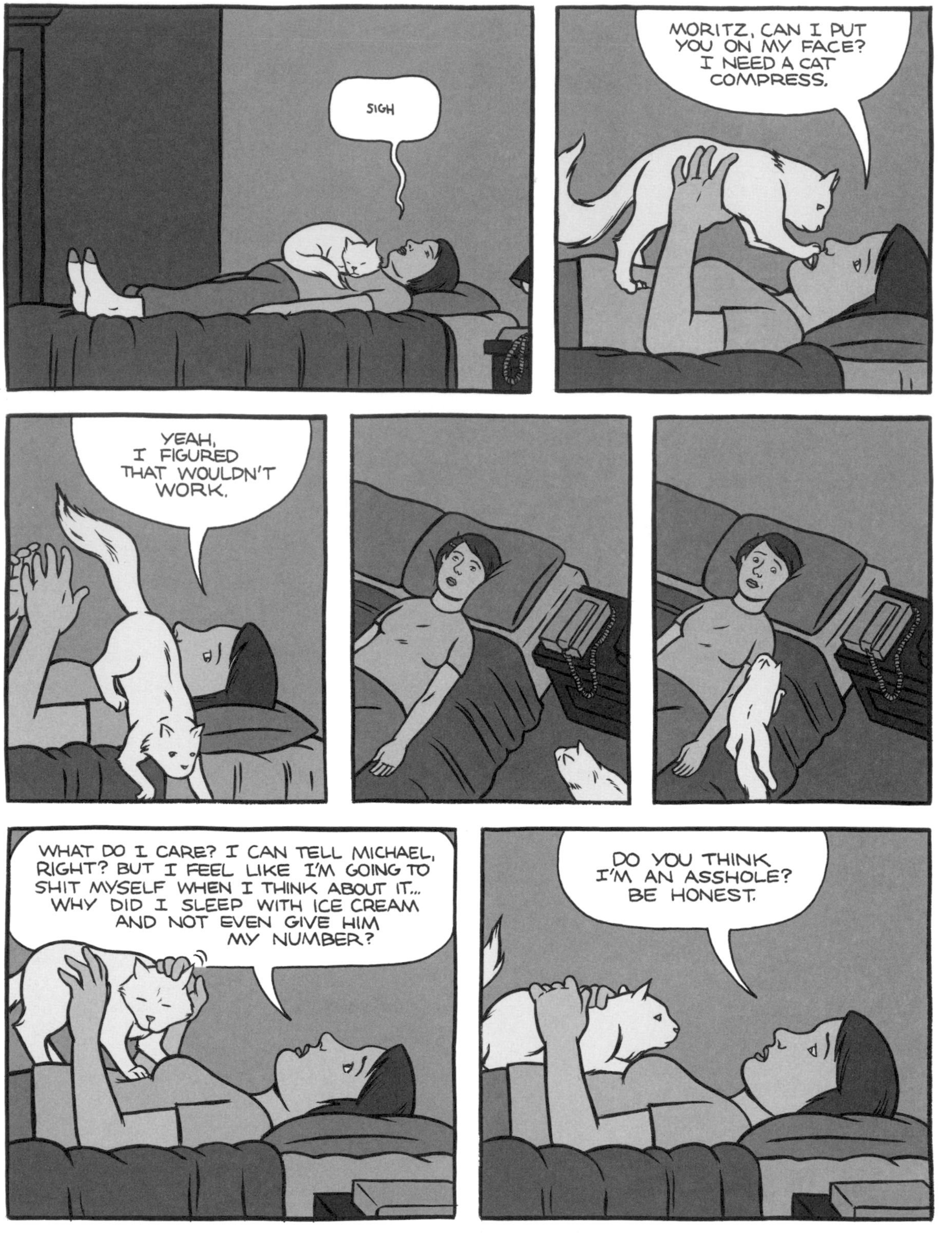
SIGH
MORITZ, CAN I PUT YOU ON MY FACE? I NEED A CAT COMPRESS.
YEAH, I FIGURED THAT WOULDN'T WORK.
WHAT DO I CARE? I CAN TELL MICHAEL, RIGHT? BUT I FEEL LIKE I'M GOING TO SHIT MYSELF WHEN I THINK ABOUT IT... WHY DID I SLEEP WITH ICE CREAM AND NOT EVEN GIVE HIM MY NUMBER?
DO YOU THINK I'M AN ASSHOLE? BE HONEST.

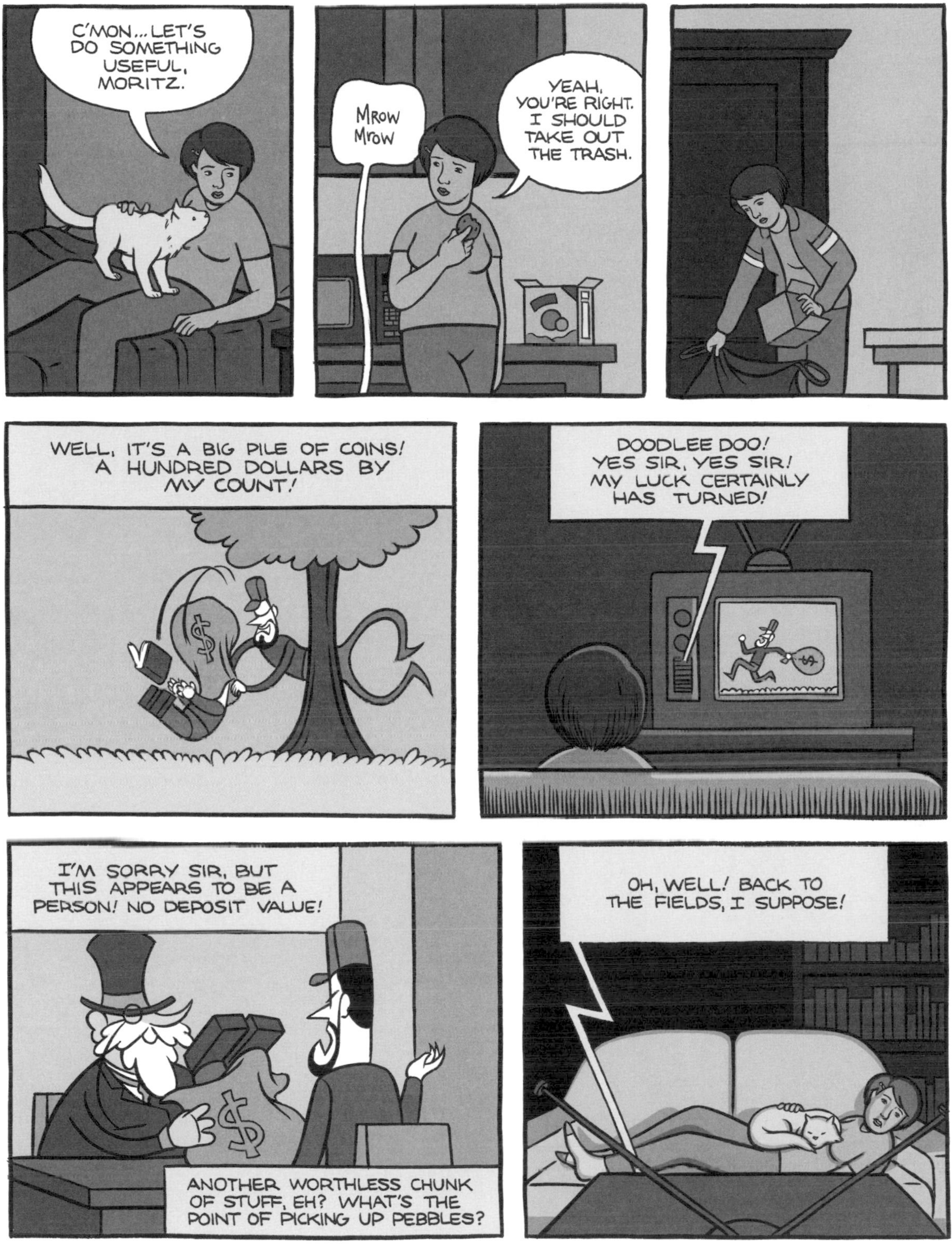

C'MON... LET'S DO SOMETHING USEFUL, MORITZ.
MROW MROW
YEAH, YOU'RE RIGHT. I SHOULD TAKE OUT THE TRASH.
WELL, IT'S A BIG PILE OF COINS! A HUNDRED DOLLARS BY MY COUNT!
DOODLEE DOO! YES SIR, YES SIR! MY LUCK CERTAINLY HAS TURNED!
I'M SORRY SIR, BUT THIS APPEARS TO BE A PERSON! NO DEPOSIT VALUE!
ANOTHER WORTHLESS CHUNK OF STUFF, EH? WHAT'S THE POINT OF PICKING UP PEBBLES?
OH, WELL! BACK TO THE FIELDS, I SUPPOSE!

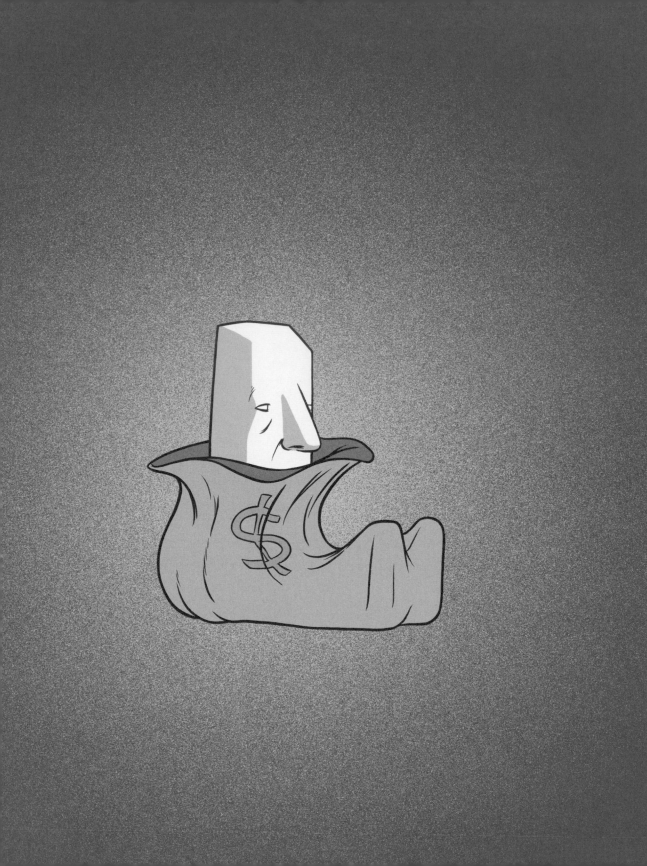

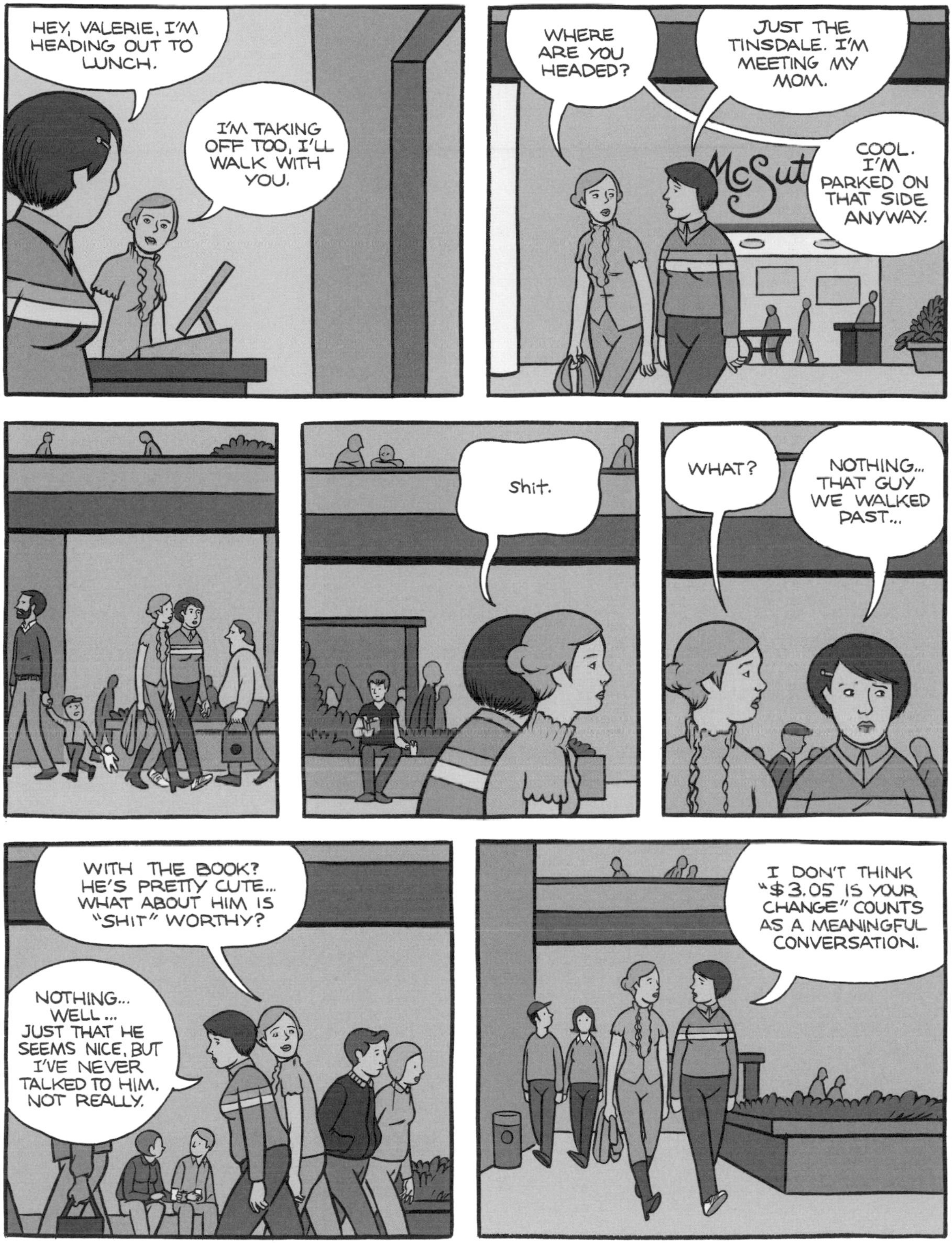
HEY, VALERIE, I'M HEADING OUT TO LUNCH.
I'M TAKING OFF TOO, I'LL WALK WITH YOU.
WHERE ARE YOU HEADED?
JUST THE TINSDALE. I'M MEETING MY MOM.
McSut
COOL. I'M PARKED ON THAT SIDE ANYWAY.
shit.
WHAT?
NOTHING... THAT GUY WE WALKED PAST...
WITH THE BOOK? HE'S PRETTY CUTE... WHAT ABOUT HIM IS "SHIT" WORTHY?
NOTHING... WELL... JUST THAT HE SEEMS NICE, BUT I'VE NEVER TALKED TO HIM. NOT REALLY.
I DON'T THINK "$3.05 IS YOUR CHANGE" COUNTS AS A MEANINGFUL CONVERSATION.

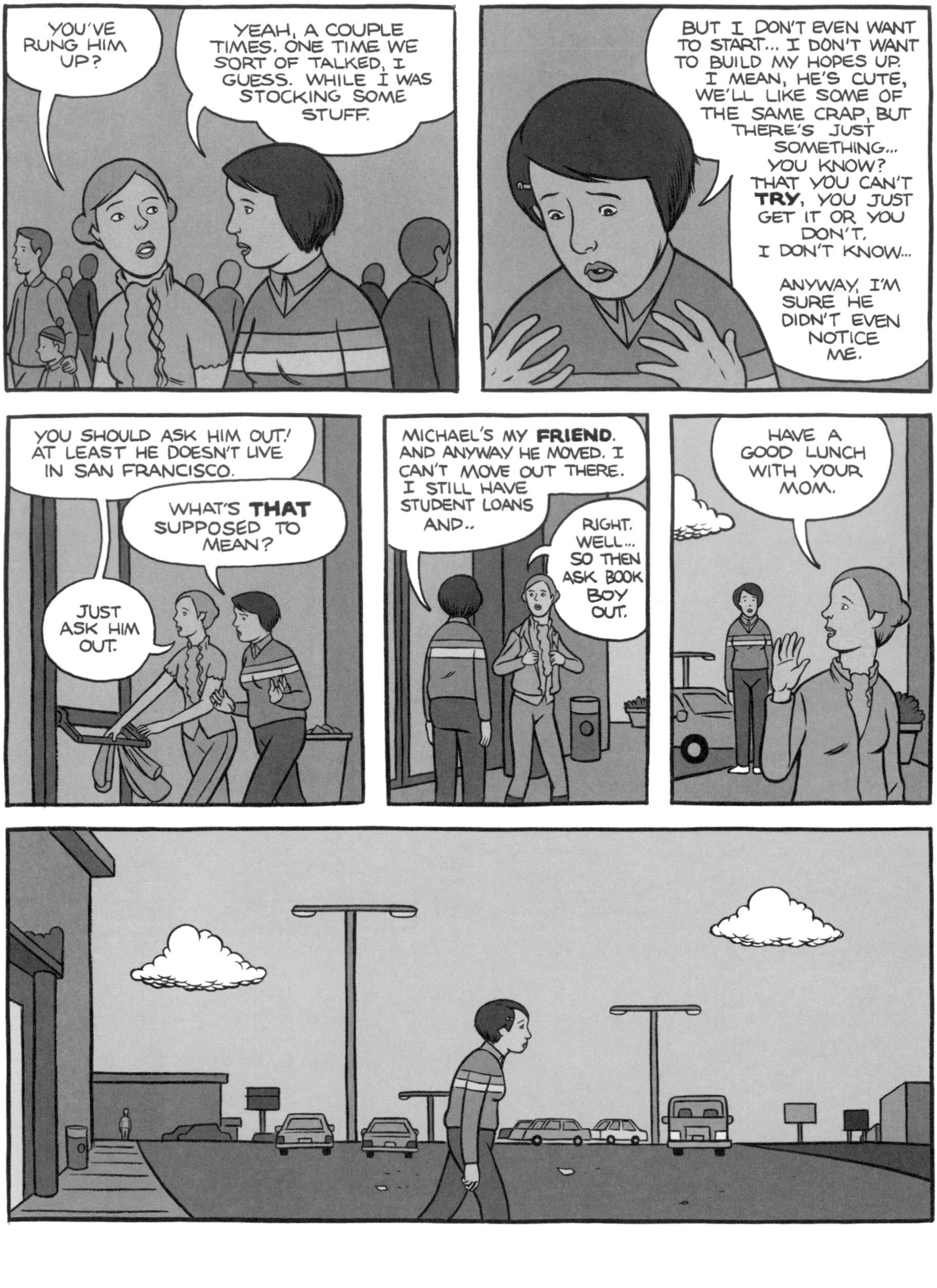
YOU'VE RUNG HIM UP?
YEAH, A COUPLE TIMES. ONE TIME WE SORT OF TALKED, I GUESS. WHILE I WAS STOCKING SOME STUFF.
BUT I DON'T EVEN WANT TO START... I DON'T WANT TO BUILD MY HOPES UP. I MEAN, HE'S CUTE, WE'LL LIKE SOME OF THE SAME CRAP, BUT THERE'S JUST SOMETHING... YOU KNOW? THAT YOU CAN'T **TRY**, YOU JUST GET IT OR YOU DON'T. I DON'T KNOW...
ANYWAY, I'M SURE HE DIDN'T EVEN NOTICE ME.
YOU SHOULD ASK HIM OUT! AT LEAST HE DOESN'T LIVE IN SAN FRANCISCO.
WHAT'S **THAT** SUPPOSED TO MEAN?
JUST ASK HIM OUT.
MICHAEL'S MY **FRIEND**. AND ANYWAY HE MOVED. I CAN'T MOVE OUT THERE. I STILL HAVE STUDENT LOANS AND..
RIGHT. WELL... SO THEN ASK BOOK BOY OUT.
HAVE A GOOD LUNCH WITH YOUR MOM.

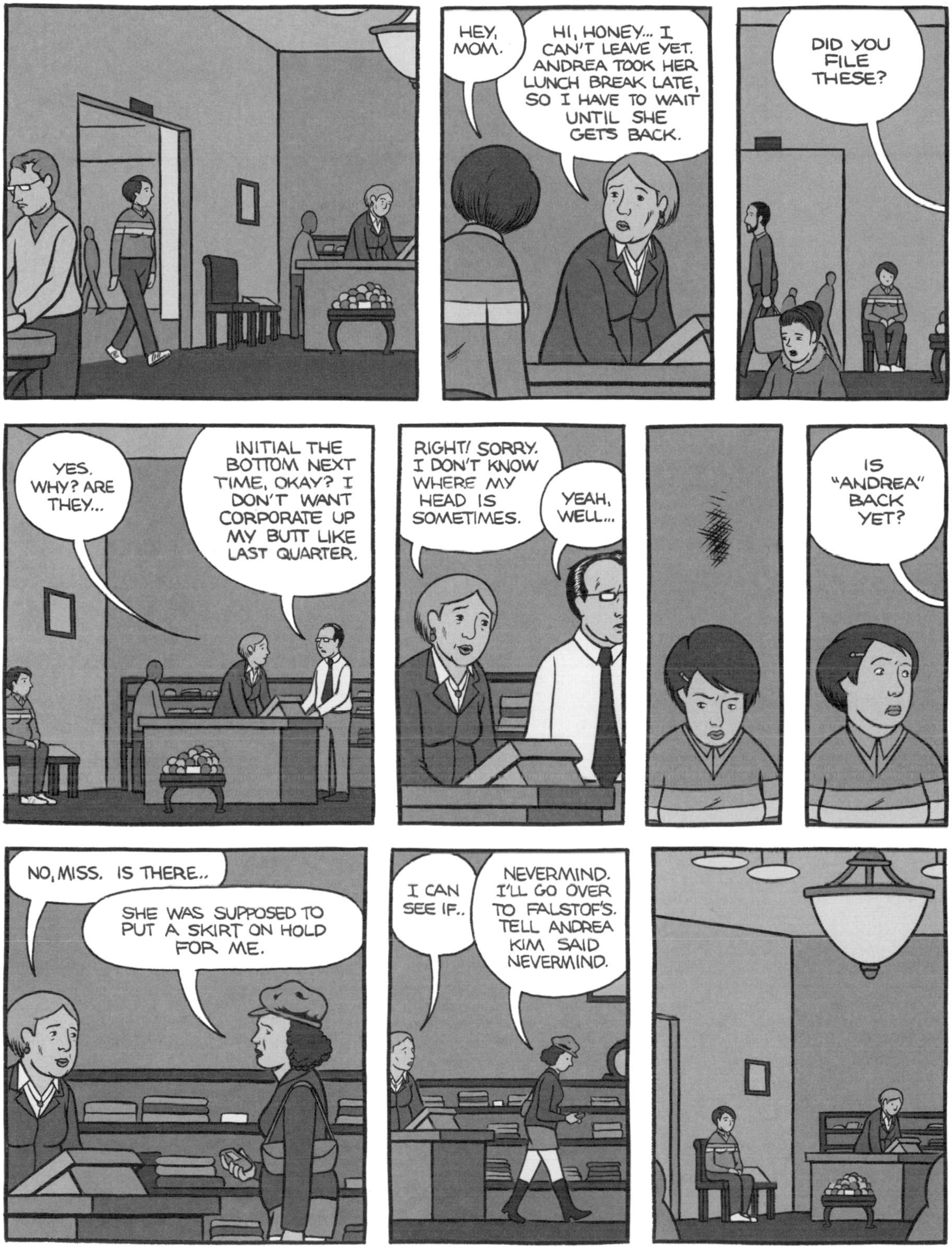
HEY, MOM.
HI, HONEY... I CAN'T LEAVE YET. ANDREA TOOK HER LUNCH BREAK LATE, SO I HAVE TO WAIT UNTIL SHE GETS BACK.
DID YOU FILE THESE?
YES. WHY? ARE THEY...
INITIAL THE BOTTOM NEXT TIME, OKAY? I DON'T WANT CORPORATE UP MY BUTT LIKE LAST QUARTER.
RIGHT! SORRY. I DON'T KNOW WHERE MY HEAD IS SOMETIMES.
YEAH, WELL...
IS "ANDREA" BACK YET?
NO, MISS. IS THERE..
SHE WAS SUPPOSED TO PUT A SKIRT ON HOLD FOR ME.
I CAN SEE IF..
NEVERMIND. I'LL GO OVER TO FALSTOF'S. TELL ANDREA KIM SAID NEVERMIND.

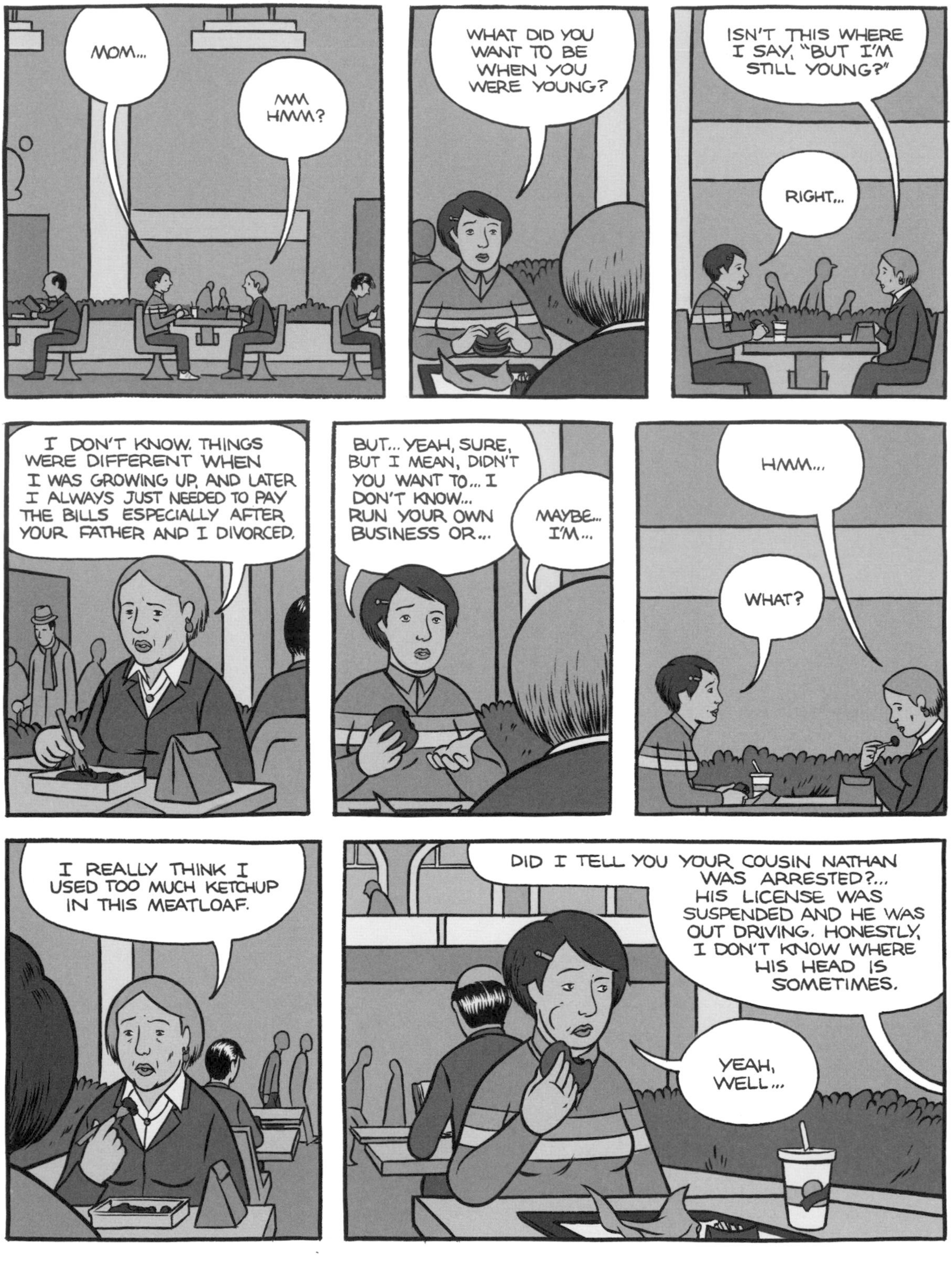
MOM...
MM HMM?
WHAT DID YOU WANT TO BE WHEN YOU WERE YOUNG?
ISN'T THIS WHERE I SAY, "BUT I'M STILL YOUNG?"
RIGHT...
I DON'T KNOW. THINGS WERE DIFFERENT WHEN I WAS GROWING UP, AND LATER I ALWAYS JUST NEEDED TO PAY THE BILLS ESPECIALLY AFTER YOUR FATHER AND I DIVORCED.
BUT... YEAH, SURE, BUT I MEAN, DIDN'T YOU WANT TO... I DON'T KNOW... RUN YOUR OWN BUSINESS OR...
MAYBE... I'M...
HMM...
WHAT?
I REALLY THINK I USED TOO MUCH KETCHUP IN THIS MEATLOAF.
DID I TELL YOU YOUR COUSIN NATHAN WAS ARRESTED?... HIS LICENSE WAS SUSPENDED AND HE WAS OUT DRIVING. HONESTLY, I DON'T KNOW WHERE HIS HEAD IS SOMETIMES.
YEAH, WELL...

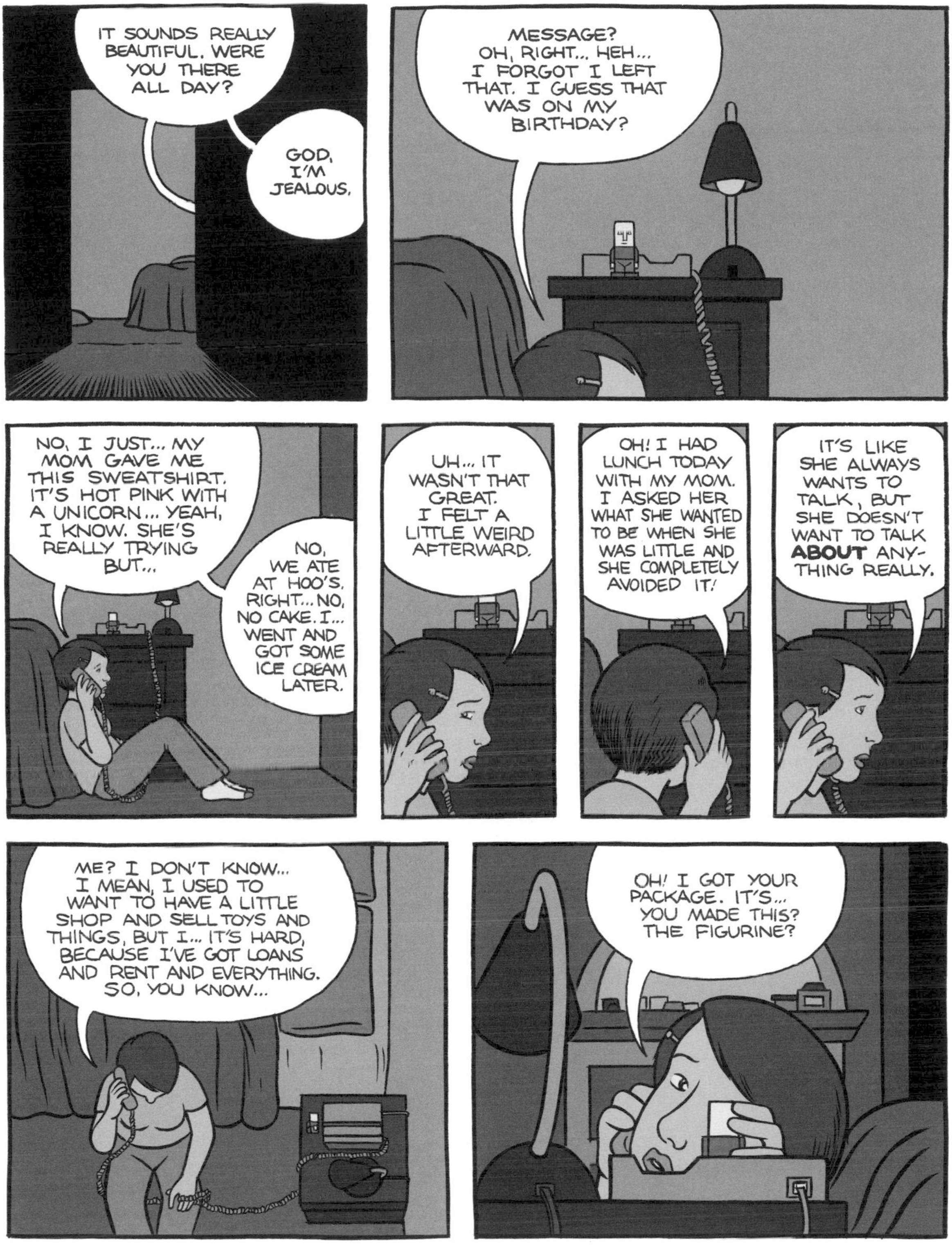
IT SOUNDS REALLY BEAUTIFUL. WERE YOU THERE ALL DAY?
GOD, I'M JEALOUS.
MESSAGE? OH, RIGHT... HEH... I FORGOT I LEFT THAT. I GUESS THAT WAS ON MY BIRTHDAY?
NO, I JUST... MY MOM GAVE ME THIS SWEATSHIRT. IT'S HOT PINK WITH A UNICORN... YEAH, I KNOW. SHE'S REALLY TRYING BUT...
NO, WE ATE AT HOO'S. RIGHT... NO, NO CAKE. I... WENT AND GOT SOME ICE CREAM LATER.
UH... IT WASN'T THAT GREAT. I FELT A LITTLE WEIRD AFTERWARD.
OH! I HAD LUNCH TODAY WITH MY MOM. I ASKED HER WHAT SHE WANTED TO BE WHEN SHE WAS LITTLE AND SHE COMPLETELY AVOIDED IT!
IT'S LIKE SHE ALWAYS WANTS TO TALK, BUT SHE DOESN'T WANT TO TALK **ABOUT** ANYTHING REALLY.
ME? I DON'T KNOW... I MEAN, I USED TO WANT TO HAVE A LITTLE SHOP AND SELL TOYS AND THINGS, BUT I... IT'S HARD, BECAUSE I'VE GOT LOANS AND RENT AND EVERYTHING. SO, YOU KNOW...
OH! I GOT YOUR PACKAGE. IT'S... YOU MADE THIS? THE FIGURINE?

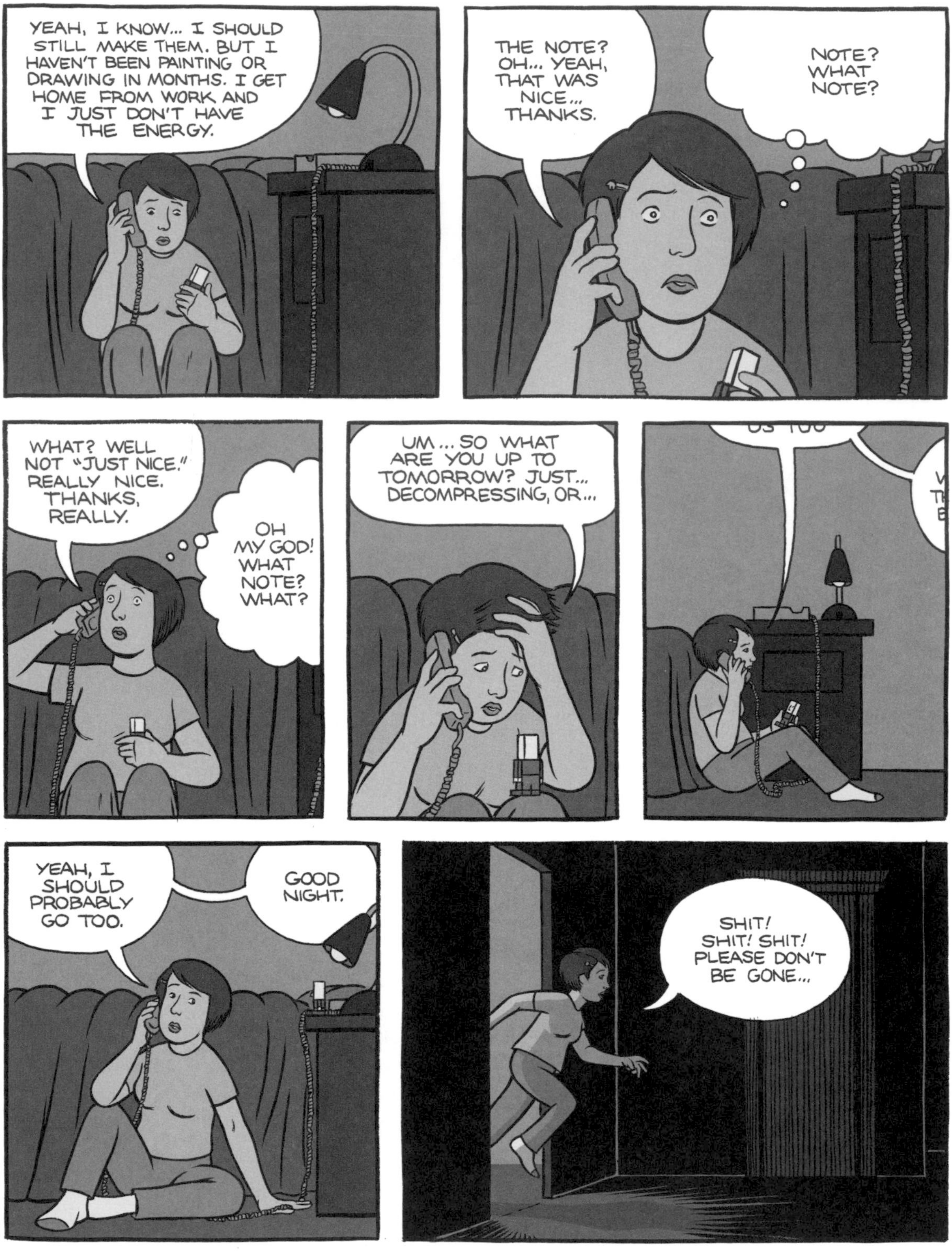
YEAH, I KNOW... I SHOULD STILL MAKE THEM. BUT I HAVEN'T BEEN PAINTING OR DRAWING IN MONTHS. I GET HOME FROM WORK AND I JUST DON'T HAVE THE ENERGY.
THE NOTE? OH... YEAH, THAT WAS NICE... THANKS.
NOTE? WHAT NOTE?
WHAT? WELL NOT "JUST NICE." REALLY NICE. THANKS, REALLY.
OH MY GOD! WHAT NOTE? WHAT?
UM... SO WHAT ARE YOU UP TO TOMORROW? JUST... DECOMPRESSING, OR...
YEAH, I SHOULD PROBABLY GO TOO.
GOOD NIGHT.
SHIT! SHIT! SHIT! PLEASE DON'T BE GONE...

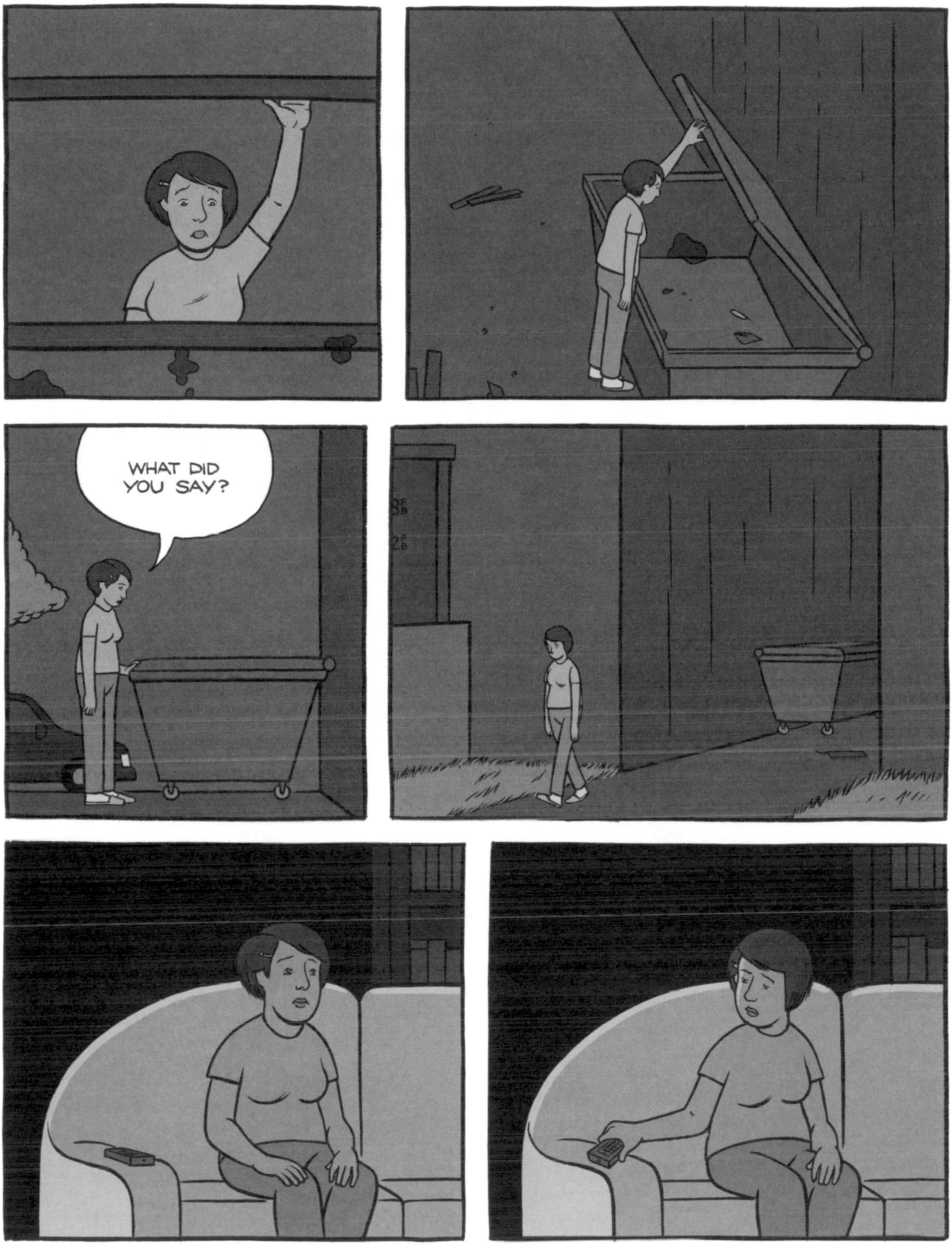
WHAT DID YOU SAY?

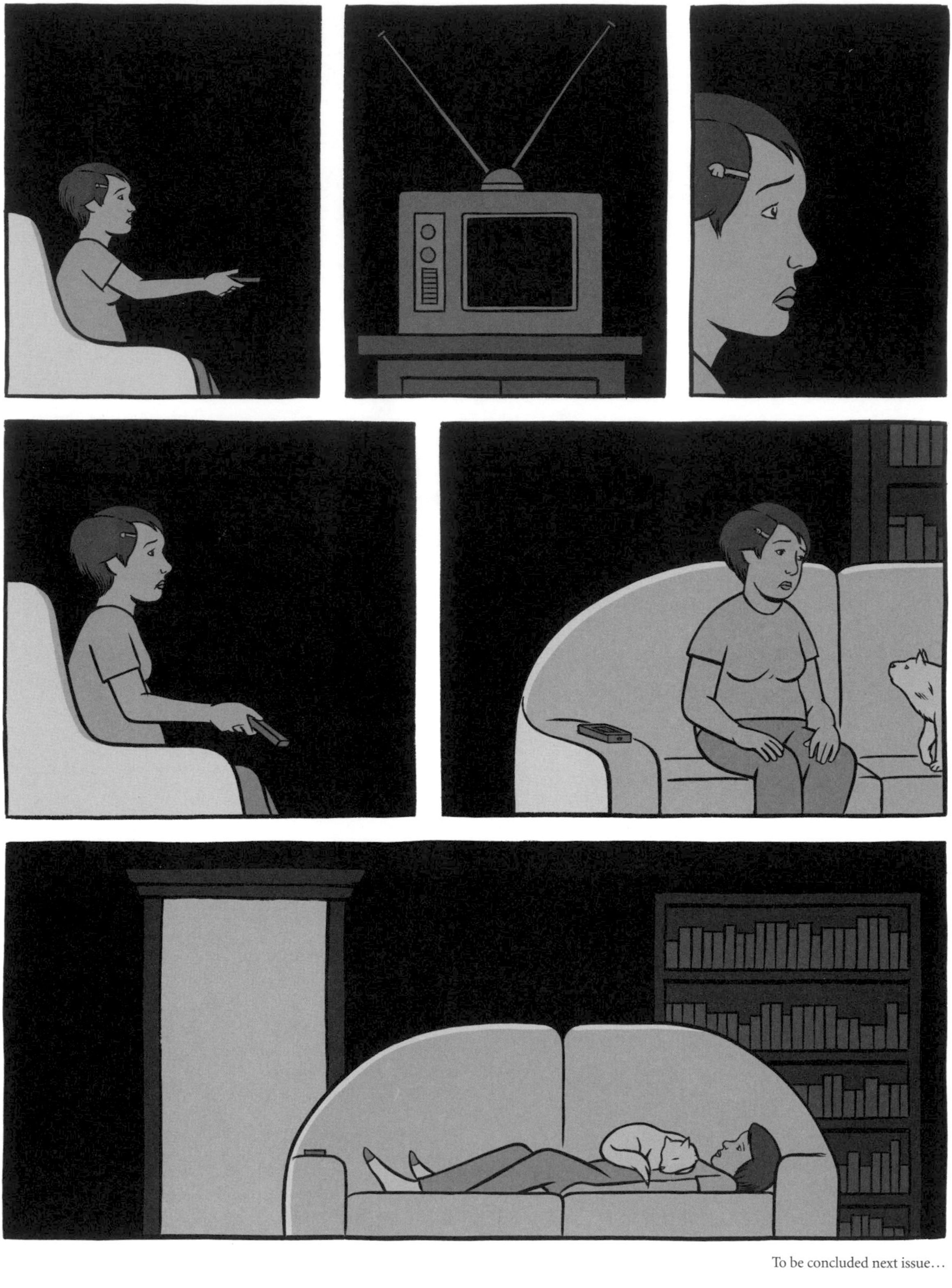

To be concluded next issue…